THE ARTS OF JAPAN

An Illustrated History

ABOUT THE AUTHOR

Hugo Munsterberg was born in Germany, the son of the famous German Orientalist, Oskar Münsterberg. He has lived in the United States since 1935, receiving his B.A. and Ph.D. degrees from Harvard University, where he followed his father's footsteps by specializing in Oriental art, studying under Benjamin Rowland, Langdon Warner, and Lawrence Sickman. After completing his doctoral thesis on Chinese Buddhist bronzes, he taught Oriental art first at Wellesley College and then at Michigan State College. He was Professor of Art History at the International Christian University, Tokyo until 1956 and is now teaching at Hunter College, New York.

In addition to many articles and book reviews on the art and culture of China and Japan, he has published three books: *A Short History of Chinese Art* (1949), *Twentieth Century Painting 1900–1950* (1951), and *The Landscape Painting of China and Japan* (1955). A new book by him dealing with the folk art of Japan is scheduled to be published by the Charles E. Tuttle Company in 1957.

Hōryū-ji, Nara

Seated Bodhisattva, Wall Painting in the Kondō (Golden Hall). Nara period.

Hugo Munsterberg

The Arts of Japan

An Illustrated History

CHARLES E. TUTTLE COMPANY

Rutland, Vermont   Tokyo, Japan

Published by the Charles E. Tuttle Company
of Rutland, Vermont and Tokyo, Japan
with editorial offices at
15 Edogawa-cho, Bunkyo-ku
Tokyo, Japan

First edition, January, 1957

Library of Congress Catalog Card No. 56–13414

Printed in Japan by
Toppan Printing Company, Tokyo

TO HACHIRO YUASA
WHO TAUGHT ME TO
APPRECIATE THE FOLK ART OF JAPAN

PREFACE

This book represents an attempt to fill a long-felt need for an account of the history of Japanese art which would deal with the crafts as well as with the so-called fine arts and carry the story of Japanese art up to the present day instead of ending with the death of Hiroshige. It was written in Japan while I served as professor of art history at the International Christian University in Tokyo and was able to examine most of the masterpieces of Japanese art in the original.

It would be impossible to list the many people who through their help and advice contributed to the completion of this book. But above all I wish to acknowledge my indebtedness to my wife, who with untiring patience revised the manuscript, my assistant, Miss Mio Onchi, who helped me with the Japanese literature, and my secretary, Miss Fumiko Tomoyama, who typed the manuscript. I am also deeply indebted to the staff of the Bijutsu Kenkyū-jo (Art Research Institute) and the Tokyo Kokuritsu Hakubutsu-kan (Tokyo National Museum) for their help in matters of scholarship. I should like to express my gratitude to the collectors who let me reproduce works from their collections and to the Art Research Institute, the Tokyo National Museum, the Sakamoto Photograph Company, the Asuka-en Photograph Company, Mr. Bunji Kobayashi, Mr. Shu Ito, Mr. Lloyd Craighill, and Mr. William Moore for supplying the photographs which are reproduced. I also wish to express my gratitude to the Bijutsu Shuppan-sha and the Heibon-sha for their kindness in letting me use their color plates.

Tokyo, Japan   Hugo Munsterberg

Contents

CONTENTS

LIST OF PLATES

COLOR PLATES

HALF-TONE PLATES

THE ARTS OF JAPAN
An Illustrated History

1

The Prehistoric Art of Japan

ALTHOUGH Japan has been inhabited for at least five thousand years, the Japanese as we know them today have probably only existed for about half that time. Who they were and where they came from are questions about which archaeologists and historians have never been able to agree. Their racial strains are varied, but it is generally recognized that the three chief components are Mongoloid, Malayan, and Caucasian. It is also agreed that waves of immigrants from the mainland, especially from China and Korea, came to Japan during the course of the neolithic period. It seems unlikely that Japan was settled before this, though archaeological discoveries may substantiate the theories of those who believe that it was inhabited during paleolithic times.

The *Kojiki* and the *Nihonshoki,* two sacred books compiled in the eighth century of our era, record myths which tell of the origin of the universe and of the Japanese people. These stories are confused in the extreme. A fantastic number of *kami* are created, spirits of every conceivable kind, such as the three *kami* called "Shore Distant," "Wave-Edge-Shore-Prince," and "Intermediate-Shore-Direction." The creation myth, retold by Post Wheeler in his book *The Sacred Scriptures of the Japanese,* is as follows:

Of old time the Sky and the Earth were not yet set apart the one from the other nor were the female and male principles separated. All was a mass, formless and egg-

3

shaped, the extent whereof is not known, which held the life principle. Thereafter the purer tenuous essence, ascending gradually, formed the Sky; the heavier portion sank and became the Earth. The lighter element merged readily, but the heavier was united with difficulty. Thus the Sky was formed first, the Earth next, and later Kami were produced in the space between them.

When the Sky and the Earth began, there was a something in the very midst of the emptiness whose shape cannot be described. At the first a thing like a white cloud appeared, which floated between Sky and Earth, and from it three Kami came into being in the High-Sky-Plain. These three Kami, appearing earliest, were born without progenitors and later hid their bodies. They were Mid-Sky-Master, High-Producer, Divine-Producer. (Some hold that the last two did not appear till after He-Who-Invites and She-Who-Invites, and that High-Producer was their child.) These first three were called the Three-Creator-Kami.

Seven generations of gods, or *kami,* followed, ending with the divine pair Izanagi and Izanami. They descended from heaven to an island in the ocean and from their union sprang the islands of Japan and all of nature. They also gave birth to various deities, among them the Sun Goddess, Ama-terasu-ō-mi-Kami, or the Heaven-Great-Shining Kami, the chief deity of the ancient Japanese, who to this day is worshipped at Shinto shrines throughout Japan.

These legends were not put into writing until a relatively late date, for no written language had existed in Japan prior to the introduction of Chinese culture during the sixth century. They therefore show certain Chinese elements which were introduced long after the original myths were created. Other elements, similar to Polynesian legends, are probably Malayan in origin. It seems likely that these stories, even in their oral form, are no earlier than the Yayoi period, that is, the second or first century B.C., for they relate the coming of a southern people and seem to bear no relationship to the original northern inhabitants.

The earliest settlers, who came to Japan at least at the beginning of the second millenium, are called Jōmon people, a name coined by modern archaeologists from the kind of cord-impressed pottery they produced. It is not clear where they came from, but the most reliable anthropologists think that they are related to the modern Ainu, who today inhabit certain parts of Hokkaido, the Kurile Islands, and Sakhalin. They are of Caucasian stock, and it is believed that they came to Japan from the Asian continent. Their

4

original home is thought to have been in northern India, and from there they migrated to Central Asia, Manchuria, and Siberia and finally, pushed farther and farther east by neolithic peoples coming from the west, to Japan. The fact that the skeletons of these Jōmon people show none of the Mongoloid characteristics present in the modern Japanese indicates that they belonged to a completely different racial group, although an admixture of Jōmon stock was no doubt absorbed by the people who supplanted them. From philological evidence, especially that of place names, it is believed that these Ainoid people originally inhabited all of Japan but that they were driven north, as conquerors from the south arrived with a higher civilization. These later people are usually referred to as Yayoi, a name taken from the street in Tokyo where the first remains of this civilization, which flourished between 200 B.C. and A.D. 200, were discovered. It is these people who are the real ancestors of the modern Japanese, although the Japanese have, of course, other racial components.

JŌMON POTTERY

The earliest art objects created in Japan are the pottery vessels known as Jōmon *doki,* or rope-design ware, and the idols (found at the same sites as the vessels) which are called *dogū,* or clay dolls. They were usually made of dark-grey clay, which was shaped by hand rather than on the potter's wheel. Both the vessels and the figures not only show a great variety of form but also have an extraordinary expressiveness. In fact, they are among the most remarkable artistic achievements of any neolithic culture, the idols in particular being without close parallel anywhere in the world. There is a feeling of mystery about them as well as a strange beauty which appeals to modern taste because it recalls contemporary expressionist and surrealist art.

No clear relationship exists between Jōmon pottery and that of the Asiatic continent although certain ornamental motifs such as the spiral design, the wavy line, and the cicada in larva form are reminiscent of prehistoric Chinese pottery and Shang bronzes. Some of the ornamental designs are also similar to those in Ainu costumes and wood carvings, although the link between Ainu and Jōmon art has not been discovered. Jōmon pottery ceased being made around the fourth or fifth century A.D., but as recently as seventy-five years ago the Ainus of the Kuriles were making pottery which was similar to Jōmon ware. It must be assumed that such designs were transmitted to the Ainu in perishable materials such as wood and cloth. Here again scholarly opinion is by no means in agreement, and it may well be impossible to establish with certainty any such connections.

The pottery vessels of the Jōmon type are often impressive both in size and ornament *(Plate 1)*. They are called rope-design pottery because of the raised, cord-like designs so frequently seen on their surfaces, patterns which were made by pressing rope, or a stick wound with rope, against the clay. The designs themselves are very irregular, not balanced or static but filled with a dynamic movement. The dominant motif is one of curves often resembling those spirals found on prehistoric Chinese vessels. The nature of these designs, depending on the age and place of origin, varies all the way from simple cord impressions to the most intricate and fantastic reliefs. Experts distinguish between Proto-Jōmon, Early Jōmon, and Late Jōmon, and there is even a final degenerate form of Jōmon which continued in northern Japan after Yayoi and Iwaibe wares had replaced Jōmon pottery in the rest of the country.

The most remarkable achievements of the Jōmon period are the clay figures representing human beings or animals, some of which are as high as one foot, while others are as short as two inches *(Plates 2 & 3)*. Human heads are also found on clay pots of the Jōmon type, resembling ones on neolithic Chinese pottery. Although the date of these images is not known, they are usually found at Middle or Late Jōmon sites, so they must come from the latter half of the Jōmon period. Most of them have been found at domestic sites, suggesting that they were idols used for worship rather than burial figures, as some scholars believe. Many of them have small perforations indicating that they might have been suspended, while others are obviously intended to be stood up. Their bodies are often covered with linear designs, commonly spirals; their facial expressions are strange, with staring eyes that suggest the magic associated with eyes in many primitive civilizations. In all these figures the human form is highly abstract, and yet, in spite of its distortions, it is clearly recognizable. Most of the figures are female deities with prominent breasts and swelling hips, and in this way

6

they are similar to prehistoric European fertility idols, such as the famous Venus of Willendorf. Professor Kidder has suggested that these figures, which were sometimes surrounded by stone circles, must be looked upon as material representations of the Ainu mother-goddess who was dedicated to nourishing the infant, protecting the child, and interceding for the adult.

YAYOI POTTERY

The Jōmon-type objects were gradually replaced by Yayoi wares, a process which probably started in the south and gradually spread to the north and the east. Since similar vessels have been found in Korea and Manchuria, it seems probable that these new immigrants came by way of Korea. Just who they were and where their original home was are not known, but since the Yayoi skeletons show Mongoloid characteristics, it would suggest that they were related to the Chinese. With their advent in the second and first centuries before Christ, the Japanese nation as we know it today was established, and the arrival of conquerors recorded in the sacred scriptures no doubt refers to these events. In China this was the period of the Ch'in rule and the establishment of the Han dynasty, and it seems quite likely that they were people who were pushed east during the disturbances in China.

Technically, the Yayoi vessels are far superior to those of the Jōmon period, although they are neither as interesting nor as expressive (*Plate 4*). They are usually dark red, their forms simple and severe, and they were not only made on the potter's wheel but they were also baked at higher temperatures than the Jōmon wares. The ornamental designs are geometrical in character, usually consisting of zigzag, undulating, parallel, dotted, or slanting lines, and sometimes there are simple incised drawings on the surface. These designs are never as bold as the ones of the Jōmon works, but the vessels themselves are more beautiful in shape. In contrast to the expressiveness of the Jōmon ornaments (something very different from anything else found in Japanese art), the restraint of the Yayoi vessels as well as their emphasis on form seems quite typically Japanese. There is a direct connection between these works and those of the following period, showing the continuity of the civilization established by the Yayoi people, who in terms of technical progress were far more advanced than the people whom they replaced. At

7

the same time there can be no doubt that after the Yayoi people had established themselves in southern and western Japan, the Jōmon people continued to live in the eastern and northern sections of the country, and we are told that even centuries later these northern barbarians continued to give trouble to the Japanese. Of course many of the Jōmon people were undoubtedly absorbed by their conquerors, and yet there is little or no influence of Jōmon art either in the art of the Yayoi or that of later periods. In spite of what some Japanese anthropologists say, it would seem that the break between these two cultures was so complete that little could be absorbed from the earlier by the later one.

During this period there were at least three main centers of culture, the first at Izumo on the Japan Sea side of Honshu, where the god Ōkuni-nushi-no-Mikoto, the *kami* of medicine, sericulture, and fishing was worshipped; the second at Ise in the Yamato region, where the Sun Goddess, Ama-terasu, had her sanctuary; and the third on the southern island of Kyushu, where various maritime cults were observed. Among these the second gradually won supremacy, and Yamato became the center of Japanese culture.

The Art of the Sepulchral Mounds

While the main archaeological discoveries of the neolithic era were found in the shell mounds of the period, the most important repositories of the art of the subsequent age were the grave mounds of the third to the sixth centuries. Their exact dates are uncertain and no doubt vary in different parts of the country, but it may be assumed that they continued to be made right into historical times. Although basically they are nothing but earthen mounds covering the graves of the rulers, they are often of tremendous size. For example, the fourth-century tomb of the Emperor Nintoku in Izumo Province measures no less than 1,620 feet in length and ninety feet in height and is surrounded by a moat. These tombs had chambers made of clay or stone, in which various burial objects were placed—jewels, mirrors, weapons and other implements of bronze or iron, as well as vases closely related to those of the Yayoi type, suggesting that there was a gradual transition from the Yayoi culture to that of the grave mounds.

The most remarkable feature of these mounds (which were covered with

8

cobblestones and had terraces and moats around them) were the *haniwa,* or clay figures which often surrounded them. Modelled no doubt upon Chinese grave-figures of the Han and Six Dynasties periods, they nevertheless are characteristically Japanese. As with the *dogū,* modern abstract taste is better able to appreciate them than the nineteeenth century, with its classical and naturalistic ideals of art. The *haniwa* were originally cylinders which were filled with dirt and set quite closely together around the base of the mound in order to secure the earth. As time went on these hollow clay cylinders became ornamented with the figures of men, women, animals, houses, as well as with all sorts of utensils. They show a great variety of form and subject matter and are often very numerous, as for example at the tomb of the Emperor Nintoku, which had no less than 11,280 such figures.

According to the *Nihonshoki,* the *haniwa* were originally made as substitutes for human beings buried with the dead rulers. We are told that when the Empress-Consort Hisasukime died, the Emperor's minister, taking pity on those who had been buried previously, ordered clay statues to be made. Similar stories are told in China at a somewhat earlier date and there may well be some truth in such accounts, although it seems unlikely that this particular story is based on historical fact. In China the grave-figures were actually placed in the tombs and must therefore be looked upon as companions who accompany the dead to the realm of the spirits, while in Japan the *haniwa* are never inside the tomb but stand on the outside, so it does not seem logical to assume that they were substitutes for the retainers and servants who were originally buried with the dead. However, this is another of the many cases where we may never be certain just what the original facts were.

The *haniwa,* which are always hollow, are made of reddish-brown, unbaked clay. They are highly abstract, but in spite of their stiff, cylindrical shape they show a considerable variety of posture. In contrast to the strange, rather mysterious *dogū,* they seem naive in expression. The emphasis with them, as with the Yayoi objects, is far more on shape than on line or ornament *(Plate 5).* Often very beautiful plastically, they are reduced to the simplest geometric form in much the same way that modern sculpture is, and it is not surprising that sculptors such as Isamu Noguchi have been greatly influenced by them. The eyes, which are cut directly into the clay, create an extraordinary contrast of light and shadow and often achieve a remarkable expression, as for example in the famous figure of a monkey in the National Museum in Tokyo. Some figures, presumably the earlier ones, consist of little more than a cylinder surmounted by a head, while others show a great deal of freedom as well as a certain natural observation in the treatment of the human or animal form. In contrast to the corresponding Chinese figures, they seem less sophisticated, their shapes rounder and simpler, their expressions more childlike and yet often more moving emotionally *(Plate 6)*. Especially if the horses are compared, the Japanese ones seem as charming and naive as large toys, while the Chinese ones are self-conscious artistic creations of great elegance and beauty.

The appeal of the *haniwa* does not lie only in their plastic quality but in their historical and cultural importance as well. A great variety of types are found—men and women in court dress, men clad in armor, a man holding a hawk, another playing a musical instrument similar to the *koto*, to mention only a few—all of which are of interest to the student of the period *(Plate 7)*. Various utensils were represented, as well as boats and houses and all sorts of animals, so a good picture of the material culture can be gained through a study of the *haniwa*. Some of the clothes and the armor of the figures is similar to that of the Chinese of the time, suggesting that already at this early date there was a close connection between China and Japan.

The influence of Han China is most clearly seen in the bronze mirrors which were often found in the tombs *(Plate 8)*. Many are actually of Chinese origin, while others closely follow Chinese prototypes. Generally speaking the workmanship is inferior to that of the Chinese and the design is usually nothing more than a crude approximation of the Chinese models. However, there are some later mirrors which show a complete technical mastery as well as an originality of design. Some of these are very abstract. with linear patterns of great delicacy and beauty, while others depict scenes from the life of the period, such as the famous mirror with battling and dancing figures, which has an animation not found in contemporary Chinese mirrors.

10

Another shows the four heavenly mansions, probably a symbol of the four directions, an idea clearly derived from China but here represented in a Japanese manner and of particular interest in showing the design used for the houses of the period.

Besides the mirrors, ornaments and ceremonial objects were also found in the tombs, among which the most typically Japanese are the *magatama,* or curved jewels, which together with the mirror and the sword are regarded as the three sacred treasures of Shintoism. Originally they were no doubt derived from the claws of the tiger or the tusk of the boar, both of which were believed to have magic power by the early Chinese. Although these particular curved jewels are regarded as characteristically Japanese, similar ones have been found in southern Korea, and even in quite recent times the claws of tigers were thought to have protective power in Korea and Siberia, so the underlying idea at least is a common one to the people of eastern Asia.

Of all the objects surviving from this period, the strangest are the bronze bells, or *dōtaku,* the origin and purpose of which are unknown *(Plate 9).* The earliest are believed to date back to the first century before Christ, but it is not clear for how long they were used. Here again Japanese archaeologists have tended to emphasize the unique character of these *dōtaku,* but excavations at Lo-lang in northern Korea, which at the time was a flourishing military outpost of the Han empire, have unearthed similar objects and their design is quite like that found on bronzes excavated in Indo-China. It may well be that the *dōtaku* did not have any utilitarian function but were considered treasures, as was the case with many of the ancient Chinese bronze vessels. Indeed it seems likely that objects made of bronze or iron were regarded as signs of wealth during the period when they were first introduced to Japan from the continent. So far no such objects from the late Chou dynasty have been found, but there can be no doubt that the contact beween Japan and Han China was very close.

The *dōtaku* vary in length from a few inches to over four feet and in make from crude casting to the most elegant and refined forms. However, what interests us most today are their simple linear designs, something like children's drawings, which represent animals such as tortoises, lizards, insects, and birds, scenes from the lives of the hunters and fishermen, and house

11

designs. These latter are of particular interest, for they show how the type of structure which is still seen in Ise Shrine goes back to the beginning of the Christian era. The designs, which may give us some idea of the painting of the period, are probably symbolic, although the symbolism is no longer understood.

Paintings from this period are very rare and those which do exist are primitive in the extreme. The most famous are the wall paintings in sixth-century tombs located in Fukuoka Prefecture in Kyushu. Executed in bright colors against a red or grey background, they consist primarily of abstract shapes such as volutes, circles, dots, wheels, spirals, triangles, and squares, which were undoubtedly symbolic in meaning. Other pictures show horses, still others portray hunting scenes and people crossing water in a boat, subjects quite common in the art of primitive people and usually connected with hunting magic and the afterlife. These pictures, artistically very crude, show that even at this comparatively late period the art of painting had not yet been developed. Besides these paintings, there are also line drawings of a childlike character, which portray human figures and animals, but these too show little artistic maturity, although they have a kind of naive charm recalling some of the work of Klee.

A new kind of pottery, one used for ceremonial purposes and called Iwaibe or Sué ware, began to be made at this period. Compared to the earlier wares it shows a marked technical advance, for it was fired at far higher temperatures and thus is much harder. The color is a dark, subdued grey and the shape is often very lovely, with a bulbous body resting upon a hollow stem into which triangular or rectangular openings are cut. The mouth is usually large and there are often additional spouts at the shoulders, or little human or animal figures, or a combination of both. The Iwaibe vessel, derived from a type first developed in China and introduced to Japan via Korea, proved very popular and was in fact used for centuries.

Ise Shrine and Early Japanese Architecture

The numerous models of ancient Japanese houses found among the *haniwa,* the designs on the *dōtaku,* and the descriptions in the *Kojiki* and *Nihonshoki* give us a fairly good idea of the type of architecture which flourished in

12

Japan prior to the introduction of Buddhism. This ancient type of building, which originally was probably a chieftain's palace as well as a sacred shrine, is preserved for us almost unchanged in Ise Shrine at Ujiyamada. Due to the fact that these buildings have been torn down and rebuilt every twenty years in their original form, the ancient design has come down to us intact. The original shrine of which the present one is a faithful replica was erected in the seventh century A.D., but the design itself, which is far more ancient, can be traced back to a much earlier period, probably to the arrival of the Yayoi people in Japan. The type of construction used shows certain affinities to the houses of Malaya and the South Sea Islands, suggesting that originally it may have been derived from some common source in the south of China, since the settlement of the South Sea Islands by the Polynesians is of more recent date than the origin of this type of structure in Japan.

The architectural style employed at Ise Shrine is known as the *shimmei zukuri*, meaning the style associated with the Sun Goddess, for it is to her that the most ancient and venerable of Shinto sanctuaries is dedicated. As the modern German architect Bruno Taut remarked, the design used here is characteristic of the very best in the Japanese artistic tradition, for it shows clarity of construction, simplicity of material, and beauty of proportion. As in so much of the best of later Japanese architecture, the unpainted and undecorated architectural members are allowed to speak for themselves. The material of the wood and the thatch is not hidden and the whole is fitted into its natural setting with great sensitivity. This is, of course, a typical expression of the Japanese love for nature in general and the Shinto worship of the forces of nature in particular.

There are actually two shrines at Ise, the inner shrine, the Naigū or Naikū, dedicated to the Heaven-Great-Shining Kami, Ama-terasu-ō-mi-Kami, and the outer shrine, the Gegū or Gekū, dedicated to the Plentiful-Food-August-Goddess, Toyo-uke-hime, which are located at some distance from each other but are very similar in style. They are surrounded by a series of fences which separate the sacred precinct from the outer world. The sanctuary itself is in this way completely cut off from the general public, who can approach but not enter it, a privilege reserved for the priests and special guests like the emperor. In this way the sanctuary is much like the Greek temple which

13

was also looked upon as a dwelling place of the god. Behind the main building are two smaller structures, which serve as treasure houses in which the sacred relics and offerings are kept. The three inner fences have gates while the outermost enclosure is approached through a torii, a kind of Shinto sacred gateway, which is still one of the main distinguishing marks of a Shinto shrine. It consists of two pillars topped by two horizontal bars. The lower one extends between the pillars like the crossbar of an H, while the upper one, which rests on the top of the pillars, projects beyond them with slanting ends. Here again the simplest of forms is combined with great beauty of proportion. Japanese tradition has it that these torii were built for birds to perch on, but obviously this is a later rationalistic explanation for something which is far more ancient, probably a ceremonial gateway of the type found in India at Sanchi and Barhut and which is common to many early civilizations.

The main building, a rectangular wooden structure with gables at both ends and a large thatched roof, was no doubt originally derived from a palace *(Plate 10)*. The building rests upon heavy piers which are rammed into the earth without laying any foundation. The floor level is raised above the ground so that there is an open space between the earth and the floor; the walls consist of simple, unpainted boards and are surrounded by an open veranda. The entrance at Ise, in contrast to other shrines, such as the one at Izumo, is on the long side rather than at the gable end, and there is a staircase leading from the ground to the entrance. The building faces south, the direction of the sun, just as the Chinese palaces and temples do.

Perhaps the most beautiful as well as the most characteristic part of the Shinto shrine is the magnificent thatched roof. Here the architect employs two features which are unique to the Shinto shrine, namely the *chigi,* or rafters crossing at the gable with the ridge lying in the angle of the crutches formed by the rafters, and the *katsuogi,* or the horizontal logs resting upon the ridge to hold it in place. Both the *chigi* and the *katsuogi* are still used in most Shinto shrines today and, together with the torii, enable even the uninitiated to distinguish between a Buddhist temple and a Shinto shrine, although there are cases when the architectural styles are mixed. This is especially true in later Shinto shrines, which absorb more and more of

14

Plate 1. Clay Vessel. Jōmon period.

Plate 2.

Head of Idol. Middle Jōmon period.

Coll. Munsterberg, Tokyo

Coll. Munsterberg, Tokyo

Plate 3. Head of Idol. Late Jōmon period.

Plate 4.

Clay vessel. Yayoi period.

Coll. Marquis d'Ajeta, Rome

Plate 5. Haniwa Dancers. Grave Mound period.

Plate 6.

Haniwa Horse's Head.

Grave Mound period.

Coll. Marquis d'Ajeta, Rome

Plate 7.

Haniwa Warrior. Grave Mound period.

Coll . Marquis d'Ajeta, Rome

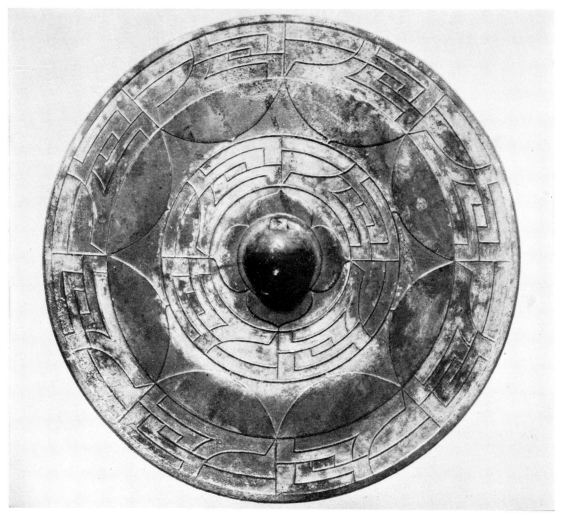

Coll. Imperial Household

Plate 8. Bronze Mirror. Grave Mound period.

Plate 9. *Dōtaku*. Yayoi period.

Plate 10.   Honden, Ise Shrine, Ujiyamada.

(based on prehistoric design).

Buddhist temple architecture. Another feature, typical of Ise Shrine and very ancient, is the additional free-standing pillar at the gable end of the building, which is designed to help support the ridge and suggests that the roof might well have projected much farther in the original structures, as is indicated by the archaic pictures on the mirrors and *dōtaku*. The interior of the shrine is extremely plain, for it was not used as a place of assembly or group worship but was looked upon as a dwelling place of the Sun Goddess, where her symbol, the divine mirror, was kept.

Although it is the most ancient and sacred of Shinto shrines, Ise Shrine is undoubtedly only one of many such shrines built at the period. A record of A.D. 737 tells us that there were no less than three thousand officially recognized shrines at that time. Of the ones surviving today, the next most famous is Izumo Shrine located on the Japan Sea coast of Honshu and built in a style known as *taisha zukuri,* which differs in some respects from the one used at Ise. The main difference lies in the fact that the entrance is at the gable end, but there is also a central pillar in the interior and the floor is somewhat higher above the ground. However, the general design and style are the same in both, although Ise Shrine is believed to be more authentic, while Izumo Shrine already shows some influence of Chinese Buddhist temples. Both, however, are typical of the native tradition of Japanese architecture. They represent the first examples of a truly national art, and it is characteristic of the traditional-minded Japanese society that they have been rebuilt again and again in the style which was first developed two thousand years ago.

2

The Beginnings of
Buddhist Art in Japan

ALTHOUGH Chinese culture had influenced Japan even during the prehistoric period, it was not until the introduction of Buddhism that the entire Japanese civilization became permeated with Chinese culture. The period during which this event took place is called the Asuka period (A.D. 552 to A.D. 645), a name taken from the place where the capital was located, or the Suiko period (593 to 628), after the empress whose rule was the most illustrious of the era. This age, which marked a complete revolution in the civilization of Japan, is important not only because of the introduction of Buddhism but also because of all the other aspects of Chinese culture, especially Confucian learning and the written language, which came in along with the religion. In fact, it may well be said that the history of Japan as we think of it today starts with the events of this period.

The arrival in 552 of a mission from the Korean kingdom of Paikché, or in Japanese, Kudara, is usually considered the starting point of this development. They brought Buddhist images, banners, canopies, and scriptures, as well as a message from their king which said in part:

This teaching (dharma) is the most excellent of all teachings; it brings endless and innumerable blessings to all believers, even unto attainment of Enlightenment (Bodhi) without comparison. Moreover, it has come to Korea from far-off India, and the peoples of the countries lying beetween are now zealous followers of it and none is outside the pale.

No doubt these gifts made a great impression upon the still backward civilization of sixth-century Japan and they were followed in succeeding years by other images, as well as monks and scholars and craftsmen. Although the origin both of the works of art and the teachings was no doubt Chinese and ultimately Indian, during this early period they all came to Japan from Korea. Records tell of monks and a nun, a temple architect and a maker of images arriving from Korea in 577, and still others followed in the course of the next decade. Among them were not only architects but also experts in casting spires, tile-makers, and all sorts of other craftsmen, who were able to give the Japanese professional training. At first the artists working in Japan were largely foreigners, whose work necessarily reflected a foreign style, but soon the Japanese began to adapt the importations to their own artistic traditions. For a time the fate of Buddhism was uncertain, but by the turn of the century the new religion was so firmly established that in 604 it was incorporated into the state code, which expressly said that the people should revere the Three Precious Things, namely, the Buddha, the Law, and the Priesthood.

This new code was the work of Prince Umayado or, to use the posthumous title by which he is better known, Shōtoku Taishi, or Sage Virtue, who lived from 572 to 621 and served as Prince Regent under the Empress Suiko. It is difficult to exaggerate the importance of this man, who was not only one of the most remarkable figures in Japanese history but also, along with the Indian ruler Asoka, one of the greatest patrons of Buddhism. His name, which is still revered in Japan today, stands beside that of Hideyoshi and the Emperor Meiji as one of the best known in Japanese history. Although his contributions were manifold, it is the temples he founded, many of which still exist today, that are of concern to us in a work of this nature.

The most ancient of these is the great temple of Shitennō-ji, or the Temple of the Four Heavenly Kings, which was started in 593 in what is today Osaka. Almost as old is the Hokō-ji, or Asuka-dera, built in 595 near Nara, but unfortunately none of the original buildings have been preserved in either of these temples. (Significantly enough, the abbot of Hokō-ji was a Korean priest, which is one of the many indications of the prominent part Korean Buddhist missionaries played in spreading the Buddhist gospel in Japan.) Of all the temples which Shōtoku Taishi founded, the most important and perhaps the most famous is Hōryū-ji, which was established in Nara in 607 in obedience to the command of the Empress Suiko. This temple, which today is a kind of museum of early Buddhist art, is preserved at least in part as it was originally built in the seventh century.

In 624, three years after the death of Shōtoku Taishi, there were no less than forty-six temples, 816 monks, and 565 nuns in Japan. In less than a hundred years Japan had become a Buddhist country and this in turn meant a complete transformation of the artistic culture, since the introduction of the Buddhist faith had from the very start gone hand in hand with the introduction of Buddhist images. When in 607 direct contact with China was established, this tendency towards a foreign cultural orientation became even more pronounced. It was a development very similar to that which took place under the Emperor Meiji in the nineteenth century, and what is most astonishing in both is that the Japanese in such a comparatively short time were able to accept and absorb these new ideas without losing their own identity.

BUDDHIST ARCHITECTURE OF THE ASUKA PERIOD

Any discussion of the artistic monuments which have survived from this early period must start with Hōryū-ji, which is not only the most ancient but in some ways also the most beautiful temple in Japan. Its exact date is a matter of conjecture, but even if the buildings are not the original ones, they are certainly based upon designs of the Asuka period. It seems most likely that the original temple (which was completed in 607 as the result of a vow made by the Emperor Yōmei and carried out by the Empress Suiko and Shōtoku Taishi) was destroyed by fire in 670, and that the present buildings were actually erected late in the seventh century. This whole problem is far from being settled, but, whatever the date of these buildings, it seems certain that they reflect the style of the Asuka period. In any case these buildings, which are over twelve hundred years old, are the most ancient wooden buildings in the world today.

The general plan of the temple may be seen in the aerial photograph *(Plate 11)*. It consists of a square precinct which is separated from the outside by a covered colonnade called *hōrō* or *kairō,* which resembles a medieval cloister. At the south side of this cloister there is a large gate, the *chūmon,* or middle gate, and on the north side is the lecture hall, or *kōdō.* To the right and to the left of the main axis which leads from the *chūmon* to the *kōdō* are, respectively, the Golden Hall, or Kondō, and the pagoda. Finally there are two smaller buildings to the west and east of the *kōdō,* namely, the *kyōro,* or sutra library, and the *shōro,* or belfry, but these last two buildings as well as the *kōdō* itself were built during the Heian period. An alternate plan, which may still be seen at Shitennō-ji in Osaka, is an arrangement in which the pagoda is in front of the *kondō* on a north-south axis leading from the gate to the lecture hall, but the Hōryū-ji plan is the more common.

Comparing the temple complex as a whole to equivalent European designs, one sees that there are three main differences, all of them characteristic of Japanese architecture. The first is the close relationship between the buildings and their natural setting. Far from denying nature or standing apart from it as Western architecture often does, Hōryū-ji, like most other Japanese buildings, is conceived as a part of nature, the buildings blending beautifully with the physical surroundings, especially with the pine trees which grow on the temple grounds. This love of and closeness to nature, which was already reflected in the Shinto shrines, is one of the outstanding characteristics of the Japanese people. Man is seen not as lord of nature but as a part of it and, in keeeping with this idea, the structures of man are related to their physical settings. The second thing which strikes one is the modest scale of this temple compared to similar structures in Europe, such as St. Peter's or Chartres. This is by no means due to the fact that Hōryū-ji was not considered important—on the contrary, it served not only as a center of worship but also, as its ancient name Hōryū-ji-Gakumon-ji, or Hōryū-ji of Learning, suggests, as a center of Buddhist study. In addition it was a kind of hospital where the Buddhist ideal of mercy and charity was practiced towards the sick and the poor. The small size of the individual buildings as well as of the complex as a whole reflects the love of the Japanese for relatively small dimensions, a love which can be seen in all phases of Japanese life and which may have something to do with the small size of the Japanese islands and with the small and graceful build of the people. The third difference is in the building material itself. Western architects usually employ stone for all major constructions, but the Japanese used wood almost exclusively, a material which their islands have in abundance and which is better suited to a country in which earthquakes are so common. The result is a lighter and simpler type of construction in which the beauty of the material is a major part of the design.

From a religious point of view the most important of these buildings is the Kondō, or Golden Hall, for it was here that the image of the deity was housed, Shaka Buddha, as is the case at Hōryū-ji, or one of the many Buddhas and bodhisattvas who were worshipped at the time (*Plate 12*). This seventh-century structure stood until 1949, when it was destroyed by a fire caused by the carelessness of a painter who was making a copy of the wall paintings, but the present building, completed in 1954, is an exact replica of the original. Its basic design is extremely simple, consisting of a rectangular stone platform to which four staircases lead, one corresponding to each door and to each direction. On the platform there are twenty-eight pillars which support the upper part of the structure and form five bays on one side and four on the other. The roof, particularly beautiful with its elegantly curved eaves, is a mixture of a gabled and a hipped roof, a development peculiar to the Far East and called *irimoya* in Japan. Beneath the main roof there are two smaller roofs. The upper one sets off the second story, which, however, does not correspond to any functional division inside, since the second floor, which is surrounded by a balcony, serves no practical purpose. The lower roof is a later one added to protect the walls and paintings from the rain. The interior consists of a rectangular chamber with walls of wood and stucco and a coffered ceiling. In the center, surrounded by a series of pillars, there is a raised platform or dais symbolizing Mt. Meru, the world mountain, on which images are placed.

This building, if compared to the sacred structures of other cultures, seems

21

most like the Greek temple in its restraint and simple dignity, although it is very different in respect to the prominent part played by the roof. In fact, it may be said that the roof which protects the interior from the frequent rains of Japan is the dominant element in Japanese architecture. Not only the size of the roof, which projects beyond the walls of the building, but also the elegant curve of the eaves and the weight and beauty of the grey clay tiles, so characteristic of Buddhist in contrast to Shinto architecture, add greatly to the impressive appearance of these temples. In Greek buildings the architect aimed at a perfect equilibrium between the horizontal and the vertical, but here the emphasis is entirely upon the horizontal. The building materials themselves, of course, are entirely different and the brilliant white marble of a temple like the Parthenon creates a very different effect from the subdued colors of the Japanese temple.

Although the construction of these early Japanese temples is quite uncomplicated, it is wholly adequate for its purpose, which is best demonstrated by the fact that these structures have survived longer than any other wooden buildings in the world. The pillars, each of which is carved from a single large tree trunk, show a swelling towards the center like that in the Greek columns, a trait which may show the influence of the Graeco-Buddhist art of Gandhara Province. They are topped by three forked brackets, on which rest the crossbeams, which in turn support the upper part of the building. Here a system of beams and rafters bears the weight of the heavy tile roof. In the early examples, all these members are quite simple, but in later temples a more elaborate design led to the multiplication of these forms and thus destroyed the unpretentious beauty of the design. Amazingly enough no nails were used in these buildings—they were held up simply by fitting the pieces together. Although the more characteristically Japanese style uses unpainted wood, at Hōryū-ji the woodwork was painted a scarlet, which today has considerably faded. The total effect of the reddish wood against the white stucco of the walls, the blue-green of the latticework covering the windows, the grey tiles, and the green pines is extremely beautiful and impressive.

Next to the Kondō the most characteristic structure of the temple complex is the pagoda, which the Japanese call *gojūnotō*, or five-storied tower *(Plate*

22

13). This typical Buddhist structure, whose purpose was to contain a sacred relic of a Buddhist saint, was originally derived from the Indian stupa, or relic mount. However, since in China it was modified by the form of the ancient Chinese watchtower, it bears little resemblance today to the Indian monument which inspired it. The Hōryū-ji pagoda has five stories, which is a common number in Japan, although three-story pagodas like that at nearby Hokki-ji, the other authentic Asuka building, also occur, as well as seven-story pagodas and in later periods even thirteen-story pagodas. The most authentic are no doubt the seven-story ones, since the pagoda represents the magic Mt. Meru, which itself has seven stories. In Japan, however, five was considered a more auspicious number because it represented the five directions, that is, the four conventional ones plus the center. Another interpretation given in Japan is that the five stories symbolize the five elements, earth, water, fire, wind, and sky. The pagoda has no real function—in fact there is usually no room inside nor are the balconies on the various floors meant to be used. It is looked upon as a symbolical representation of the universe, with the square platform on which it rests symbolizing the earth and the central pillar which runs through the entire structure symbolizing the world axis which unites heaven and earth. It is crowned by a square shape with an inverted bowl on top representing the palace of the gods and by nine umbrellas, one set above the other, symbolizing the kingship of the Buddha as the ruler of the universe. It terminates in a finial in the shape of a flaming jewel symbolizing the precious jewel of the Buddhist truth, which shines above everything. The original meaning of the flames has been lost; in Japan, where they are called *suien,* or spray, it is believed that they protect the building against fire. The pagoda as a whole symbolizes the supremacy of the Buddha and the Buddhist law which towers above the earth and its inhabitants, so it might be said that its function is similar to that of the spire in the Christian church. It is interesting to note that the central pillar is not rigidly anchored so that during an earthquake it may sway without cracking the structure. Here again, as in the Kondō, an extra roof was added later, which impairs the original design by obscuring the elegance of the ground floor. Again the most beautiful part is the gently curving tile roofs. Each is somewhat smaller than the one below, a device

23

which adds variety to the structure. the silhouette of which is visible from far off as a memorial to the Buddha.

The third authentic seventh-century structure is the *chūmon,* or central gate, which is composed of the same architectual elements found in the Kondō *(Plate 14).* Its purpose is to admit the faithful to the inner courtyard of the temple from the outer precinct, which is entered through the Nandaimon, or Great South Gate. It has five columns on each side, forming two entrances and supporting the crossbeams, and there is a double roof similar to that of the Kondō. To the right and left of the portals are two large figures of Guardian Kings, or Niō, which were supposed to keep out evil spirits. The effect of the gate as a whole with its massive roofs and fine proportions is, like that of the rest of the seventh-century buildings at Hōryū-ji, very impressive. Although few in number, these buildings not only give us an insight into the nature of Asuka architecture, but they also show how the Japanese were able to absorb what was essentially a foreign style.

Buddhist Sculpture of the Asuka Period

Buddhist images reached Japan with the very first missionaries who came from Korea, for they played a central part in the religious rites of the Buddhist church. At first the Buddhist community had to rely upon foreign importations, and even those statues actually made in Japan were largely the work of Chinese and Korean craftsmen. The earliest dated native Buddhist image is the great Buddha of Asuka, formerly in the now-destroyed *kondō* of Gango-ji and now in the Angu-in near Nara. Unfortunately this large bronze image is badly damaged and gives a very inadequate idea of the grandeur of Asuka sculpture. Far better preserved is the Yakushi Buddha image at Hōryū-ji, which is dated 607 and according to its inscription was made by order of Shōtoku Taishi following the wishes of his father. Originally it served as the main icon of this famous temple. It is believed to be the work of the Tori school, since it is very close in style to the famous "Shaka Trinity," which is now the central image on the altar of the Kondō. Since it has an inscription indicating that it was made in 623 and is the work of Tori Bushi, the grandson of a Chinese immigrant, it is of particular

24

interest both from a historical as well as an artistic point of view *(Plate 15)*.
This celebrated image, although made in Japan, shows how close the Japanese
sculpture of this period was to its Korean and Chinese prototypes, for both
in iconography and style it reflects the sculpture of China of the Six Dynasties.
In the center is the figure of the seated Buddha Shaka, the savior of Buddhism, and at his sides are two standing *bosatsu,* or Buddhist saints. Behind
him is a large flaming *mandorla* with a halo in the form of a lotus and small
images of the seven Buddhas of the Past who preceded the historical Buddha.
The representation of Shaka is characteristic of the type found in China
about a century earlier. It shows the Buddha seated with crossed legs
(the yogi position associated with meditation), and wearing a monk's
garment, a symbol of the fact that Gautama renounced the world and became
a monk. His face is serene, mirroring his inner harmony, and a smile
plays over his lips, showing the spiritual joy of one who, having achieved
enlightenment, is no longer troubled by the cares and sorrows of this world.
On his forehead is a dot called *urna,* a third eye indicating that the Blessed
One sees all, just as his large ears indicate that he hears all, and the *ushnisha,*
or raised protuberance on his head, indicates that he knows all. His hair
is short, for when he became a monk he cut off the flowing locks which
he had worn as a royal prince. He raises one hand in the *abhaya* mudra,
a gesture telling the faithful that they should have no fear, while the other
hand is held with the palm up, the so-called *vara* mudra, or gesture of charity.
He is seated upon a lotus, which in ancient Indian cosmology was a symbol
of the earth, the center of which represents the Himalayas, while the petals
stand for the four great countries of Asia, namely India, China, Central
Asia, and Iran. Thus the lotus throne symbolizes the fact that the Buddha
is regarded as the ruler of the entire world. The halo behind him and
the flaming *mandorla* are ancient solar symbols probably indicating that
originally the Buddha was a solar deity, but later merely a sign of sanctity
like the halo in the Christian art of the West. The smaller Buddhas of
the Past indicate that Shaka is only one in the long line of Buddhas which
have preceded him and which follow him at some future date. His two
attendants are represented in a smaller size, showing their lesser importance,
just as their standing position indicates their lower status. In contrast to

the central figure, they are not Buddhas, that is, beings who have achieved enlightenment, but bodhisattvas, or *bosatsu*. saintly figures who have renounced their chance at Buddhahood so that they might help save suffering mankind. In keeping with this they are shown in the garments of an Indian prince with crown, jewels, and elaborate scarfs, since Buddha, prior to his enlightenment, was an Indian prince who supposedly dressed in this manner. In their hands they hold precious jewels symbolising the jewel of the lotus, or the spiritual riches which Buddhism gives to the faithful, the same symbol which is also found on the upper part of the central halo. The faces of the *bosatsu* have the same serenity as the Buddha, a look which reflects their inner peace. They stand on lotus pedestals, which are a sign of purity, for as the lotus grows in the mud at the bottom of the lake but remains pure and beautiful, so the Buddha walked through the corruption and filth of this world but remained pure and holy. It may be seen from these brief comments how every detail of the iconography is deeply meaningful in terms of Buddhist faith, and is not the whim of the particular artist who happened to make the image. In fact the artist at this time was considered little more than a humble craftsman working for the glory of the Buddha and his church rather than as a creative person in his own right.

In keeping with the transcendental and spiritual nature of the image, the style is very abstract, for it would not seem proper to represent these other-worldly beings in a naturalistic manner suited only for creatures of this world. In order to achieve this effect the artist has flattened out the figure, placing more emphasis upon the abstract design than the plastic form, and he has created a feeling of tension by stressing the linear movement within the composition. Wherever the eye turns, be it to the hanging drapery in the center, the scarfs of the attendants, the lotus designs, or the flames of the *mandorla,* there are dynamic, moving lines, which bring out a wonderful feeling of inner tension balanced by the serenity of the facial expressions. Here again, as in the treatment of the iconography, the artist simply reflects the style of the Chinese models which inspired him and, although no such large bronze Buddhist images of this date have been discovered in China, there can be no doubt that they existed and that it was this type of image which was brought to Japan during the middle of the sixth century.

26

While the Tori Bushi trinity was made of bronze, other early images were carved in wood, a material which has been used with great skill by Japanese craftsmen throughout the ages. The most famous as well as the most beautiful of the wooden statues at Hōryū-ji is the large standing figure of Kannon Bosatsu, the bodhisattva of mercy and compassion *(Plate 16)*. It is probably somewhat later than the "Shaka Trinity," for the draperies no longer fall in winglike patterns, and the figure is far more plastic, reflecting the Chinese style of the second half of the sixth century, whereas the "Shaka Trinity" follows the style of the first half. The *bosatsu* is rendered in a graceful and moving way, expressing the compassion associated with the saint. The body is very much elongated, emphasizing the spiritual nature of the deity in a way that reminds one of the statues of medieval Europe, where the same type of elongation was used to express a transcendental feeling. One hand is extended in the gesture of charity while the other holds a bottle of heavenly nectar. The graceful carving of the fingers, especially in the hand holding the bottle, is of rare sensitivity. Equally lovely is the flowing movement of the scarf which extends in a long, curving line from the arm to the pedestal upon which the bodhisattva stands. Since he is a *bosatsu* rather than a Buddha, the Kannon is dressed in garments symbolizing a royal prince, with a crown and a long skirt and the upper part of his body bare. Another sign of his identity is the little Buddha Amida in his crown, for this deity is looked upon as the spiritual counterpart of the *bosatsu*. The Kannon stands on a lotus pedestal, the symbol of purity, and behind his head is a beautiful halo in the shape of a lotus flower. There are traces of paint on the statue, which originally must have been brightly colored with red and blue and green. The total effect of the statue, so gracefully carved and filled with such quiet serenity, is one of rare spiritual beauty. It is traditionally referred to as the "Kudara Kannon," after the Korean kingdom from which it is supposed to have come, but since there are no comparable Korean or Chinese images, it may well be a native Japanese work.

The seated image of Miroku Bosatsu at Kōryū-ji in Kyoto is no doubt of Korean origin, since there are images in Korea which are almost identical in style and iconography. However, it is impossible to tell which images were brought to Japan from the continent, which were made in Japan by foreign

27

artists, and which were made by native Japanese craftsmen who had studied with foreign teachers. Formerly, Japanese temples often ascribed works to Korean or Chinese sculptors, hoping to increase the prestige of the images, but in modern times, influenced by the rising nationalism, Japanese scholars have been somewhat reluctant to admit that any of these works were not done by Japanese artists. The truth as so often happens probably lies somewhere between, and at this point the origin of such works can not be determined with certainty. In any case, the statue of the Buddha of the Future, or Miroku, is one of the most moving and graceful Buddhist images in Japanese art. It shows him seated in deep meditation on a lotus throne with one leg hanging down, while the other one crosses it at right angles. The bare upper part of the body is smooth and round, while the lower part is covered with drapery falling in many folds. One arm is bent, with the hand resting upon the ankle of the crossed leg, while the fingers of the other touch the chin in a gesture associated with spiritual contemplation. Here again, as in the "Kudara Kannon," the carving of the fingers is particularly sensitive. Wonderfully carved also are the half-closed eyes, the sharp, curved nose, and the mouth, over which a slight smile hovers. Certainly the sculptor, whose name and career are completely unknown, was one of the great artists of the period.

The masterpiece of Asuka sculpture, and one of the truly great works of sculpture of all times is the Miroku at Chūgū-ji in Nara (Plate 17). In iconography this image is almost identical with the Kōryū-ji one, and, although according to tradition it is believed to be a representation of Kannon, it too must be looked upon as an image of Miroku, the messiah of Buddhism, for inscriptions on similar images specifically say that this type of image represented this deity. The chief iconographical difference between the two images is that instead of a headdress, the one at Chūgū-ji has two balls which represent a very stylized version of the hair style of the time. Other minor differences are the halo behind his head, the scarfs hanging from his shoulders, and the raised lotus supporting the foot which is hanging down. But the true difference is in the execution of the sculpture rather than the iconography. Like the Kōryū-ji image, the one at Chūgū-ji is carved in wood, but the surface is so smooth, and so darkened by age and incense that it looks almost like

28

metal. The form, which is both more plastic and more abstract, recalls the rounded shapes of the *haniwa,* suggesting that this is indeed a native Japanese work. It is perhaps this simplification of form which particularly appeals to the modern eye, for the sculptor has been able to combine natural observation with abstractness in a very beautiful manner. The plastic form of the torso, the rounded arms, the egg shape of the head and the balls of hair are all highly abstract, and yet they give a clear idea of the natural forms which inspired them. Every detail comes to life, not just in the figure but in the falling cascades of the drapery, which make a wonderful pattern *(Plate 18).* Most moving of all is the face, which gives perfect expression to Buddhism, with its ideal of complete inner harmony. Nowhere else has this ideal found a purer or more beautiful embodiment. The eyes are almost shut, creating a feeling of dreaminess; the mouth is slightly parted with a gentle smile playing over the lips; the expression of the whole suggests a profound spiritual peace. No words can do justice to this face, which is one of the most beautiful and moving ever created, an achievement which is doubly remarkable when we remember that this image was made by an unknown craftsman only fifty years after this type of Buddhist carving had been introduced into Japan.

There are several other Buddhist images which have come down to us from the Asuka period. Among them the most famous, perhaps, is the "Yumedono Kannon" in the Yumedono, or Hall of Dreams, at Hōryū-ji. According to tradition, it was made for the great Buddhist prince, Shōtoku Taishi, for his private contemplation, but this is no longer believed to be true. Besides this there are the Four Guardian Kings, or Shitennō, which face the four directions on the altar of the Hōryū-ji Kondō, and the six standing *bosatsu* also at Hōryū-ji. Then there is an interesting group of bronze images called the forty-eight Buddhas, as well as the charming carvings of angels and phoenixes hanging from the canopy in the Kondō at Hōryū-ji.

BUDDHIST PAINTING OF THE ASUKA PERIOD

There can be little doubt that painting flourished along with architecture and sculpture during the Asuka period, but because of the fragile nature of the material, few examples have survived. In fact the paintings on the sides of the Tamamushi Shrine, formely on the altar in the Kondō at Hōryū-ji and now in the treasure house of this temple, are almost the only authentic Asuka paintings which have come down to us. This miniature shrine was called Tamamushi after the jewel insects whose irridescent wings were originally used to decorate the lovely honeysuckle-design metalwork which ornaments the shrine. The paintings themselves are of great importance historically and iconographically, as well as being of considerable artistic merit. Executed in a mixture of lacquer and a kind of oil paint called *mitsuda,* they are the earliest oil paintings in the world. It must be added that the Japanese did not develop this technique any further, although there are some isolated examples of oil painting in the Shōsō-in from the Nara period.

On the door of the little shrine are pictures of two Niō or, Guardian Kings, like those in the *chūmon* at Hōryū-ji. Derived originally from Hinduism, they were incorporated into the Buddhist pantheon as minor deities who protected the holy place against evil spirits. On the other sides of the shrine are paintings of bodhisattvas holding lotus flowers, figures which are done in a graceful, flowing style reminiscent of the Six Dynasties period paintings at the great cave temples at Tun Huang. On the back side is a mountain landscape with three pagodas, in which Buddhas are seated surrounded by *rakan,* or holy men, Buddhist angels, phoenixes, and the sun and the moon.

The high pedestal is decorated with four additional paintings, the loveliest of which is the one showing an episode from the previous incarnation of Buddha as Prince Siddharta *(Plate 19).* This story tells how the Blessed One, when wandering upon a mountainside, sees a starving tigress with her seven cubs. Moved by compassion, he immediately decides to give up his own life so that the tigress and her young can feed upon his body. The artist, who portrays the episode in simple and naive terms, represents three different phases of the story within the same painting. In the upper part the Buddha is seen disrobing himself; in the center he is throwing himself over the cliff; and at the bottom the tigress and her young are eating his body.

The style of the painting is extremely abstract, yet at the same time the sophisticated technique suggests that this is not a primitive type of painting evolved in Japan but an adaptation of the style of painting which flourished in China during the Six Dynasties period. The treatment of space is very two-dimensional, with the black lacquer used for the background. Against this

30

Plate 11. Aerial View of Hōryū-ji, Nara.
Asuka period.

Plate 12.

Kondō (Golden Hall), Hōryū-ji, Nara.

Asuka period.

Plate 13.

Five-Story Pagoda, Hōryū-ji, Nara.

Asuka period.

Plate 14. Cloister and Central Gate, Hōryū-ji, Nara.
Asuka period.

Hōryū-ji, Nara

Plate 15. Tori Bushi Trinity. Asuka period.

Plate 16.

Kudara Kannon.

Asuka period.

Hōryū-ji, Nara

Chūgū-ji Nunnery, Nara

Plate 17.

Miroku Bosatsu (detail). Asuka period.

Plate 18.

Miroku Bosatsu. Asuka period.

Chūgū-ji Nunnery, Nara

Plate 19. Jataka Scene, Tamamushi Shrine.

Asuka period.

Hōryū-ji, Nara

Plate 20. Gilded Bronze Banner. Asuka period.

the artist has painted in different colored lacquers, using red for the garments and some of the rocks, and green and yellow for the trees and bushes and also for other rocks and parts of the figures. The forms themselves are very stylized and the elongated bodies, which recall the slender and graceful figure of the "Kudara Kannon," reflect the style of the Sui dynasty of China. Even more abstract is the treatment of the mountainside, where rocks and rolling hills are reduced to an ornamental pattern that gives the design a striking sense of movement. A further element of movement is introduced by the descending vertical of the figure which leads the eye from the upper left to the lower right and thus, both in terms of the story as well as the design, unites the different parts of the picture. The empty space of the background is brought to life by the delicate patterns of the bamboo, as well as by the falling lotus flowers in the upper half and the hanging willow and small pines at the left. The total effect is both accomplished and charming, indicating what heights Buddhist painting had already achieved by the end of the Asuka period.

The Crafts of the Asuka Period

Although very few examples have been preserved, literary accounts leave little doubt that Japan of the sixth and seventh centuries was also productive in crafts. The Tamamushi Shrine shows the skill which had been developed in the art of lacquer and metalwork, and there certainly must have been many other works in these media which have perished during the intervening centuries. The most outstanding example of Asuka metalwork surviving today is the famous gilded bronze banner, or *ban,* which was used for ceremonial occasions at Hōryū-ji *(Plate 20)*. It consists of a square canopy, strings of gems, and metal banners, the main one of which is five meters long. The design on the canopy shows Apsarases, or music-making Buddhist angels, while the hanging sections portray bodhisattvas, Apsarases, and Buddhist reliquaries. The workmanship, which is both skillful and delicate, shows a style quite similar to that of the Tamamushi Shrine—in fact the vine motif in the border is almost identical in both. This motif is, interestingly enough, a very ancient one which comes from Korea and China and was originally derived from even more distant countries. The emphasis in the bronze banner is upon the flowing, rhythmical movement of draperies and flying figures, a movement which is reinforced by the use of incised lines. The draperies swirl in charming arabesques, and the figures, which are elongated like those in the sculptures and paintings of the period, have a freedom which makes them virtually float in the air. Often a body is reduced to a simple, curving form, but it is rendered so skillfully that it creates a fine suggestion of reality. There is a strong over-all pattern, also very beautiful, which is achieved by the contrast of the gilded bronze with the cut-out areas.

In the field of pottery, the output of the Asuka period was probably much less remarkable, if we can judge from the scanty remains. Apparently Sué ware similar to that of the grave-mound period continued to be made, the body dark grey and at times covered with a greenish glaze. The quality of this pottery was not very outstanding, and there is little evidence of any new or original developments.

If the pottery was inferior, textiles seem to have flourished. Some beautiful fragments of Asuka textiles have been preserved at Hōryū-ji which show considerable variety both in design and technique. The most remarkable is the banner which, according to literary accounts, Princess Tachibana and her court ladies embroidered in 622 in memory of Shōtoku Taishi. The subject portrayed is the rebirth of the Prince in paradise, and it was hoped that his chances for eternal bliss might be furthered by this act. Only parts of the banner remain, but the quality of the silk and the needlework is very fine. Temples, human beings, lotus flowers, phoenixes, a tortoise, and the moon with the hare in it are represented. The style is similar to that of other works of this period, showing the same kind of abstraction.

The Asuka period, which was the first great creative period of Buddhist art in Japan, was a most remarkable one, for even though relatively few monuments have survived, those that have are of the highest artistic quality. Although the inspiration for the art came from China by way of Korea, the Japanese must be given credit for the way in which they responded to this new culture. In spite of the relatively primitive art which they had previously produced, in little more than a generation they were able not only to master the foreign art but to equal it in quality and variety, an accomplishment which certainly shows their artistic genius. It might also be said that since

32

many of these art forms, although originating in China, have not been pre-served in China itself, the Japanese examples are unique not only for the study of Japanese art but for that of China and Korea as well. This is especially true of the temple buildings and the wood carvings, of which no equivalents have been found in China. The fact that so much has been preserved by the Japanese is in itself indicative of the artistic culture of Japan, where, throughout the ages, works of art have been held in the highest esteem.

3

The Art of the Nara Period

THE Nara period, especially the eighth century, was the golden age of Japanese Buddhist art. This epoch, which extends from the middle of the seventh to the end of the eighth century, is usually divided into two parts, the Early Nara period, from 646 to 710, which is also called Hakuhō after the reign of the Emperor Temmu, and the Nara period proper which lasted from 710, when the capital was established at Nara, to 794, when it was moved to Heian-Kyō, as the present-day Kyoto was called. (This latter part is also referred to as the Tempyō period after the reign of the Emperor Shōmu, 729 to 748, which was the most important of the entire period.)

To the Japanese of the time, the city of Nara must have seemed unbelievably splendid. It was modelled after the T'ang capital of Ch'ang-an, and like the Chinese city it abounded in temples and palaces and broad streets which were laid out in a grid pattern. The Nara age was completely dominated by Chinese thought and Chinese culture, and the Japanese, no longer content with visiting Korea, went to the Middle Kingdom itself, which, under the powerful T'ang dynasty (618–907), was experiencing one of the great epochs in its political as well as cultural history. Just as the Japanese of the Meiji period went abroad to study the West, so the Nara Japanese travelled to the Middle Kingdom to learn from China. Contemporary records tell of scholars, priests, artists, writers, statesmen, political philosophers, businessmen, and

35

technicians who went to study in China. Many stayed for years and others never returned, so great was the lure of this ancient civilization. It must be said that T'ang China was magnificent not only by the standards of the less sophisticated Japanese but by any other standards, for the Chinese at that time were perhaps the most civilized people in the world.

Far-reaching political and social reforms were undertaken in imitation of the T'ang society, reforms which have had a profound effect upon Japanese culture. For a study of the arts, however, the influence of Chinese thought and especially of Chinese art is far more important. Confucianism, with its ancestor worship and its emphasis upon obedience to the emperor, was very influential, and Buddhism, which practically became the official religion, almost completely absorbed Shintoism. The result was a form of Shinto known as Ryōbu-Shinto, according to which the national gods were nothing but manifestations of the Buddha, a doctrine proclaimed by the monk Gyōgi (670–749), who taught that the Buddha and the Sun Goddess were really the same.

In Buddhism itself a greater diversification took place. Among the numerous sects of the period, the most important were the so-called six sects of Nara. The oldest of these was the Hossō sect which had its center at Hōryū-ji (where it still continues today) and at Kōfuku-ji. It was first introduced to China from India by the famous pilgrim Hsüan Tsang, and its central doctrine was the belief that the only true reality was consciousness. The Ritsu sect stressed ritual rather than doctrine, and its most famous exponent was the Chinese monk Ganjin, who, after six attempts, had finally reached Japan in 753, and whose teachings were very successful. Another branch, in some ways the most influential of all, was the Kegon sect, which had its center at Tōdai-ji, also called the great Kegon temple. It was based on the Avatamsaka sutra which taught that the historical Buddha Shaka is only one manifestation of the cosmic and omnipresent Buddha Roshana, or Vairocana, as he is called in Sanskrit. In the teachings of this school, the supreme Buddha Roshana is said to dwell upon a giant lotus with a thousand petals, each representing a universe and each of these in turn having myriad worlds. This doctrine appealed greatly to the people of the Nara period, and it was especially popular at the court, where the emperor was seen as the earthly counterpart of the Buddha Roshana. How important these sects had become is best seen by the fact that at the end of the seventh century the number of temples had increased to over five hundred.

The growth of interest in Buddhist thought naturally led to an increase in the study of Chinese writing and literature. In fact one might say that the ability to read Chinese, which was, of course, absolutely essential for the study of Buddhist texts as well as the Confucian classics, became the mark of a cultured man. Various copies of the sacred writings were made, many of them beautifully written and illuminated. This was done not only for utilitarian purposes, but also because it was hoped that such pious acts would accumulate merit in heaven both for the copyist and for the person who commissioned him. A secular literature developed along with the sacred one, although its progress was less rapid. The first history of Japan, the *Kojiki,* or *Record of Ancient Matters,* was compiled in 712 following the Chinese custom of writing dynastic histories. Even more important was the first great book of poetry, the *Manyōshū,* or *Collection of a Myriad Leaves,* containing more than four thousand poems, almost all of which were written during the Nara period. To this day the collection, which is regarded as the finest in the Japanese language, is read widely by all classes of people. The writing used in it is a mixture of Chinese characters read in the Japanese way and an early form of *kana,* or Japanese writing, called *manyōgana.* Although influenced by Chinese poems, particularly the *Book of Poetry,* these lyrics show a marked Japanese quality both in their spirit and form.

As for the visual arts, the contact with T'ang China could not have been more fortunate, for this period was one of the most splendid in the history of Chinese art. The Emperor Shōmu, himself an ardent patron both of Buddhism and Buddhist art, gave further stimulus to the development. In 741 he issued an edict commanding that a temple and a seven-story pagoda be erected in each province as an indication that Buddhism was the dominant religion not only at the capital but in all parts of the realm. For each of these temples he had ten copies of the Lotus sutra, or Hokke-kyō, made, and we are told that the Emperor himself copied some of the texts in golden letters for enshrinement in the pagodas. The single most spectacular event of his reign was the construction of the temple of Tōdai-ji at Nara with the image of the Great Buddha Vairocana. Unfortunately neither has survived in its original form and the reconstructions which stand today are quite inferior. The hall was the largest wooden building in the world and the giant Buddha, or Daibutsu, was fifty-three feet high and contained over a million pounds of metal. The whole enterprise, which took several decades to complete, was the most ambitious the Japanese had undertaken. The temple complex was laid out on a grand scale, comprising, in addition to the huge Buddha hall, two large seven-story pagodas, splendid gates, halls of worship and study, as well as numerous other buildings for the use of the monks. The giant image of the cosmic Buddha was begun in 747 and, after many difficulties, completed in 749, and three years later the so-called "eye-opening ceremony" took place, an event recently commemorated at the twelve hundredth anniversary of this day. There was a splendid gathering of Buddhist notables from all over Japan as well as the rest of the Buddhist world, and it is reported that no less than ten thousand monks attended the ceremony, many of them from China and Korea and even India. The celebrations surpassed in splendor anything Japan had ever witnessed, and the Emperor and his court and even the humblest of citizens took part in the magnificent pageant.

The many opportunities offered to the artists and craftsmen, and the importations from T'ang China as well as the visits of Japanese artists to the Celestial Realm proved very stimulating to the arts. The result was such a flowering of creative activity, especially in the city of Nara, that this age is justly regarded as the greatest period of Japanese Buddhist art.

THE ARCHITECTURE OF THE NARA PERIOD

Of the many buildings erected during the Nara period, few remain today. At Tōdai-ji only the famous Imperial Repository, or Shōsō-in, which is built in a log-cabin style and located on the temple grounds behind the main hall, is of eighth-century origin. Even the lovely little Hokkedō, or Sanjūgatsudō, was added to at a later date (it stands on a hillside to the east of the Great Buddha Hall), so today the original design can only be studied from the back. None of the Nara buildings are left at the famous Hossō sect monastery of Kōfuku-ji, and at Yakushi-ji, another of the great temples of the period, the only structure of Nara date is one of the two pagodas. This is of particular interest not only for the intermediate stories which were added to the three main ones, but also because it is the only authentic building from the second half of the seventh century. The most important temple for the study of eighth-century architecture is Tōshōdai-ji, which at the time was part of Nara but today is outside of the city. At this temple, founded in 759 by the famous Chinese monk Ganjin, the great teacher of the Ritsu sect, both the *kondō* and the *kōdō* have been preserved, and although the pagoda and the surrounding cloister have perished, some of the smaller buildings such as the sutra repository and the treasure house have also survived.

In contrast to the Kondō at Hōryū-ji, the Tōshōdai-ji *kondō* is a one-story structure with a large, overhanging hip roof *(Plate 21)*. The building creates a solid, rather massive impression, in which the chief element is the strong horizontal of the roof. To counteract this, the architect has put a colonnade along the front wall, the repeated verticals of which balance the horizontal, both of the roof and of the stone platform on which the building stands. The construction itself is extremely simple, quite similar to that of the Asuka-period temples except that the bracketing system supporting the projecting roof is more complicated. Instead of the four entrances found at Hōryū-ji, this *kondō* has only two, one at the front and one at the back, and the small, rather dark interior is almost completely filled by the large dais upon which the sacred images stand. The roof itself is very interesting, with its wing-like ridge ends, or *shibi,* which are thought to represent dragon tails. They were supposed to prevent fires, for the dragon, like the fish (which at other places is used instead of the dragon) was regarded as an aquatic animal which could produce water and rain. Again, the building has been fitted very beautifuly into its natural setting, and the brown wood and white plaster and grey tiles create a harmonious whole. The simplicity of the design, with its emphasis upon geometric form, is very beautiful, especially from the side, where the parts of the wall create a strong abstract pattern.

The *kōdō,* or lecture hall, at Tōshōdai-ji is the oldest building of its type in Japan *(Plate 22)*. It is belived that originally it was a part of the Imperial Palace in Nara and that when Tōshōdai-ji was built, it was donated to the temple and moved to its present site. The purpose of the *kōdō* was to serve as a meeting place, where the faithful, especially the monks associated with the temple, might gather to hear the sacred doctrines expounded. Except for the fact that the length of the building was increased to accommodate the assembly, the design is very similar to that used for the *kondō*. The interior, too, is not very different—there is an altar with images and a chancel area with a surrounding aisle, but in addition to these a place for the congregation has been added. One other feature which distinguishes the design of the *kōdō* from that of the *kondō* is that the collonade has been omitted, and as a result the design is far less satisfactory.

The other group of outstanding Nara-period buildings is found at the Eastern Temple at Hōryū-ji. The most important of these is the famous Yumedono, or Hall of Dreams, erected at the site where Shōtoku Taishi had a chapel built for his private prayers and meditation *(Plate 23)*. It is the oldest octagonal building in Japan, and although small in size it is very beautiful in design. It stands on a stone platform with four staircases leading up to entrances which face the four directions. The design of the exterior walls consists of a series of differently shaped rectangles which form a beautiful, geometric pattern, and the tiled, gracefully curved roof is crowned with an elaborate jewel symbolizing the precious jewel of the Buddhist law.

The other eighth-century building at Hōryū-ji is the Dempōdō, or Preaching Hall, which was originally Lady Tachibana's residence but was donated to the temple in 739. It is used as a *kōdō,* but it is interesting today chiefly because it gives us some idea of what a residential structure of the period was like. It is extremely plain, with a gabled roof and small doors and windows. The proportions are far less beautiful than those in the temple buildings, and its rather ordinary appearance suggests that the greatest architectural efforts were spent not on the secular buildings but on the sacred ones.

Due to the perishable materials, very few of the Nara-period buildings have survived. (In addition to the ones discussed here, there are several others, most of them modest structures in relatively isolated places.) The few which have survived give a good idea of the architecture of the period, but in order to have an adequate conception of the capital, it should be remembered that there were not just a handful of temples but hundreds of them, many of which were quite large.

THE SCULPTURE OF THE NARA PERIOD

Of all the art forms created during the Nara period, sculpture is the most important, partly because of the wealth of examples which have survived and partly because, during the Nara period itself, it was probably considered the major form of artistic expression. Hundreds of images have come down to us, images representing a great variety of types as well as materials. While the Asuka artists worked in wood and bronze exclusively, the sculptors of the Nara period added lacquer and clay, which they preferred to the more traditional media. Their images reflect in style as well as iconography the taste of T'ang China, but many types which have not been preserved in China itself have survived in Japan, and none of the Chinese examples executed in materials other than stone are as large or important as the ones which have come down from the Nara period. The stylistic changes which took place during the years between the middle of the seventh and the end of the eighth century reflect similar changes in China. The works of the Early Nara period resemble those of the beginning of T'ang, showing a cultural lag of about one generation. The Nara period proper reflects the mature T'ang style of the second half of the seventh century, and at the end of the Nara period a decline had started similar to the decline which occurred in the middle T'ang works of the eighth century. During these years Chinese sculptors came to Japan and Japanese artists visited China, but there can be little doubt that practically all of the Nara works were executed by Japanese artists in Japan.

The outstanding works of the Early Nara period are ones made in bronze, showing that this medium continued to be highly favored during the second half of the seventh century. Perhaps the most beautiful is the miniature shrine of Lady Tachibana in the Kondō at Hōryū-ji, a work whose perfection shows that the Japanese had thoroughly mastered the technique of casting bronze (*Plate 24*). In fact the subtlety of the details is superior to that found in any surviving Chinese examples of this type. The image represents the Buddha Amida, the Buddha of Endless Light, who rules in the Western Paradise, a deity who became so popular in the Japanese Buddhism of this time that he tended to replace the historical Buddha himself. He is shown

41

seated on a large lotus flower, whose stem rises out of a pond, the surface of which is covered with a delicate, beautifully rendered pattern of lotus flowers. The legs of the Buddha are crossed in the yogi position and his body is erect with one hand lifted in the *vitarka* mudra, the gesture of preaching, and the other lowered with the palm out in the gesture of charity, or the *vara* mudra, which indicates that Amida, filled with love for all mankind, is preaching the gospel to the blessed who have entered paradise. He wears a monk's garment whose folds cover his entire body with a simple, linear pattern. His head is erect, the face utterly serene and the eyes closed to the outer world. On his forehead is the *urna,* or third eye, and on his head the *ushnisha,* both marks of his superhuman perception. His hair, which is cut short, is arranged in a series of spiralling curls, and behind his head is a large halo with a lotus in the center surrounded by intricate patterns with flames on top. The workmanship of the halo is very delicate, showing the care and love which went into the design of every detail of the image.

On either side of the Buddha are two bodhisattvas. The one at the left is Kannon Bosatsu, identified by the Amida in his headdress, while the one at his right is Seishi Bosatsu, who has a sacred vessel in his crown. Both are small compared to the Buddha, indicating their lesser importance, and like the other bodhisattvas we have considered, they wear the jewels and crown and skirt which are the symbol of an Indian prince. They stand on lotus pedestals, their faces calm and their hands raised in the *abhaya* and *vara* mudras, the gestures of fearlessness and charity. Behind the figures is a screen, which for sheer loveliness of design is perhaps the most remarkable part of the whole work. At the top are the seven Buddhas of the Past rendered in high relief with little canopies over their heads, while in the lower part the souls of the blessed are seated on lotus flowers. Particularly beautiful are the flowing lines of the scarfs and the gracefully curling leaves and stems of the lotus plants, and the masterful combination of these linear patterns with the rounded forms of the figures makes this work one of the finest pieces of Japanese sculpture.

The style of the group is typical of the Early Nara period. Compared to the works of the Asuka period, its treatments of the human form is both more plastic and sensuous, and in that way it reflects the new ideals of T'ang

42

China, which in turn were influenced by Indian ideals of beauty. In India, there was no conflict between spiritual and physical beauty, and the great Buddhist carvings of the Gupta period which indirectly inspired these Nara-period sculptures combined sensuousness with spirituality. This development is similar to the one which took place during the Renaissance, when the relative abstraction of the medieval figures of Christian art gave way to a more human and naturalistic representation. In each case, the new ideal no doubt reflected a change in the culture itself, for T'ang China as well as Nara Japan and Renaissance Europe were epochs of material splendor, during which the interests of people were centered more and more upon the things of this world. In all three cultures it was likewise a time when the arts flourished, especially in the fields of sculpture and painting, although unfortunately few of the paintings have survived in the Far East.

Of the large bronze images of the Nara period, the most impressive is the recently discovered head of Buddha Yakushi, the Buddha of Medicine, which, although found at Kōfuku-ji in 1937, is believed to have originally been the image in the *kōdō* of the Yama-dera *(Plate 25)*. The work is only a fragment and even the head is imperfectly preserved, but it is nevertheless one of the great pieces of Japanese sculpture. The strong, simple lines of the hair and of the eyebrows and eyes and nose and mouth are beautifully rendered, and the entire shape is both plastic and forceful. The head shows the realism of the Nara age, and yet it is a realism which never loses itself in naturalistic detail but is tempered with a strong feeling for abstract design. Like the art of Classical Greece or Renaissance Italy, the result is a work which might be called ideal naturalism, for the elements of physical beauty are combined with the spiritual ideals of Buddhism. In keeping with this, the artist has simplified the head, leaving away much of the detail in order to emphasize the underlying form which gives the whole an impressive strength and monumentality.

Of a somewhat later date is the fine "Yakushi Trinity" at Yakushi-ji, a temple near Nara which also houses the famous "Shō Kannon," another masterpiece of the Early Nara period. The trinity consists of the seated Yakushi, the Buddha of Healing, who is flanked by the two standing figures of Nikkō and Gakkō Bosatsu, the deities of sun and moon. According to

43

tradition, this group was made to help the Emperor Temmu's consort recover from an illness. It is said that the statues were completed and consecrated in 697, and that Yakushi-ji was erected to house them. However, the fact that the style of this giant bronze is much fuller and more sensuous then that of the other Early Nara images would suggest a later date, and it has been argued by some scholars that these statues were made in 718, when the monastery was moved to Nara from its previous location at Kidono. This latter theory does seem very plausible. Whatever the exact date of this trinity, it certainly reflects the mature T'ang style of the second half of the seventh century. There is a fullness which makes the forms seem to burst with life, and they are conceived with a wonderful sense of grandeur. In contrast to the miniature forms used in the Amida trinity of Lady Tachibana, these sculptures have a monumental scale which seems even larger against the background of the kondō in which they are located, for the relatively modest size of the building tends by contrast to exaggerate the already impressive dimensions of the image. Particularly beautiful is the throne upon which Yakushi is seated. It symbolized Mt. Meru, the world mountain, with four beasts representing the four directions and little earth demons, or yaksha, which were ultimately derived from similar Indian figures, portrayed as strange, exotic creatures.

The favorite medium during the Nara period was dry lacquer, a technique which originated in China and which became so popular that it almost completely replaced plain wood. One kind of dry-lacquer statue had a solid core, either of wood or of clay, but there was another kind, called hollow dry-lacquer, in which the core was removed and replaced by a wooden skeleton, the result being a much lighter work which could easily be carried around in processions or removed from the temples in case of fire. Just why this new medium proved so popular during the Nara period is not clear, but it may be that its more pliant nature was better suited to the naturalistic and dramatic effects which the Nara sculptors tried to achieve.

Among the earliest and finest of the hollow dry-lacquer statues are the "Hachibushu," or "Eight Guardian Devas," which are believed to have been made in 734. Now in the Nara Museum, they were originally the attendants of the central Shaka trinity at the Golden Hall at Kōfuku-ji. The loveliest

44

of them is the famous Ashura, a mythological Hindu demon king who, after his conversion, was supposed to have become one of the eight guardians of Buddha *(Plate 26)*. Being an Indian deity, he is represented in a style and with an iconography very different from that found in other Japanese Buddhist figures. The most noticeable change is the bright red color of his faces and arms and legs and the dark red of his hair. Equally foreign to the Japanese artistic tradition are his multiple arms and heads, which are also typically Indian and became increasingly common in the Japanese Buddhist art of this and subsequent periods. Generally speaking, the multiplication symbolized the supernatural power of the deity, but it was also supposed to represent the many different aspects of the god. In the Ashura image, for example, each face symbolizes a different quality, just as the various hands of the statue are held in different gestures.

The style of the "Ashura Deva" shows little of the characteristic fullness of other Nara-period works. This may be partially due to the medium, for hollow dry-lacquer has a tendency to shrink, but it certainly has some bearing upon the type of the deity portrayed. In any case the figure is very graceful, and although slender it is none the less plastic, with cylindrical forms used for the arms and legs and torso. The upper part of the body is bare except for a scarf and some jewels, and the lower part has a cloth skirt covered with an ornamental design known as the *hosoge* pattern. Most beautiful are the faces and the arms. In the front face there is a kind of childlike innocence as well as a feeling of complete calm and spiritural devotion, which is also mirrored in the front hands. They are held in the *anjali* mudra, the gesture of adoration, while the side faces and arms symbolize the fiercer and more dramatic aspects of the god, who in Hindu mythology was a warrior king of the demons. The graceful, dancelike movement of the arms with their elegant gestures is particularly fine, and the total effect of the work is one of contrast between quiet and movement.

It would not be possible even to mention all the lacquer images which have come down from the Nara period. There are, for example, seven other figures in the group containing the "Ashura Deva," and another similar group of the statues representing the Great Disciples of Shaka. Other famous lacquer statues of Nara date are the majestic eleven-headed Kannon at Shōrin-ji

45

at Nara, the Vairocana Buddha in the Golden Hall at Tōshōdai-ji, and the eight-armed Fukū Kensaku Kannon at the Hokkedō of Tōdai-ji. A work which is of special interest both historically and aesthetically is the seated figure of the great Chinese monk Ganjin, who has already been mentioned both as the founder of Tōshōdai-ji and the great master of the Ritsu sect (Plate 27). It was once believed that this statue was made of papier-maché, but recent repairs have shown that it is hollow dry-lacquer supported inside by a simple wooden frame. This work is particularly interesting as the oldest portrait statue in Japan, the ancestor of a type of portrait of the great Buddhist teachers which, especially during the Heian and the Kamakura periods, became very popular. The image, which is colored in pinks and reds and greens still visible today, is modelled simply and yet with great power. What is particularly moving about the figure is the feeling it creates of utmost spiritural concentration. The body and hands and face are all completely relaxed, showing that the energies of the monk are turned inward in spiritual contemplation. His eyes are closed not so much as a sign of meditation but because he had lost his sight while making the adventurous journey from China to Japan, an experience which had only intensified his religious ardor. All this is beautifully expressed, and what is remarkable about the image is the way it combines the realism of the period with its deep religious feeling.

The other medium developed during the Nara period was clay, a technique which had been widely used in India and Central Asia and China, whence it had no doubt been introduced to Japan. It too was very popular, though it was ordinarily used for the guardian figures rather than for the main deities. In order to strengthen the statues, a rough core of wood was usually used, which was covered with rice-straw rope to which the clay was applied. The results were very durable works, which have stood up over many centuries. Here again it is difficult to decide which of the numerous fine clay statues of the Nara period are the most outstanding, but as a group the various guardian figures of the eighth century are certainly the high point in the development of clay. These deities, too, were originally Hindu gods who were incorporated into the Buddhist pantheon and used to protect the temples from evil spirits. We had already encountered the Niō who guard the

46

Plate 21. *Kondō* (Golden Hall), Tōshōdai-ji, Nara.

Nara period.

Plate 22. Kōdō (Lecture Hall), Tōshōdai-ji, Nara.

Nara period.

Plate 23.   Yumedono, Hōryū-ji, Nara.

Nara period.

Hōryū-ji, Nara

Plate 24. Amida Trinity, Tachibana Shrine.

Nara period.

Plate 25. Head of Yakushi Buddha.

Nara Period.

Kōfuku-ji, Nara

Plate 26. Ashura Deva. Nara period.

Plate 27. Priest Ganjin. Nara period.

Hokkedō, Tōdai-ji, Nara

Plate 28. Shitsugongōjin. Nara period.

Plate 29. Head of Meikira Taishō. Nara period.

Hōryū-ji, Nara

Plate 30. Amida Trinity. Nara period.

Plate 31.

Amida Trinity (detail of Kannon).

Nara period.

Hōryū-ji, Nara

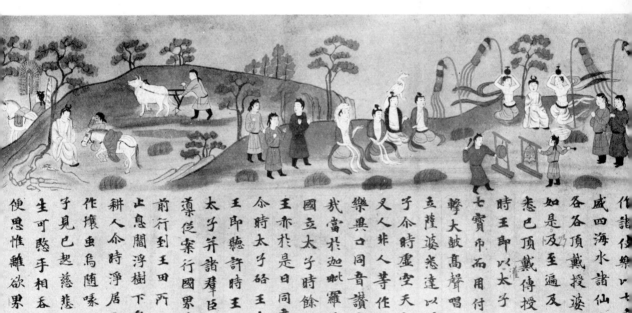

作諸伎樂以七寶器
盛四海水諸仙人衆
各各頂戴授婆羅門
如是反至遍及諸臣
悉已頂戴傳授與王
時王即以太子頂以
七寶帀而用付之又
擊大敏高聲唱言今
立薩婆卷達以為太
子尒時虛空天龍夜
樂興於口同音讚言善
我當於毗羅旃兜
國立太子時餘八國
王亦於是日同立太子
尒時太子碯王出遊
王即聽許時王即興
太子幷諸羣臣前後
藻従案行國界次復
前行到王田所即便
止息閻浮樹下看諸
耕人尒時淨居天化
作壤虫烏隨啄之太
子見已起慈悲心衆
生可愍手相吞食即
便思惟離欲果愛如

Coll. Jōbonrendai-ji, Nara.

Plate 32.   Kako-Genzai-Inga-kyō.   Nara period.

Plate 33.

Piece of Textile.

Nara period.

Coll. Shōsō-in, Tōdai-ji, Nara

Plate 34.

Gigaku Mask. Nara Period.

Tōdai-ji, Nara

entrance of the *chūmon* at Hōryū-ji, and there are similar figures at many other temple gates. They are also called Kongō Rikishi, or the strong men who hold the thunderbolt. Similar to them are the Shitennō, or Four Heavenly Kings, who are the guardians of the four directions. Another group of guardians are the Twelve Heavenly Generals, or Jūni Shinshō, who are usually grouped in a circle around the Buddha Yakushi. There are some individual guardian figures such as Vajrapani, the thunderbolt-holding deity, a Japanese version of the ancient Indian god Indra. All of these guardians were represented not only as fierce warriors but also as foreign barbarians, with large bulging eyes, wild expressions, and long curly hair, all of which were a sign of their Western origin.

Of these many statues, the most powerful is the one of Shūkongōjin, or Shitsukongōjin, which is located behind the main altar at Hokkedō *(Plate 28)*. It is a secret work only shown once a year, and as a result everything, including the original colors, is very well preserved. Although relatively small, the statue has an extraordinary power. The deity is shown in the very midst of action, his *kongō* raised aloft in one hand, while the other hand is clenched in a fist that makes the veins swell out in his arm. His face is contorted, his eyes glare, the muscles in his neck stand out—all these details, as well as the modelling of the armor, are rendered with the utmost force. The very position of the figure with one leg thrust out and the body bent at the hips is highly dramatic, and this feeling is heightened by the swinging lines of the scarf. There are many other guardian figures in China and Japan, but none equals this in power and intensity.

Another wonderful clay guardian figure is that of Meikira Taishō, one of the Twelve Heavenly Generals, at Shinyakushi-ji *(Plate 29)*. The body of this figure is not as dramatic as that of the Shitsukongōjin, but the face is perhaps even more expressive. He too is portrayed with his sword at the very moment when he cries out against his enemies. He wears the armor of the T'ang warrior, which adds to his fierce appearance, but what is most impressive is his head, especially his hair, which stands up in a wild, spiky pattern. Every detail of the face—the bulging eyes, the fierce frown, the lips drawn back to show the teeth and the tongue—reinforces the intensity of the figure. It is astonishing to think that the artists who made these

47

almost expressionist statues were the contemporaries of the ones who created the spiritual and serene figure of Ganjin, the gentle innocence of Ashura, the grandeur of the "Yakushi Trinity," and the elegant refinement of the Tachibana Shrine, but such was the creativity of this age that all these different types of expression could be handled with equal skill. The Nara period is usually regarded as the golden age of Japanese Buddhist sculpture and it may well be said that Japanese sculpture in general never reached this height again.

THE PAINTING OF THE NARA PERIOD

Although painting probably played a role equal to that of sculpture during the Nara period, few works have been preserved, and the most important of these, the famous wall paintings in the Kondō at Hōryū-ji, were damaged by fire in 1949, so today only discolored fragments remain. However, there are excellent color photographs and copies of the paintings, so it is possible to study them even now. Here again, there can be no doubt that these masterpieces, executed some time around the end of the seventh or the beginning of the eighth century, reflect the style which was current in T'ang China. This fact made these murals doubly important, for no such works had survived in China itself. Other important examples of T'ang painting as it was reflected in the art of the Nara period may be found in the Shōsō-in, where objects such as musical instruments, lacquer boxes, dishes, and screens are decorated with landscapes and figures and animals, indicating that secular painting was practiced alongside of religious painting, although the latter was no doubt the more important.

The most outstanding of these works were the magnificent wall paintings at Hōryū-ji which represented the four great Buddhas worshipped by the Hossō sect. Amida was portrayed on the west wall, Yakushi on the east, Shaka on the south, and Miroku on the north. In addition to these figures, there were eight bodhisattvas on the smaller walls, probably two corresponding to each of the Buddhas, and there were paintings of flying Apsarases and arhats below the head-beams of the outer sanctuary. These murals were all executed in a technique similar to that of fresco, although the paint was apparently applied to a smooth surface of white, dry pottery clay. The colors

48

used were red, yellow, brown, green, and blue, as well as some other pigments, but even before the fire, many of them had either darkened or been damaged so that the paintings were no longer clearly visible.

The best preserved was the Amida paradise scene. It showed the Buddha Amida in his Western Paradise, surrounded by attending bodhisattvas and the souls of the blessed who had entered his realm of endless bliss *(Plate 30)*. Dressed in a red monk's garment and seated in the yogi position on a huge lotus flower beneath a jeweled canopy, he is flanked by Kannon at his left and Seishi Bosatsu at his right. His hands are in *dharmacakra* mudra, the gesture of preaching; his face is serene; his head shows the marks of the Great Being, the *ushnisha,* the *urna,* and the large ears. The forms are full and sensuous like those of the T'ang period, and as in the great bronze images at Yakushi-ji, the artist has combined spiritual feeling with natural, sensuous beauty.

Loveliest of all are the figures of the two bodhisattvas, especially that of Kannon, the Bosatsu of Mercy, which is one of the masterpieces of Far Eastern painting *(Plate 31)*. The lower part had unfortunately been damaged, but the rest of the figure, which was quite well preserved, showed Nara painting at its best. The contours are delineated with a strong, yet flowing red line which is called iron-wire line because it is even in its thickness. Shading is employed to suggest the roundness of the body, but it is used only sparingly. Particularly beautiful are the curves of the eyebrows (which according to Indian iconography are supposed to have the shape of an Indian bow), the half-closed eyes and eyelids, the strongly modelled nose, and the full lips. Black, curly hair falls onto his shoulders, and the image of Amida in the richly jeweled crown indicates that he is the Lord of Compassion. This quality is symbolized by the willow branch, for according to legend, Kannon was filled with such love for all creatures that he could not bear even to kill insects, so he brushed them away with a fly whisk. The expression of the Kannon, as well as that of the other *bosatsu,* is one of deep spirituality and dreamy gentleness. Compared to the Buddhist paintings of India and Central Asia, from which the Hōryū-ji paintings were ultimately derived, these works seem much more linear. The style of the Indian ones is essentially plastic, and the Far Eastern artist, in keeping with his own time-honored

49

traditions, has made its abundant fullness both more linear and more abstract.

Closely related to the Hōryū-ji murals are the paintings which decorate the doors and the pedestal of the Tachibana Shrine. The pictures on the doors represent bodhisattvas and guardians done in line drawings which today are hardly distinguishable, while the paintings rendered in color on the base are fairly well preserved. They represent figures seated on lotus flowers and are believed to be the souls of those reborn in paradise. The style, which is free and graceful, is astonishingly close to that found at Ajanta in India, especially in the use of shading, which is closer to the Indian prototypes than to the Far Eastern tradition. At the same time, the thinner bodies and the long faces suggest a somewhat earlier date than the paintings on the walls of the Kondō, and it seems likely, therefore, that they date from the Early Nara period, while the wall paintings come from the Nara period proper.

In addition to these works there are at least two hanging scrolls, or kakemono, which are traditionally ascribed to the Nara period. One, which is at Yakushi-ji, is a charming representation of Kichijōten, the goddess of beauty and good fortune, done in delicate color on silk. In keeping with the T'ang ideal of feminine beauty, the goddess is shown with a full-moon-face and a plump, short body covered with an elegant, flowing garment. The rendition of the light, transparent gauze of her dress and the beauty of her face with its round, rosy cheeks, red lips, broad, black eyebrows, and narrow eyes is very characteristic of this type of beauty so prevalent during the Nara period. The colors are very subtle and, after all these centuries, astonishingly vivid. The other painting, executed on paper and showing Shōtoku Taishi with his sons, is primarily of interest as the earliest portrait of this great patron of Japanese Buddhism. The style of the painting is similar to that used for portrait painting in contemporary China, but the quality is less good. The line in particular is rather hard, and it is believed that it is not a Nara-period original but a later copy of such a work. Nevertheless it is of great interest, for it shows that portrait painting had already developed at this time.

There is one other painting which is of special importance from an artistic as well as an iconographical point of view. It is the famous Kako-Genzai-Inga-kyō, or the scroll illustrating the sutra of the Past and Present

50

Incarnations of Sakyamuni Buddha *(Plate 32)*. There were originally eight such rolls, fragments of which are now owned by Daigo-ji and Jōbonrendai-ji in Kyoto, the Tokyo University of Arts, and various private collections. All of them are remarkably well preserved, with colors as fresh as though they were painted yesterday. It is the first in the long line of *e-makimono,* or narrative handscrolls, which were so numerous during the Heian and Kamakura periods, but in contrast to the later ones, the text in this early example is written beneath the pictures so that the viewer can follow both at once as he unrolls the scroll. Although the effect is that of a continuous narrative, the paintings consist of a series of individual episodes separated by mountains or trees or some such similar device.

The style of the paintings, which is surprisingly conservative for a work of the eighth century, seems closer to that of the Six Dynasties period than to the prevailing T'ang style. However, since the calligraphy is definitely of the Nara type, it would suggest that the artist had copied the painting from an older model. As a result, these pictures have a kind of primitive naïveté which gives them a delightful freshness. This is especially true in the treatment of the landscape in which the setting is far too small in relationship to the human figures, a phenomenon also observed in Chinese painting of the Six Dynasties period. The drawing is very neat, the colors are clear and bright, the forms flat, and the result, though simple, is quite effective. The episodes vary greatly, giving a vivid picture of the life of the times, be it the court as portrayed in the scenes of Sakyamuni as Prince Siddharta, the travels as shown in the landscapes with people on horseback, or the supernatural scenes, such as the one showing the temptation of the Buddha, in which phantastic demons appear. However, despite the liveliness and charm of the pictures, they represent a kind of archaism rather than the characteristic style of the eighth century.

THE CRAFTS OF THE NARA PERIOD

Since the Nara period was not only an age of great religious faith but also one of material splendor, it was natural that the crafts should thrive along with architecture and sculpture and painting. Fortunately, thousands of authentic examples have been preserved in the Shōsō-in, the Imperial Repository at Tōdai-ji in Nara, which is a kind of museum of Nara-period crafts. Many of the objects were no doubt imported from China and reflect the culture of T'ang China, but others are certainly of Japanese origin, although closely following continental models. Since the Nara craftsmen were trying to copy the works imported from China, it is neither very important nor, in some cases, possible to determine which objects were actually made in China and which were made in Japan after Chinese models. What we can be certain of is that these were the actual utensils and materials used by the Emperor Shōmu, and dedicated by his widow at his death in 756 to the Buddha Vairocana. A detailed catalogue of the deposition was made at the time, and a record of the objects has been kept from that date to the present, a period of twelve hundred years.

Among the objects in the Shōsō-in, there are several which are particularly interesting because they preserve types of painting not found elsewhere in China or Japan. The most important of these is the six-panel screen showing Nara beauties standing under trees, a highly sophisticated work which is based on T'ang models (Color Plate 1). Delicate colors are applied to the faces and the hands and the lining of the sleeves, and bird feathers were originally stuck on the blossoms of the trees and the dresses. The paintings reflect the T'ang ideal of beauty which we have already seen in the picture of Kichijōten. The faces are full and round with heavily painted eyebrows, plump cheeks, slanted eyes, a small mouth with full red lips, a fleshy chin and neck, and an elaborate hair-do, and the clothes are loosely hanging, kimono-type garments, which with the original feather decorations must have been very striking. The style is quite free, with the brushwork creating a strong linear design, and the trees and rocks, which are shaded with different intensities of ink, show how skillful the artists were in handling the forms of nature. Far more modest in scale but of great value for the study of the development of Far Eastern landscape painting are the pictures of mountain landscapes on the biwa, a kind of musical instrument, and lacquer boxes, pictures that suggest beyond any doubt that the landscape was already fully developed during this period.

The most highly developed crafts are probably the textiles, and it has often been said that the textiles of the Nara period have never been surpassed in the entire history of Japan. A great variety of materials and designs were used, reflecting both the high level of the material civilization and the cosmopolitan character of the Nara court, for some of the designs were influenced by the art of such distant places as Sassanian Persia *(Plate 33)*. Among the typically Sassanian designs, the most characteristic is the so-called lion-hunt pattern in which four riders with bows and arrows on winged horses are arranged in a medallion around the tree of life. The circular border of the medallion has a pearl design, and the space between is decorated with patterns of the lotus and other flowers. There were beautiful silks and gauzes and dyed materials which show an amazing diversity of technique, the most important of which was batik, or wax-dye, stencil, and tie-dyeing, methods still used in Japan today. Embroidery was also very popular, especially for Buddhist banners, and there were splendid brocades. The Shōsō-in has many examples of the clothes of this period, things like garments and sashes and slippers which give a colorful view of the court dress of the time.

Next to the textiles, the lacquerwares are the most outstanding and here again a great variety of types have been preserved. Perhaps the most common are the boxes, of which there are a large number of all sizes and shapes with lacquer applied to wood, bamboo, cloth, or leather. Lacquer was also used for musical instruments, of which the Shōsō-in has several fine examples. The lacquer surface of these instruments is decorated with designs in gold and silver, oil color, and mother-of-pearl. The gold and silver was applied to lacquer in many different ways, as a sheet design, for example, or in a technique known as *maki-e,* in which the design is executed in gold and silver powder. This latter process is particularly effective and is still quite popular today. The designs on the lacquers are often very beautiful, both in their elegance and splendor. Some of the motifs consist of natural forms like flowers and birds and trees, others show human figures, many of them mythological or legendary, and still others portray imaginary animals like the phoenix and the dragon.

The art of pottery was considerably advanced, although it can not be compared with either the lacquers or textiles when it comes to variety of design or technical skill. The main new development, which also had been imported from T'ang China, was the use of colored glazes. There was the three-colored ware, in which the vessels were covered with green, yellow, and white glazes, and there were ceramics in which only one of these colors was used. The clay was rather rough and of a greyish color similar to that of the tiles, and the shapes, which are simple and strong, resemble those of T'ang China.

There are hundreds of metal objects preserved in the Shōsō-in, varying all the way from handsome bronze mirrors to such utilitarian objects as kitchen knives, spoons, and ploughs. All of these are naturally of great interest, but some of them are also rewarding from an artistic point of view. Among the most beautiful are the incised silver vessels, especially one with a hunting scene, a marvelous gilt silver platter with a reindeer pattern, and a gilt copper vase with charming designs of sages in a landscape with trees and flowers. No discussion of the metalwork of the Nara period would be complete without at least mentioning two additional works, namely, the lovely lantern with music-making bodhisattvas in the courtyard of Tōdai-ji, and the delightful flying angels in the *suien* section of the finial of the pagoda at Yakushi-ji.

Among the thousands of objects in the Shōsō-in—including such varied ones as writing paraphernalia, arms and armor, household furniture, ceremonial implements, varieties of incense and medicine, books and maps, sewing accessories, coins, pearls, and all sorts of utensils used during Buddhist services— there is a marvelous group of 164 masks. They were used in connection with an ancient dance known as Gigaku, which had originally been imported from China and was apparently performed outdoors in front of the temple. However, it is believed that the masks were used not so much for religious dances as for those performed for entertainment *(Plate 34)*. The characters portrayed are often fantastic beings with long grotesque noses and weird expressions, one of which, for example, represents Garuda, a strange bird-like creature of Indian mythology. They cover the entire head instead of just the face, and in contrast to the calm serenity shown in the Buddhist carvings they have an intensity of expression and an exaggerated emotion which is often highly dramatic. When one remembers that these relatively few objects which have survived are but a small fraction of the entire artistic output, one realizes how rich and varied the Nara period was in all fields of art.

Color Plate 1. Nara Beauty. Nara period.

4

The Art of
the Early Heian Period

THE period from 794 to 894 is often referred to as the Jōgan or Kōnin period, after two of the most illustrious reigns of the ninth century, but it is more properly called the Early Heian period, for at its beginning the capital was moved to the present-day Kyoto, than called Heian-Kyō, or the capital of peace and tranquility. Just what caused this move is not known, but since there had also been a plan to transfer the capital to Nagaoka, a place not far from Kyoto, there must have been powerful forces in favor of such a move. It is usually said that the emperor decided to leave in order to escape the political interference of the great monasteries of Nara, but since even larger and equally powerful monasteries were soon established near the new capital, this does not seem a sufficient reason for moving the entire court and erecting thousands of new buildings at a new place. Once Heian-Kyō had been established, it developed rapidly, and it has been estimated that it had no less than half a million inhabitants by the beginning of the ninth century. Like Nara, it was modeled after the Chinese capital of Ch'ang-an, with its broad streets intersecting at right angles as they still do in Kyoto today. It must have been a splendid city with its fine palaces, large official buildings, beautiful temples, spacious courtyards, and handsome gates, but unfortunately none of these have survived.

The main cultural influence continued to be that of T'ang China, only now it was the late T'ang culture of the end of the eighth century and the ninth century. The rise of esoteric Buddhist teachings, or, as the Japanese call them, the *mikkyō*, dominated the religious thought of the period, and it is for this reason that the first hundred years of Heian culture is usually treated separately, for it bears little relationship to the rest of the Heian period, during which completely different intellectual forces were at work.

The new teaching was brought to Japan in 806 by the great monk, scholar, and teacher Kūkai, better known by his canonical title of Kōbō Daishi. In Japan this doctrine was known as Shingon, or True Word, and as such it has continued to exert a profound influence upon Buddhist thinking. Like practically all Buddhist philosophy, it originated in India where these esoteric beliefs, which were extremely ancient, had been organized during the seventh century into a system contained in the tantras, or manuals prescribing proper uses and formulae, and introduced to China during the eighth century. The core of Shingon Buddhism is the belief in the essential identity of all things in the person of the Supreme Buddha, the Buddha Vairocana in Sanskrit, or Dainichi Nyorai, as he is called in Japanese. To the Shingon believer, there is no difference between the world of the senses and the world of ultimate reality, for both are manifestations of the same cosmic principle. The Western Paradise of Amida, which had played such a great role in earlier Buddhist sects and was to dominate completely the Buddhist thought of the Kamakura period, was not important in Shingon teachings, for there was no longer a difference between the world and paradise. There was also no real difference between the image and the deity, for in Shingon Buddhism the images are basically identical to the gods, and the gods themselves are merely representations of the various aspects of Dainichi. All thought, all words, and all objects are manifestations of the essential nature of the Supreme Buddha, so Shingon philosophy, the magic formula chanted by the priest, and the esoteric image are in reality the same thing.

In such a faith, the visual arts were naturally of the greatest importance, but it was a different kind of art from that which had flourished during the previous period. Unlike the Nara artists, the Shingon artists were not primarily concerned with the creation of sensuous beauty—in fact it might well be said that this was not a concern of theirs at all, for they were pre-occupied almost exclusively with the correct representations of the iconography which was prescribed in the sacred canons. Every measurement, every gesture of the image was now of the utmost importance, for it was a magic reproduction of the essential nature of the ultimate truth. Because of this, the paintings and sculptures of esoteric Buddhism are not only difficult to understand but are also lacking in appeal to the uninitiated. However, this was quite intentional, for most of the images were not shown to the public but were kept hidden in the inner sanctums of the temples. It might even be said that part of the attractiveness of Shingon lay precisely in its mysteriousness, for the court at Heian-Kyō was always ready to listen to something strange and new.

The deities themselves were also strange, their exoticness clearly revealing their Indian inspiration. There were, of course, still the Buddhas and bodhisattvas prevalent during the Nara period, but in addition to them, there were many new gods, among them the Five Great Kings, or Go Dai Myō-ō, who, as manifestations of Dainichi's wrath against evil, have fierce and terrifying forms. The most important of the Myō-ō, and for that matter, one of the main deities of the Shingon sect, is Fudō Myō-ō, originally a form of the Hindu god Shiva. He is usually shown surrounded by flames and carrying a sword and a rope with which he conquers the forces of evil, but weird and grotesque as his likeness often is, he is by no means the strangest of the various Indian gods who were introduced at this time. These super-natural beings, many of them with multiple heads and limbs, which were supposed to inspire awe and terror, are embodiments of the powers, activities, aspects, and mysteries of Dainichi, the Ultimate Buddha, of whom all reality is but an expression. The believer, if he transcends his self-centeredness, can achieve a mystical union with the Buddha and thus the microcosm of the self and the macrocosm of the universe become one.

THE ARCHITECTURE OF THE EARLY HEIAN PERIOD

The most important Buddhist temples of the ninth century were the Enryaku-ji of the Tendai sect, which was established in 788 by the famous teacher and monk Dengyō Daishi on Mt. Hiei near Kyoto, and the Kongōbu-ji on Mt. Kōya, which was founded in 816 by Kōbō Daishi as the headquarters of the Shingon sect, a position it continues to have today. None of the original buildings have survived, but Kōya-san is still a very active Buddhist center, containing no less than 120 temples. Although practically no ninth-century buildings exist today, there are records which indicate what they looked like and how they were laid out. Probably the most unique feature of the monasteries of the esoteric sects was the fact that they were located in isolated places on mountain tops and in the middle of forests. This was done to emphasize the ascetic, withdrawn character of Shingon in contrast to the old Nara sects, whose temples had been located in the capital. However, it must be said that their isolation in no way prevented them from playing a role in the world, and they soon had as much if not more influence at court than the old sects had had. In keeping with their location, the plan of these new monasteries was much more irregular, not following, as the earlier ones had, the strict symmetry of the traditional Chinese design. Furthermore, the temples themselves were often built into the mountainsides, and this in turn tended to modify the design of the buildings.

Of the monasteries in Kyoto itself, the most important was Kyōōgokoku-ji, more commonly referred to as Tō-ji, or Eastern Temple, which was established as the main Shingon temple of Heian-Kyō in 823 by Kōbō Daishi himself. Although here again none of the ninth-century structures still exist, the outlines of the original plan can still be seen. It is interesting to note that the design of this great complex, located on level ground in the capital itself, is essentially no different from the plan employed by the temples of Nara, suggesting that the changes evident at Kōya-san were dictated more by the terrain than by the nature of the Shingon teachings.

There was one respect in which the new faith did, especially during subsequent centuries, have a real effect upon the temple design, and that was in the arrangement of the interior. Two aspects in particular had a great influence upon Shingon art, namely, the more elaborate ritual objects used in connection with the service, and the different type of worship in which greater space for the attending monks was needed. Also the new emphasis upon the secrecy of certain aspects of the worship made necessary a change in the position of the chancel as well as the screening off of the *dōjō,* the innermost sanctum. During special ceremonies this area had to be screened off on all four sides because at these times the priest, making the proper gestures, using the sacred utensils, and chanting the magic formulas, confronts the supreme deity.

Of all the structures built during this period, only two are left today, the *kondō* and the pagoda at Murō-ji in Nara Prefecture *(Plate 35).* Already the location of the temple, surrounded by woodlands in a far-off mountain region, is characteristic of the Shingon places of worship. The buildings are very small, especially the pagoda, which is of quite modest dimensions, but they are both beautifully designed. The two most interesting features of the *kondō,* and ones which are indicative of the new trends in ninth-century architecture, are the kind of roof employed and the way in which the structure is built into the hillside. Prior to this, thatched roofs covered with *hinoki* (cypress) bark were only seen in Shinto shrines and the use of this material here indicates the influence which the native Japanese architectural tradition was beginning to exert upon Buddhist temples, just as Buddhist architecture was having a profound effect upon Shinto shrines. The roof is hipped with eaves which project well beyond the walls, and the exterior design is simple and strong, with the beams, the white stucco, the windows and doors forming a lovely abstract pattern. Another characteristic of the Murō-ji *kondō* is the pronounced projection of the veranda which is held up by a series of wooden supports that leave a space underneath due to the structure's having been built on slanting ground. This type of veranda was probably also found at Kōya-san and other mountain temples, and may be seen on a far larger scale at Kiyomizu-dera in Kyoto, which is believed to have been established during the Early Heian period. The pagoda, the other surviving ninth-century building, also uses *hinoki* bark for the roof, but in other respects, it is quite traditional.

Equally important in the architectural history of the ninth century were the secular buildings, especially the great palaces which were built in the new capital after the government had moved to Heian-Kyō in 794. Once again the fires which over the centuries have caused such havoc in Japan have

59

destroyed all of these structures, but the present buildings at the Imperial Palace in Kyoto, although actually built in the nineteenth century, reflect the design of the original palace even if the location and the arrangement have been changed. Among the buildings which stand today, the Shishin-den, or Ceremonial Hall, is by far the most impressive, especially since the Seiryōden was destroyed by fire in 1954 *(Plate 36)*.

It is interesting to see how this hall, in spite of the strong Chinese influence which made itself felt in the design of Heian-Kyō as a whole as well as in the palace itself, nevertheless shows marked Japanese characteristics. First of all, as at Murō-ji, the roof has the typically Japanese *hinoki* covering instead of the Chinese clay tiles. Secondly, the building is raised from the ground as Ise Shrine is, with space between the earth and the floor, and thirdly, the natural colors and plain surface of the materials is characteristic of the Japanese love for simplicity. The large gable ornamented with carved woodwork is also very much in the Japanese tradition, and so are the severity and beauty of the geometric design basic to the whole conception. The interior is also very plain, consisting of a single large chamber surrounded by screened verandas. Outside are balconies with wooden railings supported by a series of wooden pillars, a large staircase on the south side, and four smaller staircases at the four corners. The effect is dignified and beautiful in its harmony of shapes and colors, but when compared to the Imperial Palace in Peking or the great European palaces such as the one at Versailles, it does not seem very impressive, for the dimensions and the structural devices are basically very modest. It would seem as if the Japanese preference for the simple effect of relatively small wooden buildings was as characteristic of the secular buildings as it was of the temples and shrines.

THE SCULPTURE OF THE EARLY HEIAN PERIOD

The sculpture of the ninth century, when compared to that of the eighth century, shows a distinct decline both technically and artistically. Dry-lacquer and clay, which had been so popular during the Nara period, were no longer used, and bronze images became extremely rare, most of the carvings being made of plain wood. It is usually said that this development was caused by the remote location of so many of the chief esoteric monasteries, but this explanation is hardly convincing in view of the fact that the images in the Heian-Kyō temples were mostly of wood and that in China itself wooden sculpture, which was to predominate during the Sung period, became increasingly common during the T'ang dynasty. It seems more likely that it was the influence of the so-called sandalwood images which were imported from China and became very popular at this time. Another reason is that the numerous elaborate statues which the Shingon service required could be made much more cheaply and efficiently in wood, which abounded in Japan, than in bronze or lacquer. Clay had never been very suitable for monumental sculpture and it was quite inadequate for the intricate iconography which the esoteric doctrines often required.

Like the style of the architecture, the style of these carvings comes from the Nara period, but it shows certain distinct changes which in turn reflect similar changes that took place in China during the last part of the T'ang dynasty. The most important, perhaps, is a decrease in naturalism. The figures become heavier and even fuller, and the faces often have strange, rather mysterious expressions instead of the serenely harmonious smile which was so common in earlier works. The drapery is treated in a way which might well be described as manneristic, for it emphasizes the movement of line for its own sake rather than to reveal the body underneath. A good example of such a statue is the image of the seated Buddha Shaka in the Miroku-dō at Murō-ji, a large figure cut almost entirely from a single piece of wood, a method which was very common at this time (*Plate 37*). There is a massiveness and monumentality about the image which is typical of the period, and which in less successful works often degenerates into mere bulk. The forms are simple and imposing, and the drapery has the characteristic *hompa-shiki,* or rolling-waves style, which consists of a series of curving, ridge-like folds that were thought to resemble the waves of the ocean. The result is highly decorative, and the strong, sharply-cut, repeated curves have a life apart from their function as drapery. The face is full, resembling the faces of the late Nara period, and the expression, though somewhat austere, shows the inner harmony so characteristic of the Buddha. The iconography in this case is quite simple, with hands in the *abhaya* and *vara* mudras, legs crossed in the yoga position, body covered with the monk's garment, and

61

head showing the attributes of the Great Being, but the simplicity adds to the impressiveness of the statue.

Another fine Early Heian carving is the image of the eleven-headed Kannon, or "Jūichimen Kannon," in the *hondō* of the Hokke-ji at Nara *(Plate 38)*. He is shown with a bottle like that of the "Kudara Kannon," but now a long-stemmed lotus flower, a sign of purity, has been placed in the bottle. The eleven heads symbolize the fact that the Kannon looks in all directions and sees all things, and the other iconographic features such as the skirt, the scarfs, the jewels, and the crown are the traditional ones associated with a bodhisattva. The statue is carved almost entirely from a single block of what is believed to be white sandalwood, and both in this regard and in its more elaborate technique, the work shows the Chinese influence of the late T'ang period. In contrast to the Murō-ji figure, this one has a great many details, some of which detract from the effect as a whole. The more detailed treatment, combined with a certain elegance, especially in the fingers, would indicate that it comes from the latter part of the ninth century and already shows signs of the style which was to flourish during the Heian period. A sensuousness pervades the entire figure, particularly in the slight sway of the hips and the folds of flesh beneath the full chin. This suggests a strong Indian influence, and traditionally it has been said that it is actually an Indian work, but this, however, seems most unlikely. Another interesting thing about the statue is that the pupils of the eyes are inlaid with precious stones, and the eyelids and mouth are painted red, which, with the cluster of small heads in the crown, adds to the strange appearance of the figure. The drapery, which is cut in a hard, rather mannered way, creates a strong sense of movement, especially in the curves of the scarfs and their upturned ends, or *ten-e,* at either side of the body. The spiky strands of hair and the folds of the skirt add to the tension of the movement, which is counteracted by the heavy repose of the figure as a whole.

More characteristic of the iconography of Shingon Buddhism are the statues at Tō-ji, especially the carvings in the *kōdō* of the Five Kings, or Myō-ō, the fantastic Indian gods which were introduced to Japan by the esoteric sects. Their beauty as works of art may be questioned, but their expressive and awesome power is very striking. They are always shown in dramatic positions

Plate 35. *Kondō*, Murō-ji, Nara Prefecture.

Early Heian period.

Plate 36. Shishinden, Imperial Palace, Kyoto.
Style of Early Heian period.

Plate 37.

Shaka Buddha. Early Heian period.

Murō-ji, Nara

Plate 38. Eleven-Headed Kannon.

Early Heian period.

Hokke-ji, Nara

Plate 39.

Muryō Rikuku. Early Heian period.

*Hachiman-kō monasteries, Kōya-san, Wakayama Pre-
fecture*

Plate 40.

Kongo-kai *Mandara.* Early Heian period.

Tō-ji, Kyoto

with strange faces and fangs and long hair and, in many cases, with multiple arms and heads. It must be added that often more attention was paid to the correct iconography than to the sculpture as a work of art, and for this reason they can not be compared in aesthetic quality to the magnificent guardian kings of the Nara period. The same thing must also be said about the Early Heian figures of priests which lack the depth of feeling and the power of characterization which had marked the finest of Nara portraits such as the famous Ganjin figure. Besides the Buddhist sculpture, there are also some small Shinto images which date from the very end of the ninth century. They are located at Yakushi-ji and represent the god Hachiman as a Buddhist priest, the Empress Jingū as a goddess, and another female deity called Nakatsu-hime. These sculptures, though charming and colorful, lack the profound spiritual feeling which marks the best of the Buddhist works. The emergence of Shinto sculpture probably indicates that the Shintoists felt a need for images in order to compete with the Buddhists, but they were unable to develop this art, and it must be said that up to this very day Shintoism has made no significant contribution in either the field of painting or sculpture.

The Painting of the Early Heian Period

Few paintings from this period have survived, but those that have are of a quality which suggests that the output must have been remarkable. There are two reasons for this: first, the introduction of esoteric Buddhism with its need for many religious images; and second, the growth of secular painting under the influence of contemporary Chinese art. No examples of this latter type have been preserved, although something is known about the landscape and figure painters from literary accounts. As far as Buddhist painting is concerned, the situation is much better, for the Shingon Buddhists often did not permit their most sacred icons to be seen, and as a result some of the finest of the Early Heian paintings have been carefully guarded in their temples ever since the ninth century. Painting was no doubt the major artistic medium of the period, for the complex Shingon and Tendai doctrines could be expressed in pictorial terms more effectively than in those of any other medium. This in turn led to many new types of iconography, with the

63

result that the Early Heian period is one of the most interesting in the history of Japanese Buddhist art.

Among the new deities represented, the most important as well as one of the most curious is Fudō Myō-ō, the chief of the Go Dai Myō-ō, who protect the Buddhist world. The most celebrated portrayal of this god is the so-called "Yellow Fudō" of the Mii-dera on the southern shore of Lake Biwa, a temple which is one of the centers of the Tendai sect. Tradition has it that the scroll was painted at the request of Chisō Daishi, high priest of Enryaku-ji on Mt. Hiei, after he had had a vision of such a Fudō in 838. This particular representation is one of the secret images which is almost never shown, but there are many other versions of the deity. The one following this most closely both in style and iconography is the "Yellow Fudō" of Manju-in in Kyoto, and other famous representations are the "Red Fudō" of Kōya-san and the wonderful "Blue Fudō" at Shōren-in in Kyoto (*Color Plate 2*).

In all of these pictures, some dating from the Early Heian and some from the Heian period proper, when the same type of esoteric painting was continued, Fudō Myō-ō is shown as a strange and terrifying creature. He sits on a rock, his firm stance indicating that he is, as his name says, the Immovable. In his right hand he holds a sword, with which he conquers evil, and in his left he has a rope. Most striking, perhaps, is his face, with fangs at the corners of his mouth, fierce protruding eyes, thick scowling eyebrows, and stylized curls covering his head. His body, which is muscular and powerful, is ornamental with jewels, and in back there is always a flaming halo which, especially in the seated version at Shōren-in, is extremely dramatic, resembling a brilliantly colored, raging fire. In spite of his dreadful appearance, Fudō is ultimately a benevolent deity, one of the many manifestations of the great cosmic Buddha Vairocana. In works such as these, the strange doctrines of the *mikkyō,* or secret teachings, find profound and deeply moving expressions which reveal the spiritual power inherent in these Buddhist beliefs.

Another characteristic and outstanding work of the period is the picture of Muryō Rikiku owned by the Hachiman-kō monasteries in Wakayama Prefecture (*Plate 39*). This god is one of the Go Dai Rikiku, the Five Awesome

Divinities, or literally, the Five Great Ones with the Powerful Roar. He is shown performing a kind of ecstatic dance, one arm raised high with the vajra, or *kongō,* a thunderbolt indicative of power and energy, and the other lowered with the fingers making a magic sign. Like Fudō, his wrath is directed against the evil forces which might harm the Buddhist world. His face is wonderfully expressive, with a third eye in addition to the two enormous ones which stare with fierce intensity, and the dramatic movement of his body is heightened by the swirling pattern of the drapery and the colorful flames which surround the entire figure. The composition is baroque in the best sense of the word, for it shows the same combination of drama and dynamic energy on the one hand, and spiritual ecstasy on the other, which may be found in the art of the counterreformation.

The most characteristic as well as the most unique manifestation of esoteric Buddhism was the *mandara*'s, or magic diagrams of the Buddha world. The literal meaning of *mandara* is platform, but in this connection it had a meaning far more comprehensive than that of the platform upon which the sacred Buddhist images were placed. The *mandara* of the Shingon sect of the Early Heian period is no less than a visual representation of the most profound esoteric teaching. Mysteries which words cannot express are revealed in visual form and these *mandara*'s, as well as the sculptures and the other painted icons, are absolutely essential for the rituals of the *mikkyō* service.

There are two main cycles in the *mandara*'s employed by the Shingon Buddhists, one called Kongō-kai, the diamond or indestructible cycle, and the other the Taizō-kai, or the womb cycle. The first is a representation of the spiritual essence underlying all reality, and the second shows the assemblage of deities symbolising the material world. However, since both these worlds, the world of ultimate reality and the world of phenomena, are nothing but manifestations of Dainichi, the Great Illuminator, this Buddha is always placed at the focal point of the *mandara*'s. Grouped around him is the assemblage of other Buddhas, bodhisattvas, devas, rajas, demons, and spirits representing all the many manifestations of the cosmic Buddha Vairocana, who is the source and essence of all being.

The oldest of the surviving *mandara*'s are the ones at Jingo-ji in Kyoto and Kojima-dera in Nara Prefecture. Both of these works, which are painted in gold and silver on a purple ground, are of great beauty. However, the set of diamond-and-womb-cycle *mandara*'s in the great Shingon temple of Tō-ji in Kyoto represents the developed form of the *mandara* which is still used in Shingon worship today *(Plate 40)*. It is believed that these paintings, which were transferred to Tō-ji in 1176, date from the end of the ninth century and that they were originally kept in the Shingon-in which stood in the palace grounds and served as a court chapel. Although the detail lacks the subtlety and artistic refinement of the two older works, this set shows the elaborate geometrical symbolism and the strong and brilliant colors which are typical of Japanese *mandara*'s. The tendency towards formalization, which was one of the main trends in Early Heian art, finds its purest expression in these paintings, where the spiritual content is rendered in completely schematic terms.

In the diamond cycle, the surface of the *mandara* is divided into nine squares arranged in three rows, and each of the squares but one has a circle drawn inside of it. Within each of the circles in the two lower rows, there are five medium-sized circles and four smaller ones containing images and Buddhist symbols. In the center of the upper row is the large image of Dainichi Buddha, and the square to the right contains nine circles in three rows, while the one to the left has a large circle with five circles containing Buddhist figures and four smaller circles containing Buddhist emblems. The diagram as a whole represents the spiritual, indestructible aspect of the universe, while the nine squares represent the center and the eight petals of the lotus, which is the heart of the material world. The large figure of Dainichi is the focal point of the entire cycle, for in the person of the Great Illuminator the ultimate unity of the cosmic and the individual mind is contained. Vairocana sits alone on a lotus throne in an attitude of lofty composure, his hands in the *bodhasri* mudra, the sign of absolute knowledge, which symbolizes the union of the spiritual world with the material world. His head is surrounded by a brilliant halo and his entire figure is enclosed in a circle of pure white. By contemplating this magic diagram, and by identifying himself with the person of the deity, the Shingon Buddhist hoped to achieve inner harmony through union with the very essence of reality.

In addition to these Buddhist works, there was also secular painting.

Literary accounts tell of two great masters of landscape and figure painting, Kudara no Kawanari and Kose no Kanaoka, men of noble birth who were scholars as well as artists. None of their works have survived, but it is believed that they must have reflected the style of the late T'ang period, although the Chinese equivalents are also unknown. The only portraits which give us some idea of this type of painting are the two portraits of Shingon priests at Tō-ji, which were painted in 821 to complete a set of seven pictures of Shingon patriarchs which Kōbō Daishi had brought back from China. The faces express a religious devotion, and the line and the color are very delicate, but there is so little individuality of style that the works appear to be nothing more than reflections of the Chinese pictures. It is possible that there were portraits which were more typically Japanese, for when as few works remain as is the case in these early centuries of Japanese painting, those which by chance have survived may give a very distorted view of the art of the time.

The Crafts of the Early Heian Period

Almost none of the decorative arts of the ninth century have been preserved, but it is believed that the technique and style of the Nara period were continued without any great change. Undoubtedly the elaborate ritual of the esoteric sects required many craft objects, but none has survived except for a lacquer box used for storing priestly robes, which is now in the Nezu Museum and is believed to have come from the ninth century. Both its technique and design—lovely flowers and fantastic, bird-like angels—reflect the T'ang style, suggesting that the Chinese influence continued to be predominant during the ninth century. In ceramics the only important innovation was the introduction of new glazing methods from China which resulted in the development of celadon. No textiles have been preserved, but it is believed that they too continued in the Nara style.

Although the art of the Early Heian period was almost wholly dominated by the rise of the esoteric sects, landscape and portrait painting apparently were also developed, and painting in general seems to have been the major artistic medium. Sculpture and the crafts evidently suffered a decline, at least when compared to the magnificent Nara achievements, and though our

knowledge of Early Heian architecture is too limited to draw any valid con-
clusions, what has survived would indicate that here too the splendor of the
Nara age was not equaled.

5

The Art of the Heian Period

THE year 898, when the Japanese government decided to send no more embassies to the T'ang court, is usually considered the beginning of the Heian period proper, an era which lasted until 1185, when the capital was moved to Kamakura. This epoch extending over three centuries is one of the most important in the cultural history of Japan, for it was at this time that a purely Japanese art and literature was developed. It was also during the last part of the Heian period that the wars between the Minamoto and Taira clans were fought, wars which became a major subject in the literature of the Japanese theatre. However, the dominant clan of these years was the Fujiwara family, and for this reason the Heian period is also called the Fujiwara period. In fact the supremacy of the Fujiwara was so great that they were more powerful than the emperors themselves, and members of their family served as prime ministers, and daughters were married to the emperors. They ruled by their wealth and political influence rather than by force of arms and it was under their patronage that a refined and sophisticated aesthetic culture flourished at the capital. However, by the end of the eleventh century their power had waned and the latter part of the period was filled with constant wars, during which first the Taira, or Heike clan, and then the Minamoto, or Genji clan, were victorious.

The fullest and most brilliant picture of the Heian period is the one given

69

in Lady Murasaki Shikibu's famous novel, *Genji Monogatari,* which was written around the year 1000. In all of world literature there is probably no other work by a woman which is the equal of this, and few novels of any age are more remarkable. Fortunately, the translation by Arther Waley, a creative effort in its own right which some critics have even considered superior to the original, makes this masterpiece accessible to the Western reader. It is almost unbelievable that this work, with its subtle psychological observations and its skillful technique, should have been written nearly a thousand years ago, at a time when Europe was still rather crude and unsophisticated. It reveals a society almost decadent in its exquisite cultivation, a society in which the ability to write beautiful calligraphy and to compose poems, many of them on the spur of the moment, was more highly valued than the virtues of the warrior. Almost as important was the art of blending perfumes, and serious attention was given to such subtle points as the apt poetic allusion and the color of the paper to be used in writing notes. Another literary masterpiece of about the same date is the *Pillow Book,* or *Makura-no-Sōshi,* by Sei Shōnagon, which is a journal of court life. As in the *Genji Monogatari,* the impression given is that of a cultured and sophisticated but at the same time narrow society wholly preoccupied with an aestheticism in which good taste and artistic sensitivity were regarded as the ultimate values.

These works were both composed by women and written in *hiragana,* the native Japanese syllabary, rather than in the traditional Chinese characters. Both these facts are indicative of the period, for the one shows the high degree of culture which the court ladies possessed, and the other shows the growth of a native Japanese culture during these years when intercourse with China had been broken off. The relationship between the two languages in Japan of the Heian period might well be compared to that between Latin and the vernacular tongues in medieval Europe, when the clergy used the foreign language, while the literary genius expressed itself in the native idiom. In Japan, men usually wrote in a rather old-fashioned, artificial Chinese, and as a result their works have none of the vitality of those of their female contemporaries. The introduction of *hiragana,* a system of using abbreviated Chinese characters, each one of which represents a single Japanese sound, is usually credited to the great ninth-century priest, Kōbō Daishi, which is quite possible, since it originated during the Early Heian period. Its use encouraged the growth of a native literature more than did the more traditional Chinese one, and it also led to some of the most beautiful calligraphy the Japanese have ever produced.

In keeping with the new temper of the age, Buddhism underwent marked changes. The old Nara sects no longer had much vitality, and the esoteric sects had lost a good deal of their attraction, since their austere and strange doctrines did not correspond to the mood of the age. Instead, the worship of Amida, the Buddha of Boundless Light, became very popular. His cult, known as Jōdo, or Pure Land, Buddhism had first been introduced during the Nara period, but it found its chief exponent in the priest Genshin (942–1017), a great teacher and scholar who is best known for his popular religious tract, *Ōjo Yōshu,* or the *Essentials of Salvation.* The emphasis in his teaching is wholly upon faith in Amida rather than upon moral deeds or philosophical meditation. It is a simple salvation religion in which the mere chanting in the hour of death of the magic formula "Namu Amida Butsu" (Homage to Amida Buddha) is sufficient to save one's soul. In his writings the joys of paradise are glowingly portrayed, while the terrors of hell are depicted in the most horrible terms. This simple and emotional kind of doctrine suited the unreflecting spirit of the age, and it has remained popular up to the very present.

Another characteristic expression of the Heian period is the court music, Gagaku, originally introduced from China, and the accompanying dance, Bugaku, both of which were sacred arts performed only on very special occasions for the benefit of the aristocracy and the Shinto priests. Gagaku is a very refined music, and though its simplicity makes it rather monotonous, it is at the same time strangely moving. The dance is solemn and dignified, and the elegant costumes and the expressive and colorful masks worn by the chief performers are of great beauty. Today, Gagaku and Bugaku are still performed at the Imperial Palace and at the great Shinto shrines, another indication of the remarkable continuity of Japanese culture.

This sensitive and elegant civilization was wholly a product of cultured Kyoto society which, because of its wealth and birth, enjoyed all the pleasures, while by and large the provinces and the common people lived in poverty.

71

And while the Heian aristocracy spent its time writing charming poems and gazing at the moon, the provincial lords were busy amassing the military power which eventually led to the destruction of Heian society.

THE PAINTING OF THE HEIAN PERIOD

During the Heian period proper, painting—and not just Buddhist painting but secular painting as well—was without question preeminent among the visual arts. The most important development in this field was the rise of a school known as Yamato-e, or Japanese painting, in contrast to Kara-e, or Chinese-style painting, which continued to be practiced at the same time. The Yamato-e, which was typically Japanese in subject matter as well as style, broke completly from the Chinese-inspired painting, which had been popular during previous periods. It favored the narrative scroll, or *e-maki-mono,* and while this, of course, was also borrowed from T'ang China, the Japanese adapted it to their own use.

Just when this new school originated is not known, for only a very few examples of this type of painting have come down from the Heian period. However, since the first mention of Yamato-e is found in a manuscript of 999 and the earliest examples which can be attributed to it date from the eleventh century, it seems likely that the birth of this school, which was to flourish during the later part of the Heian and the following Kamakura period, took place during the eleventh century. The earliest existing work to show elements of the Yamato-e style, although still in a formative stage, is the series of paintings called "Shōtoku Taishi Eden," which represent scenes from the life of Shōtoku Taishi. Originally located on the walls of the Edono, or Picture Hall, at Hōryū-ji, they have been transferred to five two-fold screens which are now preserved in the Imperial Collection. According to the Hōryū-ji records, they were painted in 1069. In its emphasis upon a decorative style and a narrative subject matter taken from Japanese life, this work is already characteristic of Yamato-e. Even in such typical stylistic traits as the bird's eye perspective and the single-stroke technique for the portrayal of the nose and eyes, it has a marked similarity to the twelfth-century scrolls, but at the same time the rather awkward treatment of the figures and the space suggests that the new style had not yet been fully developed. Two other works attributed to the eleventh century are the land-scape screen, called *sensui byōbu,* at Tō-ji in Kyoto, and the wall paintings at the Hōōdō at Uji, which were painted between 1054 and 1056. Both of them combine a distinctly Japanese-style landscape with features which are closer to the Chinese tradition, thus reaffirming the view that the eleventh century was the formative period of the purely Japanese-style painting.

Of all the mature Yamato-e scrolls, by far the finest as well as the most characteristic is the *Genji Monogatari e-makimono* which is traditionally ascribed to Fujiwara no Takayoshi, an artist who lived during the first half of the twelfth century. Although the attribution is doubtful, the painting, judging from its style, is certainly a work of that period. The author of the *Genji Monogatari* is the greatest literary figure of the Heian period and we are fortunate in having her work illustrated by an artist who is one of the great painters of the age. (The very fact that a major artist should have been chosen for such an undertaking is indicative of the importance which secular subjects had come to have.) Although some scholars think that originally there may have been fifty-four rolls, one for each chapter of the novel, today there are only four, three of them in the Tokugawa Museum in Nagoya, and one in the Masuda Collection in Odawara. The individual scenes are painted as separate pictures divided from one another by the text, which gives pertinent selections from the novel. The surviving pictures, fifteen of which are in the Tokugawa Collection and four in the Masuda Collection, are no longer in scroll form but have been cut up and separately mounted, and, although some of them have been damaged, the preservation of the paintings is remarkably good considering that they are almost a thousand years old. The writing is of great artistic beauty, both in the quality of the calligraphy and in the delicately tinted paper on which it is written, and the exquisite refinement of the work as a whole suggests that it must have been the culmination of a long series of such scrolls.

The style of the work is a decorative and highly abstract one, in which the narrative element, although always present, is subordinate to the formal design, and the result is a typically Japanese kind of painting which has no equivalent in China *(Plate 41)*. The emphasis is upon the colorful forms, which are simplified and flattened in order to create on ornamental pattern.

73

Each shape is clearly delineated and often silhouetted against a background of a different color, so there are none of the soft transitions so characteristic of Chinese-style painting. The colors themselves are brilliant yet subtle, with silver, olive grey, and brown dominating in the background, while brilliant green, bright blue, dark red, and orange, as well as black and white, are frequently used in the figures. There is little emphasis on shading or plastic form, and the figures are organized in space through the use of parallel lines, which are especially marked in the drawing of the buildings. This type of perspective is characteristic of Yamato-e, with the scenes viewed from above and the roofs of the houses removed, so that one sees the interiors, a technique known as *fukinuki yatai*. Still another device which is considered typical for Yamato-e is the way in which the eye and nose are painted in an abstract shorthand style consisting of a straight line for the eye and a hooked line for the nose, a manner known as *hikime kagibana*. The result of this abstraction is that the artist never loses himself in illustrative detail, as is so frequently the case in Kamakura painting, but renders the essentials of the scenes with the greatest economy and the maximum emphasis upon the beauty of the formal design.

These paintings, although lovely in themselves, are conceived of as illustrations for a book, and there is a direct connection between the pictures and the selections from the novel which accompany each scene. The amorous adventures of Prince Genji, the secluded life of the court ladies, the elegance of the aristocratic world of the period are all mirrored in the pictures of these scrolls. The spirit in which they are rendered is very close to that which animates Lady Murasaki's novel, and there is the same languid yet enchanting beauty, the same sensitivity, the same melancholy, the same decadent yet exquisite sentiment. As in the novel, the paintings create a world in which people are continually engaged in playing sad music, reading love letters, or gazing at beautiful women through the openings in the screens which hide them. Even the scenes of passion or sorrow, like the death of Kashiwagi, are rendered without any strong emotion, and the movement and the colors of the pictures create the same subdued sentiment which pervades the atmosphere of the story. The Heian beauties are charmingly represented with their twelve layers of kimono, and their white faces,

Itsukushima Shrine, Miyajima

Color Plate 2. Heike-no-kyō (section of scroll). Heian period.

and their black hair flowing in a long stream down their back, and the men, too, are portrayed in a delicate, almost womanly manner, for the ideal of the time was an effeminate one, in which elegant bearing and manners were more important than masculine virtues. There are beautiful palace interiors with screens showing elaborate landscape paintings both in the Chinese and the Japanese manner, and there are delicate depictions of such characteristically Japanese plants as the plum blossoms and the various kinds of autumn grasses.

The style of the Genji paintings is reflected in two similar yet somewhat later scrolls which probably date from the thirteenth century, the *Nezame Monogatari e-makimono* in the collection of the Yamato Bunka-kan in Osaka, and the scrolls illustrating the diaries of Lady Murasaki, the so-called *Murasaki Shikibu Nikki,* which is now scattered over several private collections. Other works dating from the twelfth century which are similar to the Genji illustrations but very different in their subject matter are the Buddhist scrolls at the Itsukushima Shrine at Miyajima, which are better known as the Heike-no-kyō because they were donated to the shrine by the Heike, or Taira family. They illustrate the Lotus sutra, or Hokke-kyō, yet the pictures are by no means all related to the text. At the beginning of each of the thirty-two rolls there is a painting in pure Yamato-e style, often showing purely secular subjects, such as elegant court ladies or charming Japanese landscapes *(Color Plate 2)*. The designs are even more abstract than those of the Genji scroll, and the narrative element is completely subordinate to the decorative one. Gold and silver foil are lavishly used, and the text is written in gold and red, as well as black ink. The result is a work of the utmost elegance, mirroring the worldly spirit of the age.

The set of fans in the collection of Shitennō-ji in Osaka shows the Lotus sutra written on paper which is decorated with pictures of scenes taken from the life of the aristocracy and the common people *(Plate 42)*. Here there is no connection whatsoever between the illustration and the text, showing that even when copying sacred writings, the men of the time were more interested in the portrayal of secular life than in the contemplation of religious truths. The text is written right over the illustrations, which, to say the least, interferes with the enjoyment of the pictures, and these in turn

75

contribute little to the understanding of the texts. However, it was apparently the custom to copy sacred texts on special paper which often had splendid decorative designs, and in some cases series of pictures which were either printed or painted on the paper. The style of the Shitennō-ji set is typical of the twelfth century, although it is somewhat cruder than that found in the other paintings of the period. This gives them a simple strength, which results in a very vivid and direct portrayal of the life of the time, and they are thus of particular interest both as works of art and as documents of the period. Here again the style is typically Japanese, with its emphasis upon the narrative and the decorative, a combination which prevailed in all the most characteristically Japanese schools of painting, whether it be the Yamato-e, the Momoyama screens, the paintings of the Sōtatsu-Kōrin school, or the *ukiyo-e* woodblock prints.

Although the few works mentioned here are the only surviving examples of this kind of painting from the Heian period, there can be no doubt that this colorful, decorative style was very popular, especially during the twelfth century, and that many such scrolls must have been painted. However, even these few works give a good idea of the style during the eleven hundreds, for the Genji scroll came from the beginning of the twelfth century, the Heike-no-kyō from the middle, and the Shitennō-ji fans from the end.

In contrast to this colorful manner, the twelfth-century "Shigisan Engi" scroll represents a style of Yamato-e which depends almost wholly on line, with only slight additions of color *(Plate 43)*. This scroll, which portrays the history of Mt. Shigi, consists of three rolls which are kept at Chōgosonshi-ji in Nara Prefecture. The story represented is that of the famous monk Myōren who lived on Mt. Shigi and is said to have performed numerous miracles, the most celebrated of which is the miracle of the flying storehouse illustrated in the first roll. Briefly summarized, the story is about how, when a certain rich man refused to put food in the begging bowl of the monk, the bowl miraculously returned to Mt. Shigi carrying with it the entire store-house with many bales of rice, much to the horror of the rich man and his household, who tried frantically to follow their property. This kind of story dealing with the founding of a famous temple, or a miraculous event as-sociated with it, is very typical of Yamato-e painting, and often such scrolls form valuable pictorial records of the history as well as the former appearance of these sanctuaries.

The episode of the flying storehouse lends itself readily to a lively and dramatic rendition, and the artist has seized this opportunity in a very skillful manner. An expressive and dynamic line of varying degrees of thickness is employed, and the sense of dramatic movement is increased by having the episodes follow one other continuously, instead of being interrupted by the text as they were in the Genji scroll. Whereas the Genji scenes were decorative and quiet, these are animated and purely illustrative. The intense facial expressions often border upon caricature, so strongly has the artist stressed the emotional content of the scenes. Another aspect which differs greatly from the Genji scroll is the emphasis upon the landscape, which is remarkable not only for the skill with which it is handled but for its use of naturalistic detail.

Another painting which is usually assigned to the twelfth century and attributed to the priest Toba Sōjō is the animal caricature scroll which is owned by Kōzan-ji near Kyoto (Plate 44). There are four rolls altogether, but since the last two are of inferior quality, it is believed that they were added during the Kamakura period. The first two contain animal caricatures, whereas the third and fourth have comic representations of people. The exact meaning of these pictures is not known, but since there is a scene with a frog seated on a throne in the position of a Buddha, and others with hares chanting sutras and animals parading in priestly robes, it is said that they represent the folly and corruption of the Heian-period clergy.

The style of the paintings is superb, with an inspired line used very effectively against white paper. The result is a simple, expressive type of painting, which for sheer fluency of brush has few equals in the world. Certainly this skillful use of line must have been the result of a gradual evolution, and it has been suggested that the use of monochrome model books of Buddhist icons by the priests of the period may have been the source of this development. A tradition of vigorous ink-painting had existed in China for many centuries, and this type of painting had been introduced to Japan as early as the Nara period. In the animal scroll, instead of color, there is a delicate variation of ink tones and occasionally certain areas are blacked in or shaded.

77

The line itself ranges all the way from strong black strokes to fine, sketchy ones, and plastic form is suggested both by the different ink tones and by the variations in the line. With the very minimum of strokes the artist is able to convey an animated and surprisingly natural rendition of the animal world. Monkeys, frogs, foxes are all portrayed in a masterly fashion, and the various activities, such as the scene where the hare and the monkey are washing another monkey's back, are presented with an engaging liveliness. Equally remarkable is the way in which the painter indicates the setting by a few sensitively drawn plants, some rocks, the ripples of water, a line suggesting the edge of a hill, and similar devices.

There is one other celebrated Yamato-e scroll, the "Ban Dainagon Ekoto-ba," or the "Picture Scroll of Ban Dainagon," a work which is usually thought to come from the very end of the period *(Plate 45)*. It has three rolls, all preserved in the Sakai Collection in Tokyo. The scroll is traditionally attributed to the late twelfth-century painter, Fujiwara no Mitsunaga, which seems quite likely, for it resembles the copy of the master's famous "Nenjū Gyōji," which was certainly by Mitsunaga, although the original has not survived. The episode portrayed in the Ban Dainagon scroll is taken from the political history of the Heian period. It deals with a court intrigue during which the Great Councillor Tomo-no-Yoshio set fire to the Ōta Gate of the Imperial Palace and then put the blame on one of his rivals in order to discredit him. (The plot was discovered and Ban Dainagon was banished from court.)

The style of the work is a mixture of the two main styles of Yamato-e. In its emphasis upon line the Ban Dainagon scroll is similar to the Shigisan paintings, yet the rich but subtle colors, with brilliant reds, lovely yellows, blues, greens, orange, brown, and strong black, recall the more colorful style of the Genji pictures. The main part of the scroll is taken up with the fire and the fleeing crowds, and perhaps the most remarkable thing is the vivid facial expressions and the animated movement of the figures. A man tries to calm a frightened horse, another man pulls himself up onto the veranda instead of going around to the stairs, still another runs up the steps two at a time, and people stream through the gate in disorderly panic. The expressiveness and variety of the individual figures and the sense of move-

Color Plate 3. Blue Fudō. Heian period.

Plate 41. Genji Monogatari, Azumaya (section of scroll). Heian period.

Plate 42. Fan-Shaped Sutra. Heian period.

Chōgosonshi-ji, Nara Prefecture

Plate 43. Shigisan Engi (section of scroll).

Heian period.

Plate 44. Animal Caricature (section of scroll),
attributed to Priest Toba Sōjō. Heian period.

Plate 45. Ban Dainagon Ekotaba (section of scroll),

attributed to Fujiwara no Mitsunaga. Heian period.

Plate 46. Nehan (detail). Heian period.

Plate 47.

Fugen Bosatsu.

Heian period.

Coll.
Tokyo
National
Museum

Plate 48.
Eleven-Headed
Kannon.
Heian period.

Yakushi-ji, Nara

ment and excitement shows the great artistic power of the painter. Judging from this work it would appear that Mitsunaga, who lived at the very end of the Heian period, was able to fuse the two main streams of Yamato-e into a unified style, which formed the basis of the Yamato-e of the Kamakura period.

Although Buddhist painting no longer had the commanding position it had enjoyed during the Nara and Early Heian periods, it not only continued to flourish but it also developed along quite different lines. Shingon Buddhism declined, but works inspired by this sect were still popular, especially during the tenth century. The most famous of these are probably the wall paintings at the pagoda at Daigo-ji near Kyoto, which were painted during the middle of the tenth century. The subjects shown are various deities, the eight patriarchs of the Shingon sect, and the *mandara*'s of the two worlds, the diamond *mandara* and the womb *mandara*. The style is rather hard, resembling that of the ninth century, but the figures are less full and less sensuous, and cut-gold ornamentation is used for the first time. Numerous other *mandara*'s were painted during this and subsequent periods, but the emphasis was more on supplying aids for religious devotion than creating works of art.

How close the relationship between the esoteric Buddhist icons of the Heian period proper and those of the preceding age was is best seen by the fact that an excellent copy of the famous "Yellow Fudō" of Mii-dera was made for the Manju-in in Kyoto. It has the same fierce grandeur as the original, but the expression is somewhat less intense, and the figure does not fill the space as completely as the one in the earlier work. The most impressive Heian-period painting of this god is the so-called "Blue Fudō" of Shōren-in in Kyoto *(Color Plate 3)*. The deity sits on a rock (the symbol of strength and endurance) instead of the usual lotus throne; his legs are crossed; he holds the sword in one hand and the rope in the other. His expression is furious, his eyes bulging white against his dark face and his fangs protruding from his grim mouth. The fiery reds add to the fierce appearance of the painting, and the dark blue body stands out dramatically against the flames and the orange of the garment which he wears on the upper part of his body.

79

The most influential branch of Buddhism was the Jōdo sect which emphasized the cult of Amida Buddha, who dwelt in the Western Paradise and received all who called upon him. It is therefore not surprising that the most popular subject was the representation of Amida surrounded by his attending *bosatsu* coming down from heaven to welcome the faithful. This type of painting, known as Amida Raigō, or the Greeting of the Believer by the Buddha Amida, was very common during the Heian as well as the Kamakura periods. Many versions of this theme are still in existence, and many others were probably painted at the time. The best known and most splendid of these is without doubt the huge painting at the Daien-in of Mt. Kōya. It has been traditionally attributed to the priest Genshin, because he was instrumental in furthering the cult of Amida, but the style of the work would suggest that it comes from a later period, probably the twelfth century. The Buddha Amida, shown descending from the sky in the company of thirty-two music-making bodhisattvas, is painted in gold, while the surrounding *bosatsu* have garments of bright reds, greens, and blue against light bodies. What is brought out in this painting, reflecting the more worldly temper of the time, is the joy of paradise rather than any of the awe-inspiring aspects of Buddhism which the ninth-century painters had stressed.

Another masterpiece of Heian Buddhist painting, one owned by Kongōbu-ji on Kōya-san, is the "Nehan," or the "Death of Buddha," a very popular theme which occurs again and again in Buddhist painting of this and subsequent periods *(Plate 46)*. It is dated 1086, one of the few paintings of this period which has an exact date. What is important in this work is the human rather than the otherworldly side of Buddhism. Buddha lies as if in deep sleep, surrounded by bodhisattvas, arhats (the Buddhist hermits called *rakan* in Japanese), and other of his disciples. He alone is completely calm, for he has passed into nirvana, the realm beyond pain and suffering. The bodhisattvas express very little emotion, for although not yet Buddhas, they are saintly beings who are no longer gripped by human passion, but the arhats and disciples show their sorrow in their faces and gestures, and the most grief-stricken of all seem to be the lion representing the animal kingdom and the guardian in the foreground. The dramatic contrast between the divine serenity and the human grief is further brought out by the color scheme in

80

which the Buddha and the bodhisattvas are painted in gold with red lines, while the other figures are shown in brown or grey or white. Although there are many delicate details, such as the calligraphy, or the design on some of the garments, the painting creates the impression of a unified whole.

Perhaps the most typical Buddhist painting of the Heian period is the lovely representation in the Tokyo National Museum of Fugen Bosatsu, the bodhisattva of wisdom and virtue *(Plate 47)*. He sits on a lotus throne which is carried on the back of a white elephant, an animal which from ancient times had been regarded as the wisest of all the beasts. Here the emphasis is entirely upon the grace of the figure, and the result is that the bodhisattva looks more like an elegant Heian beauty than a Buddhist saint. The colors are lovely, with red and orange and blue and green and white, and there are exquisite details, such as the harness strung with jewel drops, and the tiny flower pattern on the saddle. The pale figures stand out sharply against a dark background over which a few flowers are scattered, adding to the loveliness of the whole.

Several other excellent Buddhist paintings have been preserved from this period, and no doubt many other fine works of this type perished during the intervening centuries. At least one other type of Buddhist painting should be mentioned, a kind which proved popular during this age and which continued to be painted during the Kamakura period, namely, the portraits of the patriarchs of the various Buddhist sects. Several individual pictures and some sets are still extant today, the most celebrated of which are the portrait of the famous Chinese priest Jion Daishi in Yakushi-ji, and the later and far more Japanese set of portraits of the teachers of the Tendai sect owned by Ichijō-ji at Hyōgo. Among these, the picture of the priest Ryūzo is outstanding for its elegance, and in this refined and worldly portrait the very essence of the Heian spirit is expressed.

There was at least one other genre which was important during this period, and that was landscape painting. Unfortunately, no examples of pure landscape have survived, but the descriptions of landscape paintings in the *Genji Monogatari,* and the screens with landscapes which appear in the Genji scroll indicate that landscape painting as such already existed at that time. The most characteristic Heian-style landscapes are those which appear

81

in Buddhist painting, as, for example, the ones on the doors and the walls of the Phoenix Hall at the Byōdō-in at Uji. The paintings, which represent the nine levels of Amida's Western Paradise, were done during the middle of the eleventh century and are thus among the oldest such works to have survived. The landscape is a very Japanese one with rounded hills and rich green foliage, and the style with its simplified forms and decorative effect is typical of Yamato-e. Even more interesting is the six-part landscape screen at Tō-ji in Kyoto. This type of screen, called *sensui byōbu,* was originally intended to be used in connection with the baptismal ceremonies of the Shingon sect known as *kanjō.* It is believed that the painting on the screen is a Heian copy of a late T'ang original which had been brought to Japan by Kōbō Daishi. Certainly the style of the scene in the foreground, in which a nobleman is shown visiting a hermit, resembles the T'ang style, but the landscape background with its undulating hills and tree-covered mountain tops seems more Japanese. The gentle spirit in which the landscape is conceived is typical of Japanese painting, suggesting again that a native school of landscape had developed.

The Sculpture of the Heian Period

Although painting was the more vital art form, sculpture also flourished, and many examples of Heian carving have come down to us. Here, too, the declining importance of Buddhism and the worldly and effeminate spirit of the age made themselves felt, and the images, although often very charming, lack both the grandeur of the great Nara-period sculptures, and the austerity and massiveness of the Early Heian works. There was a marked change in iconography, for besides Amida the most popular of the Buddhist deities were Kannon and, characteristically enough, Kichijōten, the goddess of beauty and virtue. Originally a Hindu deity called Sri devi, Kichijōten had been incorporated into the Buddhist pantheon, and during the Heian period she was represented as a beautiful and elegant lady of the aristocratic Kyoto world. Of other Buddhist deities, Yakushi and his twelve guardian kings are often found among the sculptures, and Bishamonten, the Guardian of the North, who is shown with a spear in one hand and a miniature stupa in the other, was also frequently represented.

82

Technically, the Heian images are very different from those of the preceding periods. Instead of the great variety of materials used by the Nara sculptors, the artists of the Heian period worked almost exclusively in wood. They did not carve the statue from one large block, but instead they developed a new method in which they used several smaller blocks, which were then joined together. This enabled the sculptors to work in groups, with a master and his assistants, and sometimes there were as many as a hundred craftsmen working as a team. Under this system it was possible to have a kind of mass production, for different carvers would specialize in different parts of the job, and thus they could work much faster, although the result was also a decline in quality and originality. Another important development was that the sculptors, who during the Nara period had been laymen employed by the government, which supported the great temples of Nara, were now often Buddhist priests attached to one of the monasteries. The most eminent of these was Jōchō, who was given the rank of Hōkkyō, or Bridge of the Law, and later the position of a Hōgen, or Eye of the Law, in recognition of his great contributions to Buddhist art.

The finest work of this sculptor-priest is the large wooden image of the Buddha Amida in the Hōōdō of the Byōdō-in at Uji, which Jōchō carved in 1053 near the end of his life. The Buddha sits in the familiar yogi position with his hands folded in the *dhyani* mudra, or the gesture of meditation. His face is serene, and yet it must be said that it lacks the intense spiritual expression which illuminated the faces of earlier works. In contrast to the calm of the Buddha, the *mandorla* behind the figure has a very animated design with swirling bands of clouds and music-making angels. Both the figure and the backdrop are brightly gilded, and there is an elaborate canopy above the altar. Additional carvings of music-making bodhisattvas are suspended from the walls of the hall, and the total effect of the image with its gilding and canopy and accompanying angels is very splendid.

There are many other fine examples of Heian sculpture, and it is difficult to select any one as being particularly outstanding. Very characteristic of the Heian spirit is the charming statue of the eleven-headed Kannon owned by Yakushi-ji in Nara *(Plate 48)*. Here the elegance of the age is clearly visible in the graceful treatment of the Kannon, who is no longer thought of as

83

a male god, as he had been during the Asuka or Nara periods, but rather as a female deity. The details of the statue are beautifully carved, and the gently falling draperies and the warm, rounded shape of the body are lovely indeed. The face expresses the gentleness fitting for the god of mercy, and the figure as a whole has a feminine gracefulness. In fact, it is closer to a Heian court lady than it is to the deeply spiritual images of earlier periods, and it is not surprising that this deity who possessed womanly virtues should have been so popular during the Heian period.

THE ARCHITECTURE OF THE HEIAN PERIOD

While many of the most famous Early Heian temples had been built in remote mountain spots such as Kōya-san and Hiei-san, the great monasteries of the Heian period proper were located in Kyoto itself, a change brought about by the fact that the temples were no longer looked upon so much as places of retreat but rather as centers of social activity and entertainment. For example, in *Genji Monogatari* the temples of Kyoto are referred to largely as places where the elegant world attended special ceremonies, and where dance and music festivals were held. The enormously powerful Fujiwara family was particularly lavish in building splendid temples, and we are told that their style was closely related to that of the palaces of the time. The most famous of these was the eleventh-century Hōjō-ji which was built under Fujiwara Michinaga at the very height of the Fujiwara influence. Unfortunately nothing of this has survived, and we must depend almost wholly upon the descriptions of the buildings in contemporary records. One thing is certain, and that is that the Heian-period temples were far more elaborate in layout and decorative detail than the Nara temples. It had become customary to add to the *kondō* several additional halls dedicated to such deities as Amida, or Yakushi, or the Five Myō-ō, and all of these were magnificently decorated.

The only building surviving today which gives some idea of the splendor of Heian architecture is the Phoenix Hall, or Hōōdō, of the Byōdō-in at Uji near Kyoto, which was erected by Fujiwara Michinaga's son, Fujiwara Yorimichi, during the middle of the eleventh century *(Plate 49)*. It is called Hōōdō because the floor plan resembles a giant phoenix with outstretched wings (the phoenix was regarded as a bird of good luck), and there are two metal phoenixes perched upon the gable. Although relatively small, the building is exquisite in design and construction. The central hall is dedicated to Amida and houses the large gilded Buddha discussed above, and from each side of the hall covered corridors extend, forming an L, with pavilions at their ends. The design is absolutely symmetrical, thus creating a lovely sense of balance despite the variety of lines, especially in the intersecting roofs. A third corridor extends towards the rear and forms the tail of the giant phoenix. The whole is meant to be an architectual representation of the Land of Bliss of the Buddha Amida. The pond in front of the structure in which the temple is mirrored is part of the scheme taken over from the numerous pictorial versions of Amida's paradise seen in T'ang paintings imported to Japan during the Heian period. The very style of the architecture, with its exact symmetry, its splendid decoration, and its brilliant red and white color, is closer to T'ang China than to the traditionally simple Japanese style. However, the small scale, and the refinement of the building, and above all the way in which the whole is fitted into its setting are quite Japanese.

Perhaps the most typical expression of Heian taste is the interior of the Amida Hall. Besides the paintings on the walls and doors representing the nine levels of Amida's paradise, and the gilded Buddha image and the canopy and the hanging bodhisattvas, the interior was decorated with sumptuous ornaments of lacquer, mother-of-pearl, and metalwork. This lavish display of all of the arts was combined to create a splendor worthy of the paradise of Amida himself, which it was supposed to represent. That this temple is not unique is shown by a second example of Heian architecture, the Golden Hall, or Konjikidō, of Chūson-ji at Hiraizumi in northeastern Japan. A tiny structure built as a mausoleum in 1124 by yet another member of the Fujiwara family, Fujiwara Kiyohira, it is if possible even more ornate. The outside of the building is gilded, the walls on the inside and the pillars and the altar inlaid with mother-of-pearl. Other sections are pasted with gold foil, painted with lacquer, or ornamented with metalwork, and there are intricate gold-placque designs on the sides of the altar. Considering what relatively small and unimportant structures these two buildings were, neither of them located in the capital although both built under the patronage of the leading noble family, it can be imagined how magnificent the temples and palaces of Heian-Kyō must have been. At the same time, considering the wealth of ornamental detail, it would seem as if they were more outstanding for their elaborate decorations than as great works of architecture comparable to the temples of earlier periods such as Hōryū-ji and Tōdai-ji.

Little else from the Heian period proper has survived. The most important of the buildings which remain is probably the pagoda at Daigo-ji near Kyoto, a five-story structure similar to the ones in Nara, which was built in 951. Its wall paintings have already been mentioned, and its architectural design is also very distinguished. In contrast to the pagoda at Murō-ji, which had thatched roofs, this pagoda has the more familiar tiles. Although there are some minor technical innovations such as the slope of the top roof differing from that of the ones beneath, the balcony railings being very low, and the balconies themselves lacking a floor, the design of the pagoda is very similar to that of earlier examples. In fact, the design of the pagodas in general remains remarkably constant over the centuries, and even relatively modern ones follow the traditional pattern.

In closing, a word should be said about domestic architecture. Although there are no surviving examples, numerous pictures of such structures can be found on the *sensui byōbu* and in the Yamato-e scrolls of the Heian and Kamakura periods. The most important type of building evolved was the *shinden zukuri*, a residential mansion similar in design to the Hōōdō, although the more elaborate side wings were used for functional purposes. The design itself probably owed its derivation to Chinese prototypes, but it was developed along purely Japanese lines. The raised wooden floors, the plain removable walls, and the use of unpainted *hinoki* bark for the roof already foreshadow the Japanese house of later periods. Altogether the emphasis on simplicity and lightness of construction is typically Japanese, and it must have given these dwellings a refined and quiet elegance.

THE CRAFTS OF THE HEIAN PERIOD

The interior decorations of the Hōōdō and the Konjikidō show what splendid use was made of lacquer and mother-of-pearl inlay during the Heian period, and there can be no doubt that lacquer was the most popular and highly developed Heian medium. It is rather significant that once the contact with China had been cut off, lacquer replaced pottery and other materials in many uses, showing the great love the Japanese had for this medium. The technique most commonly used in making designs on lacquer is known as *maki-e,* or sprinkled picture, a device by which a pattern is drawn in lacquer on the body of the object and then is sprinkled with powdered gold or silver or some other metal either by means of a brush or a cylindrical shaker. Sometimes this is covered with additional coats of lacquer and polished until the gold shows through, a technique called *togi-dashi maki-e.*

A great variety of lacquer objects such as sutra-boxes, chests, bottles, tables, and saddles have been preserved from the Heian period. One of the finest of these, and particularly interesting because it is the oldest surviving Japanese cosmetics box, is the one now owned by the Cultural Properties Preservation Committee *(Plate 50)*. The design is beautifuly executed in gold *maki-e* and white mother-of-pearl. It represents wheels floating in water, which is rendered in a very stylized and decorative manner. The design is varied yet perfectly balanced, showing a strong sense of abstract pattern. In this way it reveals a typically Japanese quality in contrast to the lacquerwares of the Nara period, which used a more detailed and naturalistic Chinese design. The inside of the lid is also very lovely with an exquisite design of butterflies, birds, chrysanthemums, and other flowers, and while the decoration on the outside is bold and strong, the one on the inside is more delicate.

The other crafts fared less well, especially pottery, which began to languish once the intercourse with China had stopped. Some of the earlier traditional stonewares continued to be made, but they showed no new development, and both the quantity and quality of the production did not equal that of the Nara period. The metalwork, too, although at times very tasteful and elegant, cannot compare with the objects preserved in the Shōsō-in, even granting that many of these were of Chinese origin. Nevertheless there are some very fine examples, especially among the sutra-boxes and the bronze mirrors. Interestingly enough, many of the objects of this type which have survived were excavated in mounds in which sutras and other things were buried, because it was widely believed that the age of decadence, or *mappo,* was at hand, and that one must prepare oneself for the coming of the Buddhist messiah Miroku by burying sutras. The loveliest of these objects are the bronze mirrors, which are known as *wakyō,* or Japanese mirrors. They are flatter and plainer in shape than the Chinese ones of the Nara period, and they have decorative designs of birds, flowers, and grasses rendered in a simple yet beautiful style in flat relief.

No textiles have been preserved from the Heian period, but we know a great deal about them from literary accounts, such as the many descriptions of the court dress in *The Tale of Genji* and other works of the period, as well as from the numerous representations of costumes in the paintings. The cloths were apparently very delicate with simple designs, or of a single color, since the type of dress used did not lend itself to elaborate patterns. The ladies wore the so-called "twelve-layer," or *jūnihitoe,* consisting of numerous layers of differently colored garments and a broadly spreading, pleated skirt tied around the waist. Men wore the *noshi,* a loosely fitting robe with long sleeves and baggy pants, and beneath it there were undergarments whose differently tinted layers created beautiful color effects. The elegance and decorative beauty of these clothes must have been very great, showing again the aesthetic sensitivity of the Heian period.

6

The Art of
the Kamakura Period

IN 1185, a military dictatorship was established by Minamoto Yoritomo, thus ending the civil war which had disrupted the last years of the Heian period and led to the defeat of the Taira family by the rival Minamoto clan. The new rulers were military men who moved the capital to Kamakura, a provincial town in eastern Japan, in order to protect the warriors from the effete, over-refined atmosphere of Kyoto. Yoritomo, who assumed the title of Seii-Tai-Shōgun, or Barbarian-Subduing Generalissimo, had complete control of the military forces of the country; yet in theory, at least, he and his successors continued to be subservient to the emperor, who remained the titular head of Japan. After Yoritomo's death, the actual power resided in the hands of the Hōjō family, relatives of his wife's clan, who established a regency in 1205, resulting in the strange but characteristically Japanese spectacle of the nominal ruler, the emperor in Kyoto, being ruled by the shogun, who in turn was dominated by the regent, who was a member of another clan. This type of indirect control is very typical of Japan, and retired emperors who had become monks often continued to dominate public affairs.

The new rulers, who controlled Japan for about 150 years, were warriors, whose military spirit is reflected in the culture of the time. The most dramatic event of this period was the Mongol invasion of 1281, which put the military strength of the Kamakura administration to its supreme test. The Mongols, after conquering China, had decided to subdue Japan. Two armies were assembled, one made up of about fifty thousand Mongols and Koreans which embarked from Korea, and the other containing one hundred thousand Chinese which sailed from southern China. Their initial success was great, for they succeeded in landing strong forces near Hakata Bay in Kyushu, but the Japanese, who up to this point had been bitterly divided, united in face of the common peril and, with the help of a great storm which scattered the Mongol fleet, were able to repell the invaders after about fifty days of fighting. The losses suffered by the enemy were considerable, some reports saying that four-fifths of the invading forces were annihilated, and thus ended the only major attempt until modern times at foreign invasion of Japan. Culturally speaking, this event had little influence except in so far as the conquest of China by the Mongols led to an influx of refugees who were unwilling to accept the rule of the foreign barbarians and who helped spread Chinese culture in the island empire. In fact, one of the outstanding traits of Kamakura culture was its renewed borrowing from China, especially in the realm of art, where Sung painting, sculpture, and architecture had a considerable influence.

Although the political and military power was concentrated in Kamakura, the cultural center was still Kyoto, the capital of the Heian period. Here the traditional arts continued, and in a sense it would be correct to say that Kamakura art was a direct outgrowth of the art of the Heian period. On the other hand, the spirit of the new art was quite different, for it was both more vigorous and more realistic. As time went on there was a merging of the two trends, the one reflecting the older tradition of elegance and beauty, and the other embodying the soldierly virtues of the Kamakura warriors. The samurai became more cultured and the Kyoto aristocracy was increasingly influenced by the spirit of the new age, for just as the provincial warriors admired the sophistication of court life, so the decadent Kyoto society admired the vigor and simplicity of the new rulers. Yoritomo himself was

90

by no means hostile to culture, and he spent large sums on the restoration of the great temples and shrines which had been destroyed during the wars at the end of the Heian period. This in turn had a beneficial effect upon the arts, especially sculpture. Still, compared to the Nara or the Heian period, the Kamakura period as a whole showed a marked decline in almost all fields of culture. Learning languished under the impact of the warrior tradition, and literature, which had flowered during the preceding age, was mostly outstanding for its great warrior romances such as *Heike Monogatari,* which tells of the wars between the Taira and Minamoto families.

The most important cultural development was the rise of the popular salvation sects of Buddhism, which have often been compared to Protestantism, and in their emphasis upon salvation by faith and their use of the vernacular they do indeed show a certain similarity. Directed not to the aristocracy but to the masses, they did away with much of the mysteriousness and complexity which Shingon and other esoteric sects had introduced into Japanese Buddhism. Characteristically enough, the founders of these new sects no longer wrote their treatises only in the traditional Chinese but also in Japanese, using a type of mixed *kana.* The great evangelists of the new sects, who lived in the twelfth and thirteenth centuries, were Hōnen Shōnin, who founded the Jōdo, or paradise, sect, which promised rebirth in the Western Paradise for all who called upon the name of Amida; Shinran, who founded the Jōdo Shinshū sect, which to this day is the most popular of all Japanese Buddhist sects; and Nichiren, who thought that the true teaching could only be found in the Hokke-kyō, or the Scripture of the Lotus of the Good Law. The Nara sects also experienced a revival, and the esoteric sects continued, although they were no longer of great importance. There was one other sect which arose during the Kamakura period and which was to become the dominating sect in the Ashikaga period, and that was Zen, or Meditative, Buddhism. It was established in Japan as a separate school with the founding of the Rinzai sect by the monk Eisai shortly after 1200, and it enjoyed great popularity among the samurai, to whom its emphasis on self-discipline and simplicity greatly appealed.

91

THE PAINTING OF THE KAMAKURA PERIOD

The Yamato-e school, which reached its maturity during the thirteenth century, was the most characteristically Japanese school of painting of the Kamakura period, Numerous *e-makimono,* or picture scrolls, have come down from these years, some of them consisting of as many as twenty individual rolls. Although clearly a development of the Yamato-e scrolls of the twelfth century, they show characteristics both in content and style which differentiate them from the work of the Heian period, especially at the end of the thirteenth century, when the influence of Sung China further changed the style of these paintings. Generally speaking, the main difference lies in the fact that there is a greater emphasis upon realistic detail and narrative content than upon the design or the decorative beauty. While the *Genji Monogatari* scroll was primarily concerned with the mood it created and with the beauty of its rich ornamental color patterns, the Kamakura scrolls were meant to relate a story as graphically as possible, and in some cases the text was dispensed with altogether. The result was paintings which have been much admired, especially by the nineteenth century, which tended to regard these scrolls as the culmination of Yamato-e, while the twentieth century, with its more purely aesthetic approach, has found greater merit in the scrolls of the Heian period. The subject matter itself expressed the temper of the new age, for scenes of war and episodes from the lives of the great evangelists became very popular, while purely literary subjects as well as scenes from the court were less common, and when they did occur they were painted in a style based upon Heian-period models.

Perhaps the most characteristic of these Kamakura-period paintings both in subject matter and style is the *Heiji Monogatari* scroll, depicting the battle between the Taira and Minamoto families. There are three rolls, one in the Boston Museum of Fine Arts, and the others in the Tokyo National Museum and the Seikadō. The Boston roll, which contains the section showing the burning of the Sanjō Palace, is particularly fine, and except for the scroll illustrating the adventures of Kibi in China, which is owned by the same museum, it is the only major Yamato-e scroll outside of Japan. The section reproduced here, which is from the work in the Tokyo Museum, shows the

92

emperor, who is disguised as a woman, fleeing from the palace in an oxcart to the house of Taira no Kiyomori, the leader of the Taira clan (*Color Plate 4*). The composition, both of the work as a whole and of the individual parts, is very accomplished, indicating that this scroll may well be the work of Sumiyoshi Keinin, one of the famous artists of the period, to whom it has been traditionally ascribed. Compared to the Genji scroll, the painting uses much more detail in line and color, and there is a greater realism in the figures and in their relationship to the buildings. The illustrative element is far more pronounced and yet, because of its realism, it loses much of the simplicity of abstract design which had marked the twelfth-century works. This is particularly noticeable in the battle scenes, where the carefully rendered small forms prevent the eye from gaining a unified impression, and it is also true to a certain extent in the section reproduced. While the figures in the Genji scroll had been built up of large, simple areas of color, here, especially in the soldiers, there is a certain confusion of detail. The costumes with their small, brightly colored parts, and the details of the armor and the feathered arrows make it difficult, particularly in the group in front of the oxcart, to distinguish one soldier from another. Only the figure at the right is clearly defined, with his pale blue-green robes beautifully contrasted against the strong red of the pillars. Although the individual figures are somewhat lost, the group as a whole, especially the cart, with its large black wheels, stands out crisply against the light, evenly colored ground. As narrative, the scroll is very effective, and there is a fine sense of drama in the part which shows the burning of the palace.

The most interesting group of Kamakura paintings are those devoted to the lives of the Buddhist saints. Among these, the finest is the Ippen Shōnin scroll, which was painted by the priest En-i in 1299, the year after Ippen's death (*Plate 51*). It has twelve rolls, which are owned by the Kankikō-ji in Kyoto. Ippen Shōnin, the priest who founded the Jishū, one of the Amida sects which flourished at the time, is shown traveling thoughout Japan, preaching the doctrine and doing missionary work for this new type of Buddhist teaching. How great the response was is best demonstrated in the scenes showing vast crowds coming both on foot and in oxcarts to hear the famous preacher. One of the most remarkable things about the scroll is

93

the rendition of the figures, which, along with the setting, shows the new realism of the age. The figures in the section reproduced are very small, but they are drawn in such a way that the closer you look the more detail you see. The black umbrella, the wooden clogs, the different parts of the clothes are all lucidly portrayed, and though the faces are tiny each has a definite expression. The house at the left is also carefully detailed, and the setting, although in some parts almost bare, is presented with the same distinctness. The landscape itself shows the influence of Sung China, especially in the misty space and in the pine trees, with their strong, angular strokes, yet the detailed and colorful style clearly reveals that the work belongs to the Yamato-e tradition. The primary emphasis is upon the narrative, and the artist gives a vivid picture of contemporary Japan, with its people and towns, its houses and temples, its countryside and mountains. Of all the Kamakura scrolls, only the one portraying the life of the priest Saigyō equals this in the treatment of landscape and atmosphere, which, in its Chinese influence, indicates that it also comes from the end of the Kamakura period.

Of the Buddhist scrolls in the Yamato-e style, the most curious are the ones dealing with hungry ghosts and devils, a type which became popular after the spread of the Pure Land faith during the Heian and Kamakura periods *(Plate 52)*. The unfortunate creatures in the so-called *Handbook on Hungry Ghosts* are beings who are eternally hungry but who are unable to satisfy their craving for food and drink. They represent one of the subhuman levels in the six migratory states of being, and the purpose of such scrolls was probably to warn people of what torments awaited them if they did not turn to Amida and follow the Buddhist commandments. This weird theme is presented in the most vivid and expressive way, and in contrast to the hideous ghosts the artist has introduced bits of homely Kamakura realism, such as the people squatting to relieve themselves. The old man and the child and the two women, one of whom has her back turned, go quietly about their business, utterly unaware of the ghosts who cluster around them screaming and laughing. The bodies of the ghosts are horribly emaciated except for their huge, distended bellies, and the wild growth of their hair heightens the macabre effect. Stylistically the emphasis is upon the line rather than the color, and in this way the work recalls the "Shigisan Engi"

Color Plate 4. Heiji Monogatari (section of scroll). Kamakura period.

Plate 57.

Amida Buddha. Kamakura period.

Kōtoku-in, Kamakura

Plate 58. Portrait of Uesugi Shigefusa.

Kamakura period.

Meigetsu-in, Kamakura

Plate 56.

Niō (Guardian King),

by Unkei and Kaikei.

Kamakura period.

Tōdai-ji, Nara

Coll. Yamato Bunka-kan, Osaka

Plate 55.   Poetess Ko Ōgimi (section of scroll).
Kamakura period.

Plate 54. Portrait of Minamoto no Yoritomo (detail).

Kamakura period.

Zenrin-ji, Kyoto

Plate 53. Amida Appearing Over the Mountains.

Kamakura period.

Kankikō-ji, Kyoto

Plate 51. Ippen Shōnin (section of scroll).
Kamakura period.

Coll. Tokyo National Museum

Plate 52. Hungry Ghosts (section of scroll). Kamakura period.

Plate 59.   Shariden (Relic Hall), Engaku-ji, Kamakura.

Kamakura period.

Plate 60. *Tahōtō* (Indian-Style Pagoda),

Ishiyama-dera, Shiga Prefecture.

Kamakura period.

scroll, although it is more realistic in its rendering of space and plastic form. A similar scroll is the "Jigoku-Zōshi," in which the torments of hell are portrayed in an equally vivid manner. Here again the intention of the artist was probably to frighten people into accepting the Buddhist teachings.

Only a handful of Heian scrolls still exist, but from the Kamakura period over one hundred such works have survived. It is needless to list all of them, but at least two should be mentioned, the "Kitano Tenjin Engi," which tells the tragic story of the statesman and Shinto saint, Sugawara Michizane, and the scroll representing the Mongol invasion of Japan. The last of the great Kamakura Yamato-e is the series of rolls dated 1309 and depicting the miraculous stories connected with the Kasuga Shrine. However, this already shows a hardening of style and a certain mannerism, for by the close of the thirteenth century the creative phase of Yamato-e had come to an end.

Along with the Buddhist works in the Yamato-e style, traditional Buddhist painting continued to flourish. The most typical for this period in which the cult of Amida and his paradise was so popular were the Amida Raigō paintings, especially the ones with the Buddha appearing over the mountains, a type known as Yamagoshi Raigō. These works were much sought after by those who were on their deathbed, for it was believed that if a dying person held the silk cords extending from the hands of the Amida Buddha in the picture, he would at death immediately enter paradise. The basic idea of these works goes back to the Heian period, but this particular form in which Amida appears at the horizon like a sun bringing light into the dark world is a characteristic development of the Kamakura period.

Among the many versions of this theme, the one preserved in Zenrin-ji in Kyoto is artistically the finest (Plate 53). The gold figure of Amida, surrounded by a huge halo and painted with the most delicate lines, appears over a typically Japanese landscape. Below the Buddha are his two attending bodhisattvas, Kannon and Seishi, also gold and standing on white clouds. Figures painted on a much smaller scale appear at the bottom—the guardians of the four directions in the corners, and in the middle two figures in ordinary clothes which are believed to represent Bonten and Taishakuten. In the upper left-hand corner is the Sanskrit letter "aum," indicating the influence of Shingon Buddhism even though this is an Amida painting. The picture, which is supposed to represent a vision Eshin Sōzu had on Mt. Hiei, is done in a style which reflects the tradition of Heian-period Buddhist painting. The space is flat; the mountains are conceived of as a design of undulating bands; the clouds make decorative, dragon-shaped patterns. Besides the white of the clouds and the gold of the Buddha and the bodhisattvas, the predominant colors are soft greens and browns with touches of red in the guardian figures and rose in some of the garments. Although the decorative element is certainly very strong, the work is at the same time imbued with a deep religious feeling.

Another type of painting important during this period was the *suijaku-ga*, a visual expression of the idea that the Shinto gods are manifestations of the Buddhist deities. This belief, called Dual Shinto, was already widespread during Nara and Heian times, but it was not until the Kamakura period that it was expressed in visual terms. The paintings usually represent one of the famous Shinto shrines, with the Buddhist deities with whom they are associated hovering over the site. Since they show assemblies of Buddhist deities, they are often called *mandara*'s in spite of the fact that they are not in any way connected with esoteric Buddhism. Some paintings use a symbol for the shrine instead of the actual buildings, as for example the sacred deer standing for the Kasuga Shrine at Nara, but the most common are the rather decoratively treated aerial views of the shrine, with trees in front and the sacred mountains in back. The style of these works, with their emphasis upon the decorative, is close to that of the Yamato-e, and their appeal lies as much in their beauty as landscapes as it does in their religious meaning.

The finest of these Dual Shinto *mandara*'s is the one of the Nachi Waterfall, which is preserved in the Nezu Museum in Tokyo, a work which appears to be a pure landscape but is actually thought of as a representation of the deity of the waterfall. Another landscape painting intended for religious purposes is the *sensui byōbu* at Jingo-ji in Kyoto, which, like the Heian landscape screen at Tō-ji, was used for Buddhist baptismal services. The landscape, viewed as if from a great height, represents a panorama of mountains, and the treatment of atmosphere and space would suggest that the Japanese had by this time mastered the art of the landscape, although it was not as important in Kamakura art as narrative and religious painting.

96

Another way in which the realism of the age manifested itself was in the portrait. During the Heian period it had been customary to paint likenesses of celebrated priests, such as the patriarchs of the various sects and the founders of temples, but now portraits of purely secular figures were also made. The most famous is the portrait of Minamoto no Yoritomo, the founder of the Kamakura regime, a picture attributed to Fujiwara Takanobu and kept at Jingo-ji in Kyoto *(Plate 54)*. What is remarkable about this painting is the degree of characterization with which the artist has imbued the face. The background and the robes are highly abstract, but the features, drawn with delicate lines, show a more realistic detail. The rather closely set eyes, the large curving nose, and the long face wider at the bottom than it is at the top are all individualized, though they too are done in a flat and simple manner. The result, though the picture as a whole is very decorative, is a more lifelike portrayal of a real person than any which had been done before. The artist was a contemporary of Yoritomo, and we can be fairly certain that this is a likeness of a historical figure rather than an idealized portrait painted by someone who had never seen his subject.

Far less realistic but artistically very outstanding is the series of paintings showing the thirty-six immortal poets of the Heian period *(Plate 55)*. There are many versions of this subject, both from the Kamakura and later periods, but the finest is the one attributed to the famous Kamakura portrait-painter Fujiwara Nobuzane. The painting, done in a manner which recalls the work of the Heian period, originally formed two rolls, but they are now cut up and scattered over various collections. Each shows one of the poets, some of them women, together with an account of his life and sample of his poetry. The loveliest is the section portraying the poetess Ko Ōgimi, which is now owned by the Yamato Bunka-kan in Osaka. In the Yoritomo portrait, the face, which is set against a simple ground, is the focal point of the picture, but here the face is surrounded by a sea of billowing robes. The beauty of their color patterns and the design of the different shapes, some triangular, some curving, some pleated, is more important than the face. What is stressed is not the individuality of a particular woman but the generalized type of Heian beauty, with long hair, pale, pear-shaped face, and colorful, complicated robes. Both the subject and the style are typically

97

Japanese, showing how the native emphasis which had been so important during the Heian period continued in the Kamakura period at least through the thirteenth century, though as the relationship to China became closer in the first decades of the fourteenth century this began gradually to change.

THE SCULPTURE OF THE KAMAKURA PERIOD

Sculpture experienced one last splendid flowering, only to decline as a major art form by the end of the thirteenth century. The leading patron continued to be the Buddhist church, and with the exception of a few isolated portrait-statues all the carvings of this age, as of the previous one, were images representing the Buddhist deities, primarily Buddhas, bodhisattvas, guardians, and devas. They were made for the most part in wood and bronze, but such traditional media as lacquer and clay were also used, although they never regained the popularity they had enjoyed during the Nara period.

The style expressed the same vigorous, realistic spirit as the paintings, and when compared to the Heian carvings the Kamakura works seem very forceful. There are various reasons for this new realism: the fact that the popular Buddhist sects tried to reach the common people, who understood a realistic art more readily than a refined or esoteric one; the political dominance of the military men; the revival of interest in Nara-period art, due to the rebuilding of the ancient Nara temples which had been destroyed in the civil wars; and the influence of Sung sculpture, which is apparent in the more human conception of the gods, the detailed treatment of the drapery, and the greater realism of the facial expression.

The most typical Kamakura sculptures were produced by the school of Nara artists gathered around Kōkei, his son Unkei, who is regarded as the greatest sculptor of the period, and his pupil Kaikei. The event which shaped their art was the restoration of Kōfuku-ji and Tōdai-ji, which was undertaken between 1180 and 1212. Working at these famous sites, they had an opportunity to study the magnificent works of the eighth century, and it was upon them that their style was based. It was no mere copy, but rather an inspired adaptation, and the result was works which combine the grandeur of Nara art with the realism and drama of the more typically Kamakura style.

Perhaps the most impressive of all their works are the Niō at the Great

98

South Gate, or Nandaimon, of Tōdai-ji, two giant guardian figures which, according to temple records, were made in 1203 by Unkei and Kaikei with the help of two other carvers and sixteen assistants *(Plate 56)*. The figures, measuring twenty-six feet in height, are identified as Kongō Rikishi by the vajra, or *kongō,* which each clasps in his hand. Although badly discolored, traces of pigment show that originally they were brightly painted, the hands brown, the ribbons white, the skin red, the garments in various colors with the edges in gold. What is most striking is the tremendous force of the figures. Their faces have a dramatic, glaring expression; their powerful, muscular bodies are filled with an intense movement. The figure reproduced stands with his leg thrust sharply to his right and his hips swung to his left, a jagged movement carried on by the angle of his arm and the swirl of drapery which loops up about his head. There is, of course, a close relationship between these figures and the guardians from the Nara period, but the Kamakura ones are more realistic and the movement has a greater vigor.

The most famous Buddha image of this and probably any other period is the giant statue of Amida Nyorai at the Kōtoku-in in Kamakura, popularly known as the Great Buddha of Kamakura *(Plate 57)*. Unfortunately, it is not known who the artist was, but it is fairly certain that it is the work of the middle of the thirteenth century, and the similarity between this statue and the great Buddha of Tōdai-ji indicates once again the close relationship between the Nara and the Kamakura sculptures. Originally in the main hall of the temple, it has stood in the open ever since a tidal wave carried away the wooden structure in 1495.

The style, with its strong and simple forms, resembles that of the Unkei school, although it is believed that the statue is not by any of the masters of this workshop. In contrast to the dramatic power of the Kongō Rikishi, this image, in keeping with the subject, shows the calm majesty of Buddha Amida, a feeling heightened by the huge dimensions of the statue, which is forty-two feet high. He appears in the traditional pose of the Enlightened One, his legs crossed in the yogi position and his hands in the gesture of meditation, the *dhyani* mudra. His body is covered with a monk's garment which falls in many folds, and his face expresses the serenity of one who has passed beyond the world of appearance. Besides the *ushnisha,* the *urna,* and the large ears (symbols of the Buddha's omniscience), the Buddha has a moustache, originally derived from India and used to indicate that this is a Western deity.

The most original development, and one which perfectly expressed the realistic tendencies of the age, was the growth of portrait sculpture. The most famous, perhaps, are the images at Kōfuku-ji of two great saints of the Buddhist church, Asanga and Vasubandhu, or in Japanese, Muchaku and Seshin. According to an inscription on the pedestal, they were carved in 1208 by Unkei and his sons and pupils. Although the saints had died long before the portraits were made, the statues are extremely lifelike, with a fine sculptural feeling and very expressive faces. However, some of the portraits of contemporary men are even more remarkable, especially the one of the priest Shunjōbō Chōgen Shōnin at Tōdai-ji. Chōgen was the motivating force behind the rebuilding of Tōdai-ji, and it is believed that this portrait was made shortly after his death in 1206 by a member of the Unkei school. His wrinkled face, deeply sunken eyes, and withered body are portrayed with striking realism as well as with great intensity of feeling. Among the statues of secular men, the most outstanding is the portrait at Meigetsu-in in Kamakura of Uesugi Shigefusa, the founder of the famous family of court nobles *(Plate 58)*. The style resembles that of the Yamato-e portraits such as the one of Yoritomo. The face, which gives a good idea of his personality, is even more realistic, while the treatment of the body is very generalized. From the front, the shape of the figure is perfectly symmetrical, with the exaggerated forms of the pantaloons balanced by the simple mass of the upper part of the body and the tall peak of the hat. The figure, carved out of several blocks of wood, is covered with lacquer cloth which originally was colored, and the eyes are inserted, a practice quite common in Kamakura sculptures. It is believed that the statue dates from the end of the Kamakura period, and, if this is the case, it marks the last important phase in the history of Japanese sculpture.

THE ARCHITECTURE OF THE KAMAKURA PERIOD

The rule of the samurai affected architecture as profoundly as it did all other spheres of life, and the luxurious palaces and temples of the Heian period gave way to more modest buildings. With the well-to-do patrons gone, the Buddhist temples and Shinto shrines had to depend partly upon their own resources and partly upon popular subscription, and we are told that when Shunjōbō Chōgen undertook the task of rebuilding the great temple complex at Tōdai-ji, he had to travel all over Japan to raise the money for this enterprise. The tendency towards plainer and more unadorned structures is most clearly seen in the domestic architecture, and it is the simpler Kamakura dwelling which is the forerunner of the modern Japanese house. The renewed contact with China and the importation of Zen Buddhism also influenced architecture, and resulted in a style called Kara-yō, or Chinese style, because it had come from south China. This new manner with its emphasis on simplicity proved very popular, although the older Japanese style, the Wa-yō, continued as well.

It is surprising, especially when one thinks of the wealth of European examples which have survived from the thirteenth century, how few Kamakura structures actually remain. This is particularly true of the buildings in the Chinese style, of which hardly any have been preserved. The best of these, and the only Kamakura-period building left in Kamakura itself, is the Shariden, or Relic Hall, of the Engaku-ji *(Plate 59)*. This temple, which once was one of the great centers of Zen Buddhism, was established in 1282 by Hōjō Tokimune. Characteristically enough, a Chinese monk, Tsu-yüan, or in Japanese, Sōgen, was invited to Japan to head the new establishment, and Japanese architects were sent to China to study Zen temple architecture. Unfortunately, of all the ancient buildings which made up the temple, only the Shariden is left. The exact date of its construction is not known, but it is believed that the hall, which is an outstanding example of the Kara-yō, was built in the last decade of the thirteenth century.

Despite its rather small dimensions (it is only thirty-five feet square and thirty-five feet high), the building makes an impression of solid strength. It stands on a stone platform, from which rise the slender pillars of the enclosed veranda. The most striking thing is the thatched double roof, consisting of a lower part which is quite shallow, and a huge upper part with beautifully curved eaves. The bracketing system is quite unique, with plain brackets under the eaves of the lower roof and very complex brackets in

101

the space between the upper and lower roof. Other new features imported from China are the arched heads of the windows and doors, the delicate woodwork of the window lattices, and doors swinging on pivots. The building with its sober strength and beauty is an apt expression both of the Zen spiritual ideal and of the austerity of the life of the warrior class. No doubt many such buildings were erected during the thirteenth and early fourteenth centuries for, especially in the construction of Zen temples, this style proved very successful.

A variation of the Kara-yō, which was also imported from southern China, was the so-called Indian-style, or Tenjiku-yō, which never achieved great popularity in Japan and after the Kamakura period died out altogether. It is primarily of interest in having influenced the construction of the new buildings at Tōdai-ji, which had been burned to the ground by Taira no Shigehira in 1180 for the help which the armed monks had extended to the Minamoto clan during the great civil war. When the Minamoto family emerged victorious, they decided to have the temple rebuilt, and at the insistence of Hōnen Shōnin, the founder of the Jōdo sect, Shunjōbō Chōgen was put in charge. Under his supervision, and with the help of Chinese assistants, the middle gate and the Great Buddha Hall, or Daibutsuden, were completed in 1195 and the Kaidan-in, or Ordination Precinct, the Bath House, and the Great South Gate were finished during the last years of the century. Unfortunately all of these buildings were either burned down in later years or reconstructed in a different style, with exception of the Nandaimon, the only pure example of the Tenjiku-yō which is left today. It is marked by a grand scale, solid construction, and great boldness. However, it lacks the simple beauty which is characteristic of many of the finest buildings in Japanese architecture, and it is not surprising that within a generation or two its style was forgotten. Its chief structural innovations are the bracket arms which are inserted through the body of the columns, and the use of brackets in front and back but not at the sides. As a whole, the effect is very impressive, but compared to the center gate at Hōryū-ji, it lacks subtlety of design and proportion.

Most of the buildings erected during this period were built not in the newly imported Chinese style but in a more traditional manner based either

102

on Nara-period models or the Wa-yō, which was really a Heian version of the T'ang style. Practically all the surviving Kamakura structures are built in one of these manners, or in a mixed style which by the end of the Kamakura period had become dominant. A good example of the return to the traditional styles may be seen at Kōfuku-ji in Nara, which had been destroyed during the civil war and was then reconstructed. The Northern Octagonal Hall, or Hokuendō, and the Three-Storied Pagoda, or San-jū-no-tō, were rebuilt in the Heian style, while the Tōkondō, or Eastern Main Hall, and the Five-Story Pagoda were rebuilt in the Nara style. The present structures are Muromachi reconstructions, but this example shows how strong the hold of traditional architecture was upon the builders of the time.

Of the more typical Kamakura buildings erected in the Japanese style, the most interesting is the *hondō* of the Rengeō-in in Kyoto, popularly known as the Sanjūsangendō, which was erected in 1266. It is the longest of all Japanese temples, measuring no less than 384 feet in length, although it is only thirty feet deep. It was designed in this manner to accommodate one thousand images of Kannon, and, characteristically enough, its veranda served as a shooting range for the samurai archers. Its construction is extremely simple, with a curved tile roof in the peculiarly Japanese shape known as *irimoya zukuri,* a combination of a hipped and a gabled roof. The woodwork is painted red, forming a lovely contrast with the white plaster and the grey tiles, and in spite of its great length its proportions are very harmonious and pleasing.

There is one other monument which should be mentioned, partly for its uniqueness and partly because it reflects still another facet of the architectural activity of the time. This is the stupa, or *tahōtō,* of Ishiyama-dera at Ōtsu near Lake Biwa, a type of structure which goes back to the Heian period and is always associated with Shingon temples *(Plate 60).* This example, however, is the earliest of the ones which have survived. Basically, it is a pagoda of a type which more nearly resembles the Indian stupa than the traditional Japanese pagoda, thus indicating the close relationship which existed between esoteric Buddhism and India. Instead of five or three stories, it always has two, the lower one square and the upper one circular, with a square roof on both levels. At the top, there are the same elements as the ones in the pagodas—the pole, the nine umbrellas, and the flaming jewel. Originally the stupa was no doubt derived from the Indian relic chamber and burial mound, but in esoteric Buddhism it is considered a symbol of the two aspects of the universe, the Kongō-kai, or diamond world, and the Taizō-kai, or matrix world. Its appearance is quite exotic and yet in that way it is very characteristic of Shingon Buddhism, which, in spite of the rise of the Jōdo sects and Zen, had by no means died out. However, the Chinese-style buildings which the Zen monasteries favored and the more traditional Japanese style used by the popular sects are more characteristic of the architecture of the period.

THE CRAFTS OF THE KAMAKURA PERIOD

It is not surprising, in view of the military spirit, that the Kamakura period was not outstanding for its crafts. Kyoto continued to be the center of such activities and by and large the style followed the pattern of the Heian period. However, the quality of the production deteriorated, partly because the craftsmen did not have the discriminating patronage which had been a mark of the Heian court. Then, too, the realistic tendencies were not so successful when carried over into design, and the decorations of the lacquer boxes and mirrors had little of the elegance which the Heian objects had possessed.

Of all the crafts, probably ceramics was the field in which the Kamakura period most excelled. The center of pottery manufacture was the town of Seto in the vicinity of Nagoya, which to this day is the leading ceramics center of Japan. The origin of this development goes back to the trip which the potter Katō Shirozaemon, better known as Tōshirō, made to China in 1223. Interestingly enough he went there as the attendant of the Zen priest Dōgen, and ever since the Kamakura period there has been a close connection between Zen Buddhism, the tea ceremony, and Japanese pottery. The wares he particularly admired were the Sung celadons and the *chien* ware, or *temmoko*. In imitation of these, he and other Kamakura potters made black and brown wares resembling *temmoku*, and stoneware jars, dishes, bowls, and vases with green or occasionally yellow glaze, which were modeled after the celadons and sometimes decorated with lovely incised flower and grass designs. Although still crude, these wares, which marked the beginning of Japanese ceramic manufacture, had a tremendous influence upon the work of later periods.

Among the other decorative arts, lacquer and metalwork were the most outstanding. Generally speaking, the lacquer objects, although less sophisticated, were similar to those of the Heian period in technique and design. However, there was one new development, and that was the origin of a technique known as Kamakura *bori*, a type of lacquerware with plain colors and simple patterns. It probably originated in an attempt to imitate Chinese lacquers in the red relief style which had been brought to Japan during this period. The design is carved into the surface of the wood and covered with a thin layer of red, or red and green, lacquer, and the result, though it lacked the refinement of *maki-e*, often had a plain, rather strong beauty. Of Kamakura textiles little but fragments have been preserved, but judging from the costumes in contemporary paintings the clothes were less elaborate than Heian clothes, and the designs were bolder.

Like the other arts of the period, the crafts reflected the general cultural climate. In contrast to the Heian objects, they showed a new vigor, although along with this there was a decline in technique. While the Heian culture was typically Japanese in its emphasis upon an abstract decorative beauty, the Kamakura period showed a strong Chinese influence, which, at least during this particular age, expressed itself in a pronounced trend towards realism. It is difficult to evaluate different artistic epochs, but as far as originality and subtlety are concerned this period cannot be compared with the previous one.

7

The Art of
the Muromachi Period

DURING the first part of the Muromachi period civil wars again disrupted the country. These years from 1333 to 1392 are usually called the Epoch of the Northern and Southern Dynasties, for during this time there were two rival emperors, one in Kyoto and one south of Nara. Various clans fought with one another for power and land, and only gradually did the Ashikaga family gain control. However, even after the dynastic struggle had been settled, the Ashikaga shoguns were never able to exercise the authority which the Hōjō regents had had. Still, they did manage to stay in power, and they ruled fairly efficiently until 1467, when the Ōnin civil war started, plunging the country into chaos and destroying Kyoto. The Ashikaga, or Muromachi period (named after the quarter of Kyoto in which the Ashikaga shoguns had their headquarters) lasted until 1573, but the last hundred years, called the Sengoku Jidai (age of the country at war), were filled with violent strife. Strange as it may seem, this period in spite of its wars and instability was very remarkable in its culture, which had a profound influence upon all later periods. The Zen monasteries became great centers of culture, perhaps because men of learning took refuge in the temples, or because of the renewed contact with China.

The high points of this cultural renaissance were achieved under the third shogun, Ashikaga Yoshimitsu, and the eighth, Ashikaga Yoshimasa. The former, who in 1395 abdicated and retired to his famous villa, the Golden Pavilion, or Kinkaku-ji, led a life of elegance and luxury, in which connoisseurship of ink-painting and calligraphy, and skill in the tea ceremony were considered crowning achievements. The military aristocracy, who no longer practiced the austerity of the Kamakura warriors, were eager for the refinements of Kyoto life, and as a result the military and the court society were no longer so clearly separated. Trade with China, where the Mongol rulers had been overthrown and replaced by the native Ming dynasty, also had a great effect upon the period, and the latest Chinese fashions in art, literature, and Zen Buddhism were eagerly embraced. It may well be that the motivating force behind these artistic developments was the passionate desire for everything new that came from abroad (a sentiment shared by the Nara and Meiji periods as well), rather than any religious or artistic beliefs. In fact purely religious elements played less and less of a role, and the cultivation of artistic sensitivity for its own sake became far more important. The mark of a gentleman was his refined taste, and the aristocracy, when it was not at war, engaged in poetry-writing contests, tea-tasting parties, and the study of Sung and Yüan masterpieces of painting and porcelain. It is not surprising that, just as in the Heian period, the rulers neglected the affairs of state, and as a result their regime ended in disaster.

Although the traditional sects declined, Buddhism continued to thrive in the form of Zen, or Meditative, Buddhism. The importance of this sect during the Muromachi period was so great that in a way it became the official religion, and Zen priests acted as advisors to the shogun in matters of state as well as religion. In fact, since Zen priests were often sent as emissaries to China, they were not only in charge of religious and cultural matters but also of diplomacy and trade. This last was of great consequence, for among the things which the Japanese imported from the mainland were books and paintings and textiles, and whoever controlled this trade would in turn be able to influence the culture. (In addition to raw materials, fans, lacquerware, and swords were exported from Japan to China.)

It is impossible to explain Zen in a few words, for its illusive and mystic doctrine prides itself on the fact that it canot be transmitted in writing or through ritual or images. It speaks directly, and only when one realizes that the Buddha is in one's own heart as well as in all nature can one attain true insight. According to Zen, even good works are futile, and one must turn one's gaze inward to achieve enlightenment. It is believed that this doctrine was first introduced to China in 520 by the Indian monk Bodhidharma, known in Japan as Daruma, and from there it reached Japan during the Nara period. Both the Tendai and the Shingon sects had incorporated certain aspects of Zen, but it did not become an independent sect until the monk Eisai founded the Rinzai sect around the year 1200. During the thirteenth century it was taken up by the Kamakura warriors, and it became the most popular and influential school of Buddhist thought among the aristocracy of the Muromachi period. Today, it is the one Buddhist sect which enjoys a certain amount of prestige among educated Japanese, and even people who have never studied Zen are profoundly influenced by its spirit of restraint, its emphasis upon contemplation, and its distrust of ritual and dogma, as well as the many things it brought in its wake, such as the tea ceremony, flower arrangement, and the cult of ink-painting. Japanese children pay unwitting homage to Zen, for one of their favorite toys is the Daruma, a round, red doll who is always legless because the sage is said to have meditated for so long that his legs fell off.

The importance of this age in the cultural history of Japan is best illustrated by the fact that many of the concepts and ideals which were introduced during the Muromachi period from Sung and Yüan China are today looked upon as typically Japanese by the Japanese themselves as well as by many foreigners. The love for extreme simplicity and restraint, the emphasis upon subdued colors, the dislike of gorgeousness and ostentation are not at all typical of the characteristically Japanese phases of Japanese culture such as the Heian, the Momoyama, and the Edo periods, but are Chinese importations which were introduced by the Zen monks of the fifteenth century. Today, however, they have been so completely absorbed that they are looked upon as a part of the native tradition, and the world at large thinks of the tea ceremony and ink-painting and flower arrangement as peculiarly Japanese, although they are really Chinese in origin.

THE PAINTING OF THE MUROMACHI PERIOD

Chinese-style ink-painting of the Sung period, called *suiboku,* or *sumi-e* in Japanese, had already been introduced to Japan during the second half of the Kamakura period, but it was not until the Muromachi age that it became so prevalent that it transformed the entire artistic tradition. This influence proved so cardinal that the history of fifteenth-century painting in Japan is little more than the history of ink-painting, and in the Kanō school it has continued up to the present day.

At first the subjects were either Buddhist or representations of trees, grasses, and rocks, but later the artists of this school devoted themselves primarily to the landscape, and it was in this field that they celebrated their greatest triumphs. All of these works were thought of as an expression of Zen Buddhism, and most of the early *suiboku* painters were Zen monks rather than professional artists. The first of these, and one of the most gifted in the rendering of Buddhist subjects, was Mokuan, who lived during the middle of the fourteenth century and spent the latter part of his life in China, from which he never returned. In style he was very close to the celebrated late Sung painter, Mu Ch'i or, as the Japanese call him, Mokkei, and he was therefore known as the second Mu Ch'i. A typical example of his work is the picture of the gay wandering monk Hotei, who to the Zen believers symbolizes the carefree life of one who has found peace in the study of Zen *(Plate 61).* Mokuan portrays him as a rotund little figure with short legs, bare belly, and a sack hanging from a stick which he carries over his shoulder. The line is strong yet sensitive, and the ink tones are skillfully handled, with blurred greys, the sharp black of the stick, and the sketchy black of the rough lines delineating the garment. The background is left bare, and the empty silk heightens the power of the simple, expressive little figure.

Under the influence of Sung painting, new subjects were treated by the Buddhist painters, especially those working for Zen temples. The most important of these were the paintings of Buddhist hermits, the arhats, or *rakan.* Sets of these holy men became extremely popular, the most common number being a group of five hundred hermits painted on a set of fifty kakemonos.

110

三會龍華未厭當
長衒短耑恣徉在
帀裹裹許宪卝大
桯丈頭過日月長
兜率陀天乖居扳
尼盧攊閜水靈郷
為言我是真弥勒
家醜無耑向外揚
玉几　正印蔣黃

Plate 61.

Hotei, by Mokuan.

Muromachi period.

Coll. K. Sumitomo,
Hyōgo Prefecture

Myōchi-in, Kyoto

Plate 62. Portrait of Muso Kokushi (detail), by Mutō Shūi. Muromachi period.

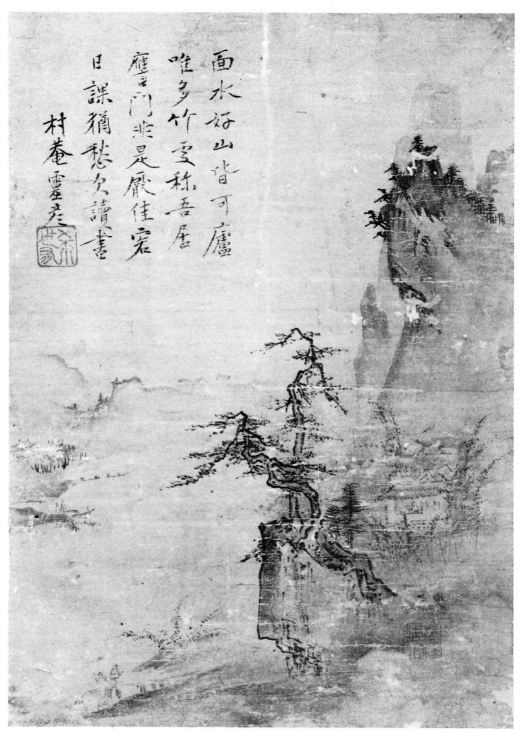

面水好山皆可廬
唯多竹變稱吾居
庭言門非是嚴佳宦
日課猶愁欠讀書
村菴靈彥

Coll. Tokyo National Museum

Plate 63. Landscape with Sage Reading in a Hermitage,
by Shūbun. Muromachi period.

Coll. Tokyo National Museum

Plate 64. Winter Landscape, by Sesshū.

Muromachi period.

Coll. Tokyo National Museum

Plate 65. Landscape, by Sesshū.

Muromachi period.

Nanzen-ji, Konchi-in, Kyoto

Plate 66. Landscape with Pavilion at Lake,
by Kanō Motonobu. Muromachi period.

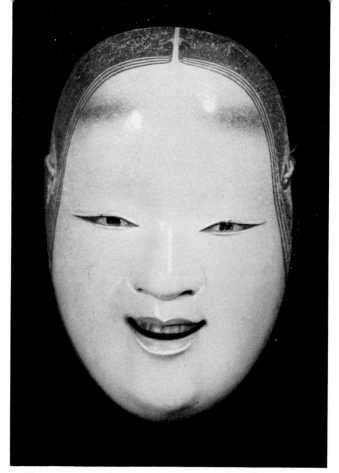

Plate 67. Ko-omote Mask.

Momoyama period.

Coll. I. Kongō, Tokyo

Plate 68.

Shikami Mask, by Shakuzuru.

Momoyama period.

Coll. Nara Museum

Plate 69. Kinkaku-ji (Golden Pavilion),
Rokuon-ji, Kyoto.
Muromachi period.

Among the artists devoting themselves to this subject, the most outstanding was Minchō, also called Chō Densū, who lived from 1352 to 1431. The hermits in such works are usually seen against a landscape, either individually or in groups, and they are shown meditating or performing some miracle. The style is extremely detailed, and from a purely artistic point of view, many of the *rakan* paintings are quite inferior. Far more rewarding aesthetically are the portraits of famous monks, a type which also owed its origin to Chinese models but which the Japanese developed in a very beautiful way. The finest of these is probably the portrait of the priest Musō Kokushi in the Myōchi-in in Kyoto, a work painted in 1349 by Mutō Shūi, who is supposed to have been one of the disciples of the Zen master portrayed in the painting *(Plate 62)*. The Zen doctrine, which rejected the worship of idols, made no use of traditional Buddhist paintings, substituting for them the portraits of famous religious teachers and Zen masters. These pictures are deeply moving, interpreting the holy men in such a way that the unique personality of each stands vividly before us. The style is realistic in so far as the rendition is based upon a model whom the artist has not beautified, but at the same time, by omitting all that is not essential, the artist gives these portraits a remarkable simplicity and strength. Compared to the Kamakura portrait of Yoritomo, the painting of Musō Kokushi is less formalized, especially in the treatment of the robes, where there is more linear detail. Strong, simple lines mark the contours and folds of the garments, but as in the earlier picture the head, distinct against a bare background, remains the center of interest. The face is somewhat more individualized than in the Yoritomo portrait and the line used for the features, in contrast to the line used for the robes, is very sensitive. The features stand out clearly, the eyes with their wrinkled lids and the mouth turned down at the corners being particularly moving, and the whole suggests a spiritual, rather melancholy man of great sensitivity.

The most important development in *sumi-e* was the growth of Chinese-style landscape painting, a form which was apparently established by Josetsu, a Zen monk connected with Shōkoku-ji, a famous Zen monastery in Kyoto, and perfected by Shūbun, who was a priest at the same temple. Both were active in the early part of the fifteenth century. Today there is only one painting which can be attributed to Josetsu with any certainty, and that is

111

the famous hanging scroll of a man trying to catch a catfish with a gourd. The subject is typical of Zen, indicating that it would be as hard to express the ultimate truth in words as it would be to catch this fish with a gourd. The style of the painting, with its subtle tonal values, its economy of means, and its suggestion of a deep and mysterious space, is typical of the Chinese painting of the Sung period. Even more important than Josetsu was Josetsu's pupil Shūbun, to whom a great number of works have been attributed. Most of these are probably later paintings done in the manner of Shūbun, for it is customary both in Japan and China not only to paint pictures in the style of some celebrated artist of the past, but also to sign them with the seal and signature of the master. The Shūbun works which today are regarded as the most authentic are the scroll in the National Museum called "Reading in a Hermitage in a Bamboo Grove," and the mountain landscapes in the Fujiwara Collection in Tokyo. They reveal Shūbun as a brilliant *suiboku* painter who followed the Chinese masters of the thirteenth century very closely, especially Hsia Kuei and Ma Yüan *(Plate 63)*. The theme is always the same: the hermit scholar in a little hut at the foot of the mountains meditating upon the grandeur and beauty of nature. In keeping with Zen pantheism, the onlooker was supposed to identify himself with this tiny figure, so that by losing his individuality in the vastness of the cosmos, he might find his true self. In the National Museum landscape, a haze obscures one half of the picture, and in the other half a steep, craggy cliff looms against the sky. A few peaks appear like shadows in the distance, and there are some tiny roofs and fishing boats in the middle ground, and in front a bridge and two small figures. The water melts into the haze and the haze melts into the sky and against this cloudy space stand two large gnarled pines, which dominate the picture. Behind, sketched in faintly, is the scholar's hut, with the little figure of the scholar just visible through the window. Both the theme and the spirit of the work are very close to that of Sung painting, and the skillful brush as well as the atmospheric effect are worthy of the tradition he was following.

While the work of Shūbun and his contemporaries was little more than an imitation of the Chinese style, Japanese ink-painting achieved a native character in the work of Sesshū (1420 to 1506), Shūbun's pupil and fellow

112

Zen priest at Shōkoku-ji. His fame and influence have been extraordinary, and although it may be an overstatement to say, as many critics have, that he is the greatest painter Japan has ever produced, he is certainly the most outstanding of the artists working in *sumi-e*. Like many of the monk-painters of the period, Sesshū went to China, where he received high honors and according to one report was even asked to decorate a room in the Peking palace. It is interesting to note that while Sesshū, whose own artistic style had been formed by studying the landscapes of Hsia Kuei and other Sung masters, was fascinated by the actual landscape of China, he had little use for contemporary Chinese painters who were working in the more realistic Ming style.

Of all the many works which today are attributed to Sesshū, the finest is the famous landscape scroll in the Mōri Collection in Yamaguchi. The painting, which is fifty feet long, portrays the changing seasons starting with a spring landscape and ending with a winter one. Painted in 1486 when the artist was sixty-six years old, it shows the full measure of his genius. What is particularly impressive is the strength and boldness of his brushwork and the variety of his compositions. His lines are often heavy and angular; his forms, such as those of the buildings, are very abstract. A work in which these qualities are brought out very clearly is the winter landscape in the collection of the National Museum in Tokyo, one in a series of four paintings of the seasons, of which only two have survived (*Plate 64*). A thick, forceful line marks the contours of the trees and rocks, and the bare twigs are drawn with great boldness. This charged, expressive line, now black and heavy, now thin, is balanced by the empty areas of the sky and the hills at the left, which, except for some shading, are almost bare. The building is indicated with a few quick strokes, and in the middle of the lower part a figure, sketched in with half a dozen lines, is seen climbing some stairs which disappear behind the hill. In contrast to Shūbun, who imitated the mysterious, misty depth of Chinese painting, Sesshū tended to flatten out the space and emphasize strong linear patterns. Still, the underlying conception in his work of the insignificance of man in the lonely splendor of nature is typical of Chinese-style landscape painting.

A work of his which has been greatly admired and which illustrates a completely different aspect of his genius is the hanging scroll, or kakemono, of 1496, which is now in the National Museum *(Plate 65)*. This landscape, painted at the end of his life as a present for his pupil Shūen, is done in a manner known as the splashed-ink technique. In contrast to the Mōri scroll which is rather detailed in line and form, the work is extremely abstract, recalling the style of the late Sung painter Ying Yü-chien. The artist uses a very wet brush, splashing the ink on the paper quickly and freely. This technique is closely connected with Zen, which taught that enlightenment came not as a result of a long, thorough study but in a momentary flash, and it was this feeling which the artists working in the splashed-ink manner wished to convey. The subject of the Sesshū painting is so abstractly rendered that at first it looks like nothing but blots of ink splashed near the bottom of some blank paper. A closer study reveals a rocky mountain with bushes and trees, a small building, and the line of a boat with two miniature figures. Most of the surface is left bare, for it is the relationship between the empty paper and the greys and sharp blacks of the ink which gives the work its expressive power. Here again the use of nothingness as a positive element, and of suggestion rather than statement, is typical of Zen and shows how such a painting, although on the surface merely a landscape, is ultimately a visual expression of the pantheistic spirit of Zen.

Numerous other paintings are attributed to Sesshū, most of them landscapes but some representing figures, birds and flowers, or animals. In addition to the kakemonos and the *makimono*'s, there are some screens, or *byōbu*. Many of these, however, must be looked upon as school pieces, for Sesshū had a large number of pupils, and artists for several generations after his death regarded themselves as his disciples. There was, in fact, a whole school of painters who called themselves the Sesshū or Unkoku school, the latter being the name of the temple in which Sesshū's studio was located. So great was his fame that even a man like Hasegawa Tōhaku, the most outstanding painter of the following century and a very original artist in his own right, signed himself Sesshū of the Fifth Generation. However, most of the artists of the Unkoku school did little more than imitate the manner of the master without contributing anything new or original of their own.

114

The only painter who caught the spirit of Sesshū and at the same time transformed it into his own style was Sesson, who lived from 1504 to about 1589. Although he was too young to have studied with him, he modeled his style upon Sesshū and referred to himself as a pupil of the master. The finest of his surviving works and one of the masterpieces of Japanese *suiboku* painting is his small picture of the stormy lake scene in the Nomura Collection in Kyoto. Here the strong brush strokes with which the artist has rendered the gale-swept trees and the rolling boat give a wonderful feeling of the storm. Only touches of color are used, for here again it is the quality of the ink against the paper which gives the painting its expressive power. Unlike the imitators of Sesshū, Sesson does not blindly copy the master but infuses his style with his own individuality, thus giving the painting an intensity of feeling which, in this example at least, almost surpasses Sesshū himself.

A school of painting which originated at this time, although it was of far greater importance during the Edo period was the Kanō school, so called because its founders were Kanō Masanobu and Kanō Motonobu, and the painters of the school were either actual or adopted members of the Kanō family. Kanō Masanobu (1434 to 1530) was a contemporary of Sesshū and is said to have been a pupil of Shūbun's, but unlike these artists Masanobu was a professional painter who belonged to the warrior class. Few of his works have survived, but those which remain would suggest that he was a rather mediocre painter who followed the Chinese tradition without any of the originality of a Sesshū. Nevertheless he became court painter to the shogun, and it was his position at the court which made the Kanō school so influential.

The true founder as well as the outstanding exponent of the school was Masanobu's son, Kanō Motonobu (1476 to 1559). He was a painter of great versatility, but in spite of his talent he was little more than an eclectic who tried every manner but excelled in none. Some of his works are in the style of Mu Ch'i, others in the style of Hsia Kuei or Ma Yüan, still others in the style of the Yüan as well as the Ming period, and he even painted in the Yamato-e manner. However, his most typical works, such as the landscape in the collection of the Konchi-in in Kyoto, show a style ultimately based

115

upon Sung painting, a manner in which he had been trained but which he modified in so far as he introduced a certain decorative element and a more realistic detail *(Plate 66)*. It has often been said by Japanese critics that this constitutes a Japanization of the Chinese ink-style, but in view of the fact that this same development was taking place in Ming-period China, it would seem more logical to assume that Motonobu, who after all was fifty years later than Sesshū, was inspired not only by Sung models but also by contemporary Chinese painting. The only way in which he can be said to be characteristically Japanese is that he sometimes introduced the bright, decorative color of the Tosa school into the *suiboku* style.

Yamato-e, which had been so important during the Kamakura period, was almost completely supplanted by the new ink-style, and only a few historical scrolls or stories of temples were still painted in this manner. The school which continued the Yamato-e tradition was the Tosa school, which was founded by Tosa Yukihiro, who in 1407 was given the title Tosa no Kami. It reached its greatest fame under Tosa Mitsunobu (1434 to 1525), who was appointed chief of the office of painters at the Imperial Court. Even in later centuries the Tosa school enjoyed a privileged position at the court in Kyoto, while the Kanō school became associated with the court of the shoguns in Edo. Mitsunobu's contribution was that he combined the colorful tradition of Yamato-e with the prevailing taste for Chinese-style painting, and the result was that his work is a rather unsatisfactory mixture of both. Later Tosa painters who were more frankly eclectic succeeded rather better in creating works which, although not original, kept alive the memory of a glorious past.

Besides these various schools, traditional-style Buddhist painting continued to be practiced, and although the artists made no original contributions they were often able to recapture the spirit of the older types of Buddhist painting. However, the age of Japanese Buddhism was drawing to a close, and even Zen, which had been the last sect to flourish, had declined by the end of the Muromachi period, and religious painting as Japan had known it for a thousand years gave way to purely secular painting.

THE SCULPTURE OF THE MUROMACHI PERIOD

Sculpture, which had deteriorated after the end of the thirteenth century, never regained the dominance which it had enjoyed for over seven hundred years. It may seem strange that a nation which had already shown a remarkable plastic sense in the prehistoric period and had so quickly and successfully taken up the Buddhist sculpture imported from the continent should then lose its creativity, but similar examples could be cited from other civilizations. It is enough to mention here that Chinese sculpture, which for almost two thousand years had been among the world's greatest, suffered a hopeless decline after the end of the Sung period. There would seem to be three principal causes for this strange phenomenon, although in the last analysis artistic creativity defies this type of rational explanation. The first is no doubt the falling off of Buddhism, which had been the great patron of sculpture throughout the previous centuries. Here, as in Europe, after the church ceased giving the sculptors commissions, their work was no longer so much in demand, resulting in a decline of the sculptor's profession. Second, the increasing realism of Japanese sculpture brought about a deadening of imaginative power, particularly noticeable in the religious images, and third, the growing emphasis upon pictorial rather than plastic elements led to a deterioration of the art of sculpture. Interestingly enough, these very same factors could be cited as the reasons for the decline of Chinese sculpture and to a lesser extent, of European sculpture as well. In all of these civilizations, as sculpture deteriorated, painting assumed an ever greater importance, becoming the form which dominated all other types of artistic expression.

The only kind of Buddhist sculpture which showed any vitality during the Muromachi period was portrait sculpture. Statues of Zen priests were particularly common, for it was the custom in Zen Buddhism to have images of famous Zen figures instead of icons of Buddhist deities. Among these, one of the most interesting is the representation of Musō Kokushi, whose portrait painted by Mutō Shūi has already been discussed. This statue, which is in the Founder's Hall of Zuisen-ji in Kamakura, shows the famous abbot in a large chair, his hands folded in the gesture of meditation, his face completely tranquil. The head is very realistic, yet even this image, which is

117

from the beginning of the Muromachi period, when the Kamakura tradition was still strong, shows a lack of plastic quality, especially in the drapery.

Far more successful are the Noh masks, which were first made during this period. Noh, a classic dance drama of Buddhist inspiration, is one of the most traditional and purely aesthetic art forms existing anywhere in the world today. Like Gigaku and Bugaku, it requires masks, although they are smaller, covering only the front of the face, and not all the actors in a given play wear masks. They combine abstract symbolism with a realistic portrayal of different types, and they are carved in such a way that an actor can express different moods through the mask *(Plate 67)*. All sorts of women are represented, beautiful young ladies, middle-aged women, old women, mad women. The masks for men include youths, warriors, court nobles, priests, blind men, and these general groups can be broken down into more specific types such as a humble old man or a noble warrior. In addition to the human masks there are various supernatural ones, such as ghosts, demons, and gods, many of which are rendered in a very fantastic manner *(Plate 68)*. The same types recur over and over again, and they are carved today in exactly the same way as they have been carved for the last several centuries, the profession of making Noh masks, as is so frequent in such traditional arts, often being handed down from father to son. However different they are in type, they all combine in a strange and moving way the beauty of abstract design with a profound expression of human emotion, usually of a tragic kind, for the spirit underlying Noh is a deeply pessimistic one, springing from Buddhist philosophy, with its emphasis upon the tragic and fleeting character of human existence.

THE ARCHITECTURE OF THE MUROMACHI PERIOD

Although there was a good deal of building during the Ashikaga period, especially in and around Kyoto, which had once again become the center of government, few of the palaces and temples survive today. This is largely because of the destructive Ōnin civil war which raged during the second half of the fifteenth century and destroyed half of Kyoto. As can well be imagined from the character of the rulers, who were aesthetes and men of refinement, the style of architecture was marked more by elegance than innovation or grandeur. The Chinese style declined in importance, except for Zen temples, whose architecture remained more closely linked to the mainland, and the dominant style was largely based upon the Japanese Wa-yō, with the addition of certain Chinese features. But generally speaking this age was not out-standing in its architectural design, and few if any imporant contributions were made. Perhaps the most significant development took place in resi-dential architecture, for as the age became increasingly worldly, this type of building became ever more luxurious. Unfortunately hardly any of the mansions and palaces are left today, but old paintings and descriptions in contemporary texts enable us to form a fair idea of the style used for the domestic architecture of the period. Even more important in the history of Japanese culture were the landscape gardens which were constructed under Zen auspices, and which originally came from China, although they were developed by the Japanese in a very beautiful way. Fine examples of Muro-machi landscape gardens are still in existence, such as those at Saihō-ji, Ryō-an-ji, and the Daisen-in of Daitoku-ji.

Of all the monuments of Muromachi architecture, by far the most famous is the Golden Pavilion, or Kinkaku of Rokuon-ji in Kyoto *(Plate 69)*. This temple was originally a villa built by the great art patron, Ashikaga Yoshi-mitsu, as the place of his retirement, but after his death it was turned into a Buddhist temple. Unfortunately most of the buildings were either destroyed by fire or moved to other locations, leaving only the pavilion at the original site, and in 1950, this last remaining structure was burned down by a crazed monk. It is now being rebuilt, and, since there are excellent photographs and detailed architectural drawings of the pavilion, an attempt is being made to construct it in its original style. Although modest in scale, the building was very charming, with trees forming a screen in back and the lake mirror-ing the villa, the rocks and trees and water all carefully arranged so that with the building they made a harmonious whole. This combination of landscape gardening with architecture is very effective, and it is a typical expression of the pantheistic spirit, which under the influence of Zen Bud-dhism permeated so much of the thinking of this age.

The villa was a three-story structure which combined a simple over-all design with luxurious ornamentation in the detail. The total effect was one

119

of graceful elegance rather than the gaudy splendor that became fashionable in the following period. The lowest story, which served as living quarters for the shogun, was built in the purely Japanese style of domestic architecture called *shinden zukuri*. The second floor was built in a similar style, but it had colored paintings on its ceilings, and was used for the poetry and musical parties given by Yoshimitsu for his friends. The top story was used for religious worship, and it is believed that it originally contained an image. It was built in a Chinese Zen style, the Chinese influence being particularly noticeable in the arched windows. Its interior and exterior were originally covered with gold leaf, which some scholars now think may have actually covered the whole building, but in any case it was this decoration which gave the villa its name. The roof, which was pyramidal in shape, was made of cypress bark and crowned by the gilt bronze image of a phoenix. In front of the first floor there was a projecting veranda which extended over the pond and was used for viewing the scenery, indicating again the typically Japanese attempt to use the surroundings in such a way that, together with the building, they become a part of an artistic whole. The villa, which combined in a very successful way features of religious architecture with others of domestic architecture, is a beautiful example of the Muromachi style.

The other famous building of this type is the Ginkaku, or Silver Pavilion, which was built as a country villa for Ashikaga Yoshimasa, the second great art patron among the Ashikaga shoguns. After his death it became a temple which was called Jishō-ji, although it is popularly known as Ginkaku-ji. Erected in 1489, it was modeled after the Golden Pavilion, which had been built almost a century earlier. In contrast to the former, which was located in the northern part of Kyoto and thus called Kitayama-dono, the Silver Pavilion was built in the eastern part of the capital and was therefore known as Higashiyama-dono, and Yoshimasa's rule was often referred to as the Higashiyama era, a name which has come to signify a period of aestheticism and refinement. Compared to Kinkaku-ji, Ginkaku-ji is more modest in dimensions, with only two stories instead of three, the lower one being in a Japanese and the upper one in a Chinese style. The villa, also very lovely in its simple elegance, is surrounded by a magnificent landscape garden, which is said to have been designed by Sōami, one of the greatest artists of

120

the age. Close to the pavilion there is a small structure called Tōgudō, containing a tiny tea room, which served as a model for all the later rooms used for the tea ceremony. Although the mature tea-ceremony house did not come into being until the following century, this room points in the direction in which it was to develop, and in the same way the living quarters at Tōgudō anticipate the type of design which was to be used for the Japanese house in subsequent periods. Features such as the alcove, or *tokonoma,* and the sliding doors, or *shōji,* as well as the general simplicity and restraint, are already a part of this fifteenth-century structure.

The most important buildings of the period were the great Zen temples, especially those of Kyoto, which exerted a tremendous influence upon the spiritual and cultural life of the time. Among the most famous were Tōfuku-ji, Nanzen-ji, Daitoku-ji, and Myōshin-ji, but almost none of their original buildings have survived. The only exception is the main gate, or Sanmon, at Tōfuku-ji which is an excellent example of contemporary architecture, showing a mixture of traditional Japanese and continental traits, in contrast to the great gate at Tōdai-ji, which had been built in a purely Chinese style. Of particular interest is the position of the gate in the general plan of the Zen compound, for the arrangement of the buildings was quite different from what it had been in older times. It consisted of the following elements, which were usually organized along a straight axis: first, a small gate known as the Sōmon; then the Sanmon, a two-story main gate like the one preserved at Tōfuku-ji; next the Buddha Hall, or Butsuden, and then the lecture hall, or Hattō. To the right and the left of these were smaller buildings like the sutra hall, the belfry, and the bathhouse, while the living quarters of the priests were usually behind the lecture hall. A pagoda was not part of this scheme, although at times one was added.

Among the other remaining Muromachi buildings, the most interesting are perhaps the pagoda and the Tōkondō at Kōfuku-ji in Nara, one of the great temples of the Nara period, which had been largely destroyed. These eight-century structures, which had been burned down repeatedly and then built up in the same style, were during the Muromachi period once again reconstructed in a pure Nara style. However, this was rather exceptional, and far more typical of the Muromachi period was the Kinkaku-ji and the

Ginkaku-ji, which combined elements of traditional Japanese architecture with others imported from China. However, only a very few of these buildings remain, and most of the others are minor structures in provincial locations.

THE CRAFTS OF THE MUROMACHI PERIOD

As in the other arts, Zen Buddhism affected the development of the crafts, particularly those associated with Cha-no-yu, the tea ceremony which had been imported from China by Zen priests and became one of the favorite pastimes of the Ashikaga aristocracy. The crafts used in connection with this highly ritualistic cult were pottery, iron casting, lacquer, and bamboo-making. The guests, in order to enter into the spirit of the ceremony, were supposed to appreciate the beauty of the utensils in contemplative tranquility. A class of tea masters was created, as well as sensitive connoisseurs, whose aesthetic perception was heightened by the practice of Cha-no-yu, which was perfected under Ashikaga Yoshimasa, the shogun who built the Silver Pavilion.

Among the utensils employed by the tea masters, the most important were the *chawan,* or tea bowl, and the *cha-ire,* or tea caddy, both often of real beauty, and fine examples are prized as great artistic treasures. They were originally imported from China and Korea, and a Chinese pottery called *chien yao,* or *temmoku* in Japanese, was favored, a heavy, rather coarse stoneware with a thick brown or black glaze. During the later part of the Muromachi period, a new school of tea ceremony called Wabi arose, which emphasized rustic simplicity. Under the influence of this school, the plain and often coarse Korean tea bowls became popular, and this led to the development in Japan of new kinds of pottery which were characterized by crude simplicity, in contrast to the highly finished products of China. The leading kiln sites at this time were Bizen near Okayama, and Shigaraki in Shiga Prefecture.

Although the *chawan* and *cha-ire* were the most important implements in the tea ceremony, they were by no means the only ones. Various other utensils were used, among them the *mizusashi,* or water container, little boxes used for keeping incense, and plates to hold the cake. The tea kettle was also very important. Made of cast iron, it was frequently decorated with beautiful relief designs, and its strong, simple shape reflects the spirit of austerity which is so characteristic of Cha-no-yu. The most famous place of their manufacture was Ashiya in Fukuoka Prefecture and they are therefore called Ashiyagama. Even the bamboo utensils used in connection with the tea ceremony—the tea spoon, the whisk, and the dipper—are very much prized, and great care is devoted to their manufacture.

The most important of these utensils were usually made of pottery, but at times some of them were made of lacquer, especially the cake plate and the incense box. Because of these and other uses, lacquer thrived during this period, although it did not reach the heights it had attained under the Heian rule. Here again the Chinese influence was pronounced, particularly of Ming lacquers, which had become very popular. The decorations used were often copied from contemporary paintings or designed by famous painters, and these landscapes or bird-and-flower pictures were rendered in *maki-e* and highly stylized, so they fitted the decorative nature of the various objects, such as writing or cosmetic boxes, for which they were intended. Textiles were also important, but only a few examples have been preserved, most of which are found at Shinto shrines. These garments are subdued both in color and pattern, and their refined beauty perfectly reflects the artistic ideals of the age. Towards the end of the period, foreign textiles were also imported, mostly from China but also from other Asian countries, as well as the Near East and Europe.

Of all the epochs of the last thousand years, it was the Muromachi period which was most strongly under the influence of China. Many of the artistic traditions of Japan, such as ink-painting, flower arrangement, tea ceremony, and landscape gardening, were introduced from China by Zen monks, who saw them as an expression of their pantheistic philosophy, yet the Japanese not only absorbed these arts, but, in the tea ceremony and the flower arrangement and garden designs, surpassed their teachers.

8

The Art of
the Momoyama Period

THE Momoyama period, although it only lasted from 1573 to 1615, was one of the most important in the entire history of Japan, for it was during this time that the foundations of modern Japan were laid. When it opened, the country had just emerged from a period of struggle and confusion, and four decades later, at its close, Tokugawa Ieyasu had established himself as the undisputed ruler of a united nation.

This period, in contrast to the refinement of the Ashikaga age, was one of exuberance and vitality. It was dominated by three military men, each a giant in his own way. The first, Oda Nobunaga, who lived from 1534 to 1582, was the founder of this new, unified realm, and the second, Toyotomi Hideyoshi (1536 to 1598), brought to a climax the splendor of the period, which was named after the palace Hideyoshi built on Momoyama, or Peach Hill, near Kyoto. It was he who undertook the invasion of Korea with an army of twenty thousand men, and who made plans to conquer China, a campaign which ended with his premature death in 1598. The third of the great leaders was Tokugawa Ieyasu (1542 to 1616), the founder of the Tokugawa Shogunate, who, after Hideyoshi's death, defeated his rivals

125

at the battle of Sekigahara in 1600. He was appointed shogun in 1603, and after the seige of Osaka, where Hideyoshi's son had been holding out with his supporters, he became the absolute ruler of the country. Although perhaps a less inspiring figure than Nobunaga or Hideyoshi, his influence on the history of Japan was in some ways even greater, for he consolidated for centuries to come what they had built up.

Perhaps the most characteristic symbol of the Momoyama period was its huge fortress-castles. The first of these was the one at Azuchi near Lake Biwa, which was erected between 1576 and 1579 and served as Nobunaga's military headquarters. Built of wood and clay upon a massive stone base, it was over seventy feet high, and it had a solidity of construction and vastness of scale unknown in previous Japanese buildings. There can be little doubt that this type of fortification was profoundly influenced by Western models, for Portuguese priests and merchants, who had come to Japan around the middle of the sixteenth century, had taught the Japanese Western methods of warface, such as the use of firearms, which made necessary stronger and more extensive fortresses. Even more impressive were the huge castles which Hideyoshi built after he succeeded Nobunaga in 1582. The greatest of these, and one which later served as a center of the Toyotomi forces, was the Osaka castle, but the most splendid were the Jurakudai, or Mansion of Pleasures, and the Fushimi Palace on Momoyama, the first built in 1587 and the second in 1594. Although only fragments remain, we can visualize their splendor from contemporary descriptions as well as the views of them in paintings. It is said that in building the Osaka castle, no less than thirty thousand laborers worked every day for three years before it was completed in 1586, for not only was it tremendous in scale, but its interior was magnificently decorated. Celebrated artists were employed to cover its walls with paintings and provide sumptuous screens lavishly ornamented with gold and silver. The beams were decorated with polychrome woodcarvings which made up in gorgeousness what they lacked in refinement, and yet it must be said that in spite of this great display the art of the period never degenerated into more vulgarity, for the new rulers, although not of the traditional aristocracy, were men of culture.

It seems strange, at least to the Westerner, that these great military dictators, one of whom (Hideyoshi) was actually of peasant origin, should also have been patrons of the arts. In fact, this combination of the man of action, ruthless in the pursuit of his own ends, with the man of learning and sensitivity is a peculiarly Japanese type, which is still encountered in modern Japan. These men sponsored not only palatial arts, like the gorgeous screens, but also refined arts, like the tea ceremony. Hideyoshi was particularly interested in Cha-no-yu, and one of his favorites was the great tea master Sen-no-Rikyū, who was also an expert in flower arrangement. Interestingly enough, the only lasting effect of Hideyoshi's ill-fated Korean expedition was the introduction of Korean potters and pottery to Japan, which greatly stimulated Japanese ceramics.

Alongside the growth of a more worldly culture, there was a further decline of Buddhism and Buddhist art, and it may well be said that from this period on Buddhism ceased to be a major factor in the artistic development of Japan. Nobunaga, the first great leader of the Momoyama period, was openly hostile to the Buddhist temples which had resisted his rise to power, and the most notorious but by no means the only example of this hostility was his destruction of Hiei-san in 1571. All three thousand buildings of this monastery, one of the holy places of Japanese Buddhism, were totally destroyed by fire, and most of the thousands of monks and other persons attached to it were killed either by fire or sword. Its land was confiscated, and at the foot of the mountain Nobunaga had a fort built to guard against the revival of the monastery. The only sect which continued to enjoy a certain amount of favor was Zen, which was still the chief sect of the samurai, and even continued during the Tokugawa period, when Confucianism became the official state cult. Confucianism largely supplanted Buddhism, and even today most Japanese, whether they know it or not, are Confucians at heart.

The vitality of the Momoyama period was no doubt partly because of the abilities of its three great leaders, and partly because of the prosperity which was the result of the country's being unified and at peace. The old court aristocracy had been invigorated by new blood from the warriors and the common people, and the merchant class became more prosperous and influential than it had ever been before. Most important of all, perhaps, was the contact with the West, which had been established in 1542, when Portuguese traders were driven ashore by a typhoon. Other Portuguese ships came, and a few years later Jesuit missionaries arrived, among them the great Spanish priest St. Francis Xavier, who landed in Kagoshima in Kyushu. In 1568 the Jesuits were received by Nobunaga, who was quite sympathetic to them. On the whole, their reception was favorable, and by 1582 it is reported that one hundred and fifty thousand converts had been made, most of them in Kyushu. However, the real reason why the Jesuits were well received had little to do with religion, but was rather because of the desire of the Japanese for Western technical knowledge and trade. European clothes and ships and weapons and mechanical objects soon became the vogue, and the feudal lords who welcomed the missionaries did so more for worldly considerations than spiritual ones. Nevertheless, the Christian faith spread widely, and it might well have been generally accepted if it had not been for the restrictions and frequent persecutions which, after the death of Ieyasu, led to its complete suppression. Considering the population of Japan during this period, the result of these few decades of proselytising is more impressive than the outcome of the hundred years of missionary labor during the nineteenth and twentieth centuries. However, it is a sad commentary upon the Christians themselves that two of the main reasons for their persecution were the struggles among the various religious orders, and the influence of Dutch and English Protestant traders who persuaded the shogunate that the Catholics were trying to establish a hold in order to conquer Japan. During the Momoyama period itself, the restrictions upon missionary activity were not too severe, and even during the years of the most cruel persecutions many of the Christian converts stood up admirably. Thousands payed for their faith with their lives, and even after Christianity had been stamped out it continued secretly in certain isolated villages.

The Painting of the Momoyama Period

The most brilliant achivement in the arts was the paintings which adorned the castles of the military rulers. Although few remain today, we know that Nobunaga's castle at Azuchi had paintings on its walls and screens, and that Hideyoshi's castles and palaces were ornamented in a magnificent manner. The style was very bold, with bright colors against backgrounds of pure gold. In their size and splendor, these works were quite in keeping with the spirit of the age, and they were ideally suited for the grand setting of the castles. The very scale of the paintings was indicative of the new tendencies; yet they were never simply ostentatious, for even at their most sumptuous, these Momoyama works show considerable taste.

The origin of their style is by no means certain, but evidence would suggest that three traditions are combined in these works. The decorative emphasis, and the flat, abstract patterns of brilliant color are certainly the heritage of the Japanese Yamato-e, which had continued in the form of the Tosa school (whose center was no longer exclusively in Kyoto, where Chinese-style ink-painting prevailed, but in provincial places such as Sakai near Osaka). At the same time the vigor of the brushwork shows that these artists were trained in ink-painting, and they did in fact work in the black-and-white as well as the colorful Momoyama style. Often the very same artist used both types together as Kanō Eitoku did in decorating the Azuchi castle. Generally speaking, however, the more ornate type of painting was reserved for the official halls, while the monochrome style was used in private chambers and the *tokonoma*. Finally, Western painting, which was introduced at this time, may account for the grandeur of these Momoyama works, a supposition which seems quite likely in view of the fact that the castles themselves show a good deal of European influence.

The founder of this new type of painting is believed to have been Kanō Eitoku, the grandson of Kanō Motonobu, who lived from 1543 to 1590. Although he studied under his grandfather, he soon developed a style which bears little resemblance to the eclectic work of the former. His great opportunity came when Nobunaga called upon him to undertake the decoration of his castle at Azuchi, and after Nobunaga's death Hideyoshi had him decorate the Osaka castle and the Jurakudai Palace. We are told that every story of these castles was adorned with huge paintings, some of which were on the walls, while others were on the *fusuma* (sliding screens) and *byōbu*. (At the Momoyama castle alone there are supposed to have been no less than one hundred pairs of folding screens.) It is said that Eitoku worked with a large brush made of straw, and that he produced works on a scale and in a quantity greater than anything which had been done before. Unfortunately

129

very few of them are still in existence, but from those which remain we can imagine the splendor of these palaces, which are such a striking expression of the Momoyama period.

Of the surviving works attributed to Kanō Eitoku, the most impressive are the pair of six-part folding screens representing hawks on pine trees in the collection of the Tokyo University of the Arts, and the "Lion Screen" in the Imperial Collection. The subjects are based on Chinese motifs, but they are executed in a manner completely unlike anything which the Chinese had ever done, and it is in works such as these that a truly Japanese quality is expressed *(Plate 70)*. The main characteristics, which are also found in Heian art, are the emphasis upon the purely decorative, the use of bright colors, the flat space, and the simplification of form. However, the paintings of the Heian period, which used Japanese subject matter, were quite small, while these works usually have Chinese subjects and are on a very large scale. Eitoku in his hawk-and-pine screens clearly exemplifies the Momoyama style. The space is so flat as to be nearly two-dimensional, and though there is a certain amount of detail in the bird and the rocks and the tree trunk, other areas are almost wholly abstract, especially the clouds and the foliage, which have been turned into decorative patterns. The design is very bold, with the strong vertical of the trunk and the curving horizontals of the branches and foliage, and there are splendid colors, of which unfortunately the reproduction gives no idea. The clouds are gold, the water is deep blue, the foliage is green, and there are sharp black lines which strengthen the decorative pattern.

It may seem strange that this new colorful style of painting should be the product of the Kanō school, but it must be remembered that Motonobu himself had worked in the Japanese as well as the Chinese style, and that in Japan belonging to a certain school does not necessarily mean that the artist follows the same style as every other member of the school, but that he continues a family tradition. It must also be said that Eitoku, although his most original works were in the new Momoyama style, also painted in the Chinese tradition. However, the work he did in the *suiboku* style of his grandfather lacked the subtlety of really good Chinese painting, and contemporary critics called it coarse and rough. It has the same boldness which marks his other work, but this manner was less suited to Eitoku's genius, and he is far less outstanding in the *suiboku* style than he is in his decorative screens.

After Eitoku's premature death in 1590, numerous followers and students carried on his work, most notably Kanō Sanraku, who was born in 1559 and died in 1635. He lived into the Edo period, and his work in many ways reveals the eclecticism of the Edo Kanō painting rather than the boldness of Momoyama art. The emphasis in his work on realistic detail interferes with the decorative beauty and the largeness of design which was so characteristic of Momoyama painting, and the result in most cases is a very unsatisfactory type of painting, in which there is a strange mixture of flat gold backgrounds with detailed naturalism in the trees and birds and rocks. However, other works of his continue the more abstract style of Eitoku, and they are not only more typical of the Momoyama period but also more successful as works of art.

The greatest painter of this period, however, was not a member of the Kanō school and for this reason was neglected until his rediscovery in recent times. He was Hasegawa Tōhaku, the founder of the Hasegawa school, who lived from 1539 to 1610. Like Eitoku, he worked in the traditional Chinese manner as well as the typically Momoyama style, and he created masterpieces in both. At first he regarded himself as a follower of Sesshū, the great fifteenth-century master, but then he turned to Mu Ch'i, the famous Chinese artist of the Sung period, whose work he studied at Daitoku-ji. A beautiful example of Tōhaku's black-and-white painting is the "Monkey Screen" in the Shōkoku-ji in Kyoto *(Plate 71)*. In Eitoku's hawk-and-pine screen, everything is explicitly stated, and every part, whether it is the mountain in the background or the stream in the middle, is brought out with the same clarity. In the "Monkey Screen," exactly the opposite is true: everything is suggested. Instead of a clear, flat space, there is a haziness, through which the tree is only partly visible. The composition of the tree, however, is very similar to that of the Eitoku hawk-and-pine screen, and there is the same emphasis on the foreground, with the tree brought to the very front of the picture. While Eitoku crowds space with flat, sharp-edged areas of color, Tōhaku leaves much of the screen bare, and unlike the hawk, which has a pattern of clear,

131

small, decorative details, the monkeys are painted in a soft, rather blurred style. Even more beautiful, perhaps, are Tōhaku's pine tree screens in the collection of the National Museum, in which isolated groups of pines appear partly obscured by the mist. Works like these are sensitive re-creations of the spirit of Mu Ch'i, and yet, particularly in the pine tree screens, they combine this soft-ink style with a very original and more characteristically Japanese conception.

Tōhaku also painted in the colorful Momoyama manner, and it is in this style that he created his most brilliant works. Particularly beautiful are the series of fusuma paintings in the Chishaku-in in Kyoto (*Color Plate 5*). They are believed to have been painted in 1591 when the temple was built at the command of Hideyoshi, and they have traditionally been attributed to Tōhaku and his pupils. These works are the masterpieces of Momoyama painting, for nowhere else does the bold decorative spirit of this age find a stronger or lovelier expression. The various screens show the different seasons, such as spring, with the white glory of the cherry trees against a golden ground, and fall, with the delicate, red-leaved maples. The reproduction is an autumn scene with flowering hibiscus, green grasses, some chrysanthemums and bamboo, and a pine, whose rugged trunk makes a broad diagonal leading from one part of the *fusuma* to the other. The white hibiscus flowers are balanced by the crisscrossing grass on the one side and the solid areas of green needles on the other, and the clouds and sky make a setting of rich gold. Here, the Japanese love of nature is combined with their decorative genius, and this fusion, expressed in all the splendor of the Momoyama style, results in some of the finest paintings in Japanese art.

Besides the works in the Chinese and the more typically Japanese styles, Western-type painting was also produced. Although the lasting effect of these works was not great (they were largely destroyed at the time of the persecution of the Christians and the banning of Westerners from Japan in the early seventeenth century), there was quite a vogue for them during the Momoyama period. Most of them were probably religious works painted for the use of the growing Christian congregations, but some were secular, showing the life and fashions of contemporary Europeans. They have little artistic

132

merit, for they are simply copies of the European models, but they are interesting as social documents and often have a naive charm which makes them rather appealing. Almost all the religious works perished during the persecutions, but some of the non-religious paintings still exist, and they illustrate how well understood the Western style was in the Japan of that time.

Far more interesting and successful are the so-called Namban Byōbu, or screens showing "Southern Barbarians," as the Westerners were then called because they had first come to Japan from southern regions such as the Philippines. The pictures, which show the Europeans in Japan, record their strange looks and peculiar dress. They are painted in a typically Japanese style with gold clouds and flat decorative patterns, but the main emphasis is upon the portrayal of the foreigners who, to the Japanese, were grotesque and exotic. A screen in the Imperial Collection is particularly interesting, for, besides the foreigners, it shows the interior of a Christian church built in the Buddhist-temple style *(Plate 72)*. On one side of the screen, priests and monks are shown worshipping before a Western-style painting of Christ, and on the other side, in the courtyard in front of the church, there is a group of Europeans in strange hats and baggy pants. They have moustaches and narrow beards and long, exaggerated noses, and some of them are so tall that they look as if they were standing on stilts. Although this particular screen is believed to be early Edo, it shows the same style and content as the ones of the Momoyama period. Others depict the arrival of foreign priests, or the merchants in their splendid ships, and all of them record in great detail the customs and looks of these foreigners, who were so fascinating to the Japanese.

The Namban pictures indicate yet another interest of this period, and that is genre painting, for the Momoyama artists did not only portray the strange customs of the foreigners but, like the Yamato-e painters of the Kamakura period, they illustrated the life of their own time. The growth of a more popular culture stimulated the genre painting, for the newly rich merchants of Osaka and the port cities were not so much interested in the aristocratic culture of Kyoto as they were in the more vital civilization of their own day and their own class. Interestingly enough, the artists who painted these

133

pictures side by side with the more official Chinese-style ink-paintings often did not bother to sign them (they were considered a lesser art), yet in some cases it is upon these spontaneous and informal works that their fame rests today.

Here again, it is difficult to make a clear distinction between the Momoyama and early Edo works, for the style and the spirit of these paintings remain much the same during the first half of the seventeenth century. The scenes are usually portrayals of the festivals and amusements of ordinary people rendered in a very simple and decorative manner. No attempt is made to idealize them, and the result is that the paintings are often extremely interesting not only as works of art but as documents reflecting the culture of the time. Some of the pictures also show scenes from domestic life, and still others, dancers, musicians, and beauties of the day, and it is from this type of genre painting that *ukiyo-e* developed during the Edo period. Certainly the choice of these subjects was not chance but reflected a change in the structure of Japanese society, a change which was to be even more pronounced during the Edo period, and it has often been said that the Momoyama period marks the beginning of modern Japan, when a popular culture supported by the new merchant class supplanted the aristocratic culture of ancient Kyoto.

THE ARCHITECTURE OF THE MOMOYAMA PERIOD

The most characteristic expression of the age was the large castles and palaces built by Nobunaga, Hideyoshi, and Ieyasu. Unfortunately, none of these castles have been preserved in their entirety, and the remnant of the Osaka castle seen today is a modern reconstruction preserving little of the original design. However, some portions of Hideyoshi's palaces were removed to temples and in them something of the magnificence of these Momoyama buildings is still preserved.

The most impressive of these structures are the Audience Hall of the Shiro, the Noh stage, the adjoining reception rooms, and the Chokushimon, or Imperial Envoy's Gate, all from Hideyoshi's Fushimi Palace and now part of Nishi Hongan-ji in Kyoto. The Audience Hall is a perfect example of the interior of this kind of architecture, for it is ornamented with splendid

Color Plate 5. Pine Tree with Grasses and Flowers Screen, attributed to Hasegawa Tōhaku. Momoyama period.

paintings of pine trees and cranes as well as ancient Chinese rulers and sages, all against gold backgrounds, and there are elaborate carvings of cranes and golden clouds in the *ramma,* or frieze, between the pillars and the ceiling. The gate, designed in the Chinese style, is also very impressive, with rich carvings and an elegantly curved outline. A similar gate, the Karamon, is now at Daitoku-ji, and it is believed that it was originally a part of Hideyoshi's Jurakudai Palace, which seems likely, in view of its style. It combines simplicity (especially in the thatched roof and the pillars) with ornateness in the elaborately carved and graceful curved gables. Also from the Jurakudai Mansion and now located on the grounds of Nishi Hongan-ji is the Hiunkaku, or Flying-Cloud Pavilion. It is a garden villa modeled after the Golden and Silver Pavilions of the preceding period, but it lacks the elegance of the earlier buildings, for grandeur rather than refinement was the strong point of the Momoyama period.

Of the palaces, the only one of which a substantial part remains is the Nijōjō, or Nijō Palace, in Kyoto *(Plate 73).* These buildings, which were originally part of a larger complex, were the dwelling of the lord of the castle, whose residence was in the second fortress, or *ni-no-maru,* and it is believed that they were erected during the first decade of the seventeenth century. Since it is the only example of palace architecture from the Momoyama period, it is of great interest historically as well as artistically. Here again the basically simple Japanese design of the plain, geometric walls with their white plaster and the severe verticals and horizontals of the brown beams is combined with a huge curved roof, the gables of which are embellished with intricate designs in metalwork and carved wood. As in the paintings, the splendor is controlled by artistic taste, so the buildings are never ornate in a vulgar sense, as is the case with the Edo-period structures at Nikkō. Even more impressive is the interior of the palace, especially the Audience Hall, which the famous Kanō school painter Kanō Tanyū adorned with pictures of huge pine trees against backgrounds of gold *(Plate 74).* The paintings are very large, yet they fit beautifully into the room, their strong, curving patterns counterbalanced by the equally strong lines of the beams, which are set into the walls. If the ceiling is richly garnished, the floor, with its *tatami* mats, is almost severely plain, and the simplicity of the

135

unadorned parts of the room is an effective and necessary contrast to those parts which are lavishly decorated. At the end of the room there is a raised alcove, or *tokonoma,* which is still one of the chief characteristics of the Japanese house, although in a somewhat different form. To the right is a much smaller alcove with *tana,* or shelves, and a *shoin,* or window, at the left, which served for reading, features found not only at the Nijōjō but in all Japanese buildings in the so-called *shoin* style. In spite of the brilliance of the paintings on the walls and on the sliding screens, the effect of the room as a whole is relatively simple, when compared to the great European palaces like Versailles, showing how the underlying Japanese tradition of honesty and simplicity in architectural design prevails even in an age noted for its splendor.

The best-preserved castle from the Momoyama period is the Himeji castle west of Osaka in Hyōgo Prefecture *(Plate 75).* Originally built by Hideyoshi as a military strong point for western Japan, it was enlarged by the lord Ikeda Terumasa at the command of Ieyasu during the early years of the seventeenth century. It consists of a series of walls and moats copied from Western fortifications, and it is crowned by a huge six-story tower, or keep, called *tai-tenshu* in Japanese. (In addition to this central tower there are three smaller ones known as *ko-tenshu.*) In times of trouble, the keep could be used as a residence for the lord instead of the palace in the outer part of the castle like the one at Nijōjō, but its main purpose was to serve as a final holdout in case the outer fortifications fell. Of these there were usually two in addition to the inner portion known as the *hon-maru,* namely, the *ni-no-maru,* like the one preserved at Nijōjō, and the outermost one, called *san-no-maru.* The appearance of the castle is very impressive, with its huge stones at the base of the white walls, and on the hilltop, dominating the landscape, the imposing white towers, with the handsome tile roofs marking each story.

Castles such as the one at Himeji were very important, not so much for military reasons, since they were rarely used in that capacity, but rather as centers of commerce, for traders supplying the lord and his retinue established themselves in the area, and markets grew up and towns crystallized around the castles. Many of the great cities of Japan still have their castle or the remnants of one as a reminder of the fact that they originally grew up around the castle of the feudal lord of the region. Unfortunately few of them retain much of their original appearance, for some, like the Osaka and Edo castles, were burned down and rebuilt in modern times, and others, such as the Nagoya and Hiroshima castles, were almost completely destroyed by bombs during the Second World War. However, some provincial castles have survived, and today they still stand in the middle of the towns which once sprang up about them.

The energies of the period were spent on the castles and palaces, and Buddhist architecture fell into a decline. Neither Nobunaga nor Hideyoshi were at all sympathetic to Buddhism, the former having actually destroyed many of the ancient temples. However, Hideyoshi, although not a believer, used Buddhism for his own political ends and characteristically enough he built Hokō-ji, a huge temple in Kyoto, to rival or even surpass the great Nara temple of Tōdai-ji. This structure was the largest temple ever built in Japan, just as the statue in its main hall was the biggest Buddha, and here again it was the size and grandeur of the undertaking which was stressed. Built in 1587, it was destroyed in 1612, rebuilt, and destroyed again in 1798, so the present edifice, which is small in scale, is quite modern.

Of the surviving Momoyama-period temples, the most beautiful is Zuigan-ji, a Zen monastery at Matsushima near Sendai. Although it adds little to the traditional style of Buddhist architecture, it is very lovely in its design and execution, and the ornamental carvings are particularly fine. Another outstanding example of Momoyama architecture is the Sanbō-in, or Abbot's Quarters, at Daigo-ji, a famous Shingon temple near Uji. These quarters were rebuilt, along with the beautiful garden, in honor of Hideyoshi, who had come there for a flower-viewing festival. The proportions of the building are very beautiful, and the rooms, such as the *shinden,* or reception room, are perfect examples of this type of Japanese interior, combining an over-all simplicity with a richness of painted decorations.

THE CRAFTS OF THE MOMOYAMA PERIOD

In the crafts as in the other arts (except sculpture), the Momoyama period was of great importance, and it might well be said that all the rich developments which occurred in the Edo crafts were based upon the artistic ideals of the Momoyama period. Since it was an epoch of wealth, it is not surprising that the crafts should have expanded, and there were many new centers of production, not only in the traditional places such as Kyoto and Seto, but in provincial centers as well. The rise of the merchant class in the rapidly growing cities added a new group of patrons, and the contacts with the outside world, especially Europe, through the Portuguese and Spanish traders and priests, and Korea, through Hideyoshi's military expedition, proved very stimulating, with the result that there was a marked increase not only in the quantity of craft production but also in the quality and variety.

* In many ways the Momoyama period was the golden age of Japanese pottery, and outstanding pieces from this time are regarded as national treasures. The chief reason for this flowering was the importance of the tea ceremony, which created a demand for tea bowls that could no longer be met by importations from Korea and China. The greatest of the tea masters, Sen-no-Rikyū (1521 to 1591), was patronized both by Nobunaga and Hideyoshi, and the simple, rather severe taste associated with the Wabi school influenced the aesthetics of that time, just as it still does today.

The traditional sites of pottery manufacture had been Seto near Nagoya and Karatsu in Kyushu, but for finer glazed wares the Japanese had looked to Yi-dynasty Korea, which was far more advanced in the manufacture of ceramics. Both in style and technique these Yi-dynasty vessels left their mark upon the ceramic production of the time, and most of the outstanding wares of the Momoyama period, particularly the Karatsu and Raku wares, but also the Shino and Oribe-type pottery were strongly influenced by Korean models. However, the more native Japanese wares such as Bizen, made in the neighbourhood of Okayama and outstanding for its plain unglazed body, and the similarly plain Iga and Shigaraki wares continued to be made and were further developed, but after Hideyoshi brought back Korean potters and pottery from his military expedition, the Korean influence became even more pronounced.

The finest of these Korean-type wares and in the eyes of many the most beautiful pottery Japan has ever produced were the Shino wares made at

Kujiri in Mino Province not far from Seto *(Plate 76)*. Although the best ones were produced during the Momoyama period, Shino ware continued to be made during the Edo period and many early Edo pieces are just as fine as the Momoyama ones. The most outstanding characteristic of this type of pottery is the heavy translucent white glaze which was put on very thickly and unevenly. Often the surface is decorated with simple abstract designs in iron oxide which is reddish in color and adds greatly to the beauty. This kind is known as *e*-Shino, or painted Shino, and then there is the red Shino and the grey Shino, so called because of the color of the glaze, but actually the different types are very similar in technique and style. The forms are usually ones associated with the tea ceremony, such as the *chawan* (tea bowl) or *kashiki* (cake plate). In all of them the simple strength of the shape, the beauty of the glaze, so thick and irregular, and the restraint of the abstract design are remarkable. This type of plain, rather crude ware has had a particular influence on present-day potters both in Japan and in America, and leading modern potters such as Rosanjin have done some of their best work in the Shino style.

Another type of pottery made in the Mino region (now Gifu Prefecture) was Oribe ware, named after the celebrated tea master Furuta Oribe, who is supposed to have originated it *(Plate 77)*. In contrast to Shino ware, it shows considerable variety in both shape and ornament, especially the *e*-Oribe, which is often very imaginative in its decorative design. Although originating in the Momoyama period, this ware continued to be produced throughout the following centuries, and it is still made today. Its distinguishing characteristic is the use of a greenish glaze covering only a part of the vessel, and a design which is painted against a light, neutral-colored ground. These decorations, like the stalk of grass on the wine bottle reproduced, are very abstract, and like the designs on the Shino ware they bring out the shape of the vessel itself.

Perhaps the most famous of the tea-ceremony bowls are those of the Raku type, which are named after Hideyoshi's palace, the Jurakudai. They were produced in Kyoto (the traditional center of tea ceremony) by the Raku family which today still continues to make pottery as it has for fourteen generations *(Plate 78)*. However, the most famous pieces of Raku ware, which have been celebrated for centuries and have even been given personal names, such as Mt. Fuji or White Peak, are those made by Kōetsu, one of the great geniuses of Japanese art. His tea bowls have a grandeur of design and beauty of workmanship seldom equaled and never surpassed even by the potters of the Raku family itself. This type of ware is usually black in color, but red Raku and white Raku also exist. The shapes are strong and plain, for the ware was used exclusively for the tea ceremony, and they create a feeling of somber, brooding strength, which in the West would never be associated with a teacup.

Of all the Momoyama wares, the one which most clearly reveals the Korean influence is the Karatsu ware made in the Hizen Province in Northern Kyushu, where Korean potters were actually brought in order to teach the Japanese the superior methods of Yi-dynasty pottery manufacture. The most beautiful are the *e*-Karatsu, which are decorated with very free, very lovely abstract designs *(Plate 79)*. The glaze is usually brownish-grey and crackled, but there are white and dark brown ones as well, and the shapes, which are close to those of the Korean models, are particularly graceful. This pottery, which was much in demand for the tea ceremony, continued to be made during Edo times, and many of the best examples come from the early part of this period.

Textiles also flourished, for it was only natural that the splendor of Momoyama life should find expression in gorgeous materials. If the kimono of the Heian period was more elegant with its many layers of different colors, the Momoyama kimono has never been surpassed in its richness and beauty of design. Yet here again, as in the Momoyama *byōbu,* the artist does not lose himself in the garish display which is not uncommon in later Edo-period textiles, for he is always governed by a sense of simple over-all design. These kimonos, so typical of the period, are among the finest works of art ever to come out of Japan and as textiles are hardly rivaled by cloths anywhere in the world.

The style of the costumes had changed, for, while since Heian times the aristocracy had worn many layers of solid-colored kimonos which hid the body and depended upon beauty of color and arrangement rather than the pattern of the cloth, the fashionable garment was now a short-sleeved kimono called *kosode,* which was worn directly over the body. In addition to being more natural, this new garment was also better adapted for the use of ordinary people, a fact which indicates the freer spirit of the age. In contrast to the colored materials which were popular with the earlier aristocracy, the new rulers favored bright designs, which were usually executed in costly embroidery and resulted in kimonos which for variety and splendor have never been surpassed.

A fine example of a Momoyama garment, which at one time was owned by Hideyoshi himself and is now in the collection of Mr. Akashi in Kyoto, is the man's cloak, or *dōfuku,* with paulownia and arrow designs *(Plate 80).* The darker part around the shoulders and beneath the knees is dyed in purple, while green is the other dominant color. The design is very strong, showing flat abstract patterns which preserve the two-dimensional surface of the cloth. It is precisely in this awareness of the fact that a decorative design on a kimono should never be a painting that the effectiveness of the Momoyama kimono lies, but in later times more ornate and illusionistic designs were used, which, by their very nature, were not suited to the medium.

Even more typical for the Momoyama period are the marvelous Noh costumes, in which the bold, decorative sense of the age is perfectly expressed. The designs are always simplified, and various techniques are employed, such as embroidery with colored silk and gold and silver foil. A beautiful example of such a Momoyama Noh garment is the one in the National Museum showing clementis blossoms and fans *(Plate 81).* This type of kimono with two completely different designs on the two sides is called *katami-gawari,* and was quite popular at the time. In this kimono, it is used with a great imaginativeness, for the patterns put together seem at first glance completely unrelated. The one of the flowers is a small, rather delicate all-over pattern on a dark ground, while the other uses large fans, which are differently colored and differently decorated. It is a balance of opposites, and its bold and unexpected combinations show a sense of design very unlike that of the West. Since the Noh theater is traditional, these kimono designs have been continued right up to the present, and even relatively modern ones preserve much of the beauty found in the ancient Noh costumes.

The other craft which was very popular during this period was lacquer

141

and *maki-e*, the technique of making a design by sprinkling powdered gold on the lacquered surface, was much in favor. This type of Momoyama lacquer is usually called Kodai-ji *maki-e*, for the finest examples are found in the temple of that name, which the widow of Hideyoshi had built in Kyoto from the remains of the Fushimi Palace. Here again, the designs are clear and strong, usually with rich gold against a black lacquer ground. A common subject is the pampas grass and the chrysanthemum, both typical of the Japanese autumn and reminiscent of the magnificent wall paintings at the Chishaku-in. In contrast to the descriptive character so often found in the designs of Muromachi lacquers, these are purely decorative and like the textile designs are perfectly suited to the medium. Other lacquer objects reflect both in shape and design the renewed contact with the outside world, some showing Namban, or Westerners, and others mirroring the lacquers of Ming China. The most important development, however, was the revival of painting on lacquerware, which had flourished during the Asuka and Nara periods. Red, yellow, green, and black were used on a brilliant red ground. The brushwork is very free, with the strokes light and delicate, and the result is a charming type of art which is very much in keeping with this gay and worldly time. Here again, as in pottery and textiles, the Momoyama period prepared the way for the Edo period, and the same artistic style continued during the remainder of the seventeenth century.

Coll. Tokyo University of Arts

Plate 70. Hawk and Pine Screen,
by Kanō Eitoku.
Momoyama period.

Plate 71. Monkey Screen,

by Hasegawa Tōhaku.

Momoyama period.

Plate 72. Namban Screen.

Edo period.

Plate 73. Entrance and Gable of Roof,
Nijō Castle, Kyoto. Momoyoma period.

Plate 74. Audience Hall, Nijō Castle, Kyoto.

Momoyama period.

Plate 75. Himeji Castle, Himeji, Hyōgo Prefecture.

Momoyama period.

Coll. Tokyo National Museum

Plate 76. Shino-Ware Tea Bowl.

Momoyama period.

Plate 77. Oribe Bottle.

Edo period.

Coll. Marquis d' Ajeta

Plate 78. Black Raku Tea Bowl, by Kōetsu. Edo period.

Coll. N. Murayama, Hyōgo Prefecture

Plate 79. E-Karatsu Jar. Edo period.

Coll. K. Uchimoto, Fukuoka

Plate 80. Man's Cloak (*Dōfuku*).
Momoyama period.

Coll. A. Akashi, Kyoto

Plate 81. Noh Costume.
Momoyama period.

Coll. Tokyo National Museum

9

The Art of the Edo Period

In 1615, with the fall of the Osaka castle and the annihilation of the Toyotomi forces, Tokugawa Ieyasu, who for some time had been consolidating in
power, was left the complete master of Japan. Having observed the fate
of the houses of Nobunaga and Hideyoshi, neither of whom had been able
to keep the succession in their families, Ieyasu had long been determined
to establish himself so firmly that the ruling power would pass on to his
descendants. With this in mind, he had set up a powerful police state in
which every aspect of political and social life was carefully supervised by
the government. Although the emperor remained the head of state and
lip service was paid to his divine descent, the power rested entirely in the
hands of the shogun, and, although Ieyasu himself died in 1616, the shogunate
he founded ruled the country for some two hundred and fifty years.

The new political and cultural center of the country was Edo, the present
Tokyo, and for this reason the epoch is usually called the Edo period, its
other name being Tokugawa. The population of Edo, which increased
steadily, soon outnumbered that of Kyoto and Osaka. By the middle of
the eighteenth century, it had no less than half a million inhabitants, and
by the end of the century Edo, with one million people, was not only the
largest city in Japan but also in the entire world. The growth of cities such
as Edo and Osaka contributed to the rise of a wealthy merchant class who,

although politically disenfranchised and in theory at least at the bottom of the social scale, nevertheless succeeded in gaining financial control over much of the economic life of the country. They were also important socially and culturally, but the dominant class was the samurai, or warriors, who were considered the true rulers of the Tokugawa society.

One of the most important, and for Japan the most tragic, results of this new policy of strict supervision was that Japan was almost completely isolated from the rest of the world. By 1640 this policy of national seclusion had gone into full effect, all the missionaries and traders having been either banished or executed. Christianity had been outlawed and cruel measures were taken to ferret out and punish those who still clung to the faith. The only outlet for foreign trade was a tiny Dutch settlement and a Chinese trading mission on Deshima Island in Nagasaki harbor in Kyushu, but great care was taken that these foreigners would not in any way interfere with domestic matters.

Such complete isolation could not be maintained forever, and under the Shogun Yoshimune (1715 to 1746), the edicts against Occidental learning were relaxed in order to encourage the growth of science and industry. Since the Dutch were still the only Westerners who were permitted on Japanese soil, it was Dutch scientific knowledge which was studied, as well as Dutch books on practical subjects such as shipbuilding, navigation, anatomy, and astronomy. Young scholars came to Nagasaki for the express purpose of acquiring Western knowledge, and in 1745 a Japanese-Dutch dictionary was produced. The contacts with China were also increased, and Chinese scholars who had fled to Japan after the defeat in 1644 of the native Ming dynasty by the barbarian Manchu rulers, helped spread Chinese learning and Chinese art in Japan.

Literature was one of the most characteristic expressions of this age, which especially in the brief but splendid Genroku period (1688 to 1704), produced some of Japan's most outstanding writers. Poetry was marked by the development of the *haiku,* a short poem of seventeen syllables in contrast to the classic form, which used thirty-one. Its greatest practitioner, and still Japan's most popular poet, was Matsuo Bashō (1644 to 1694), who was of samurai descent, although he led the simple life of a priest. He was a master of the

144

art of compression, and he was able to put into this brief poetic form a wealth of observations on life and nature. His type of poetry, although originating with the nobility and the scholars, soon became popular with all classes of society and there were merchants and even farmers who not only enjoyed *haiku* but also composed them.

Another great writer, one who started out as a *haiku* poet but made his most significant contribution in the field of the novel, was Ihara Saikaku, who lived from 1642 to 1693. Interestingly enough, he came from the merchant class, and instead of dealing with the life of the court or with the warfare between the great feudal clans, Saikaku's novels were drawn from the world of the new bourgeois society. The work with which he established his reputation was *The Man Who Spent His Life at Love-Making,* a gay and sometimes pornographic novel, which in many respects shows the author's indebtedness to *The Tale of Genji.* The character of his stories is usually quite realistic, and the themes for the most part come from the life of the times, especially the stories dealing with love adventures, and the rise and decline of the well-to-do families. Works of this type were referred to as *ukiyo* literature, or literature dealing with the floating world, a term which was also used for the painting showing the same aspects of contemporary city life.

The third great literary figure was the dramatist Chikamatsu Monzaemon (1653 to 1724), who has often been called the Shakespeare of Japan. It was the masterful texts of Chikamatsu which raised the puppet show from the level of a popular entertainment to the dignity of dramatic art. This puppet theatre, or Bunraku, which is still seen in Osaka today, is one of the most important dramatic forms of the Japanese stage, and one of its memorable features is the chanted text, known as *jōruri,* which is accompanied by the samisen, a three-stringed musical instrument. Chikamatsu's plays may be roughly divided into two categories, those dealing with historical events and those treating domestic tragedies, unhappy love stories ending with a double suicide being particular favorites.

As successful as Bunraku was, Kabuki already during the Genroku period was even more successful, and it has far outshadowed the puppet theater today. Kabuki, which was more realistic and more exciting than the aristocratic Noh, was really a people's art developed by the merchant classes of the great urban centers. At first the samurai regarded it with contempt, but even they could not help but be attracted to it, and Kabuki became the national drama of Japan. It has often been said that the growth of this colorful, highly dramatic art (as well as the appearance of the gay quarters) was due to the suppression of the people, who used this theatre as an outlet for their emotions. Certainly Kabuki played a great part in the culture of the time, and scenes from Kabuki drama as well as portraits of famous actors were common subjects in the art.

The dominant philosophical school was Confucianism, which became the official philosophy of the Tokugawa state, since it served the purpose of the regime, with its emphasis upon loyalty and obedience. In fact Confucian philosophy of government and Confucian ethics completely colored the thought of the Edo period, and even today it is the single most important factor in the fabric of Japanese society. Japanese institutions such as emperor worship, the importance of the family as the primary social unit, the cult of the ancestors, the social stratification of the different classes, and the great emphasis upon etiquette are merely expressions of this Confucian point of view, which, even if not conscious, is still held by most Japanese today. Buddhism on the other hand had ceased to be important, a decline evident in the lack of vitality which Buddhist architecture, sculpture, and painting exhibited during the entire Edo period.

One of the results of the supremacy of Confucianism was the strengthening of nationalism, for interest in Confucianism led to greater emphasis on historical studies, which in turn revived the cult of the emperor and the Japanese past. The myths and legends of old Japan as related in the ancient chronicles, the *Kojiki* and the *Nihonshoki,* were again studied, and Shinto scholars reintroduced the educated public to these traditions. Hand in hand with this went the idea that the emperor was the true head of the state, whose position had been usurped by the Tokugawa shoguns, and that it was the obligation of these nationalists and imperialists to restore the son of heaven to his rightful place. By this time, the vigor of the Tokugawa regime had ebbed, and since the economic conditions of the country had also deteriorated, the time was ripe for a change. When Commodore Perry appeared with his

146

famous Black Ships in 1853, this set in motion a train of events which led to the overthrow of the Tokugawa regime.

THE PAINTING OF THE EDO PERIOD

Of the many different schools of painting which were current during the Edo period, the most traditional was the Kanō school. Since it expressed the Confucian spirit so well and was in keeping with the conservative character of the regime, it is not surprising that the Tokugawa rulers chose it as the official school, a position which it held throughout the entire period. Its most famous early Edo artist was Kanō Tanyū, the grandson of Kanō Eitoku, who lived from 1602 to 1674. Unlike the earlier painters of the Kanō school, Tanyū lived in Edo where he served as court painter to the shoguns. He was a gifted, facile artist whose output was enormous, but in the last analysis he was little more than an eclectic who used the manner of his predecessors such as Motonobu, Eitoku, Sesshū, and the great Chinese masters of the Sung dynasty without contributing much that was distinctive or new. His most impressive work in the bold, decorative Momoyama style is the series paintings depicting huge pine trees on the walls of the audience hall at Nijō Palace. His more subdued manner is illustrated in works such as the *fusuma* at Daitoku-ji in Kyoto *(Plate 82)*. The trees in the screens reproduced are reminiscent of Sesshū with their black, angular lines and bold twigs, and the simplicity of the whole is typical of the Chinese style of painting of the Kanō school. So is the theme, with its vast expanse of the winter landscape, its gnarled trees and tiny figures, but there is a hardness of line and an emphasis upon the decorative element which would not be found in Sung painting.

An artist who was neither as famous nor as prolific, though he was probably a more sensitive painter, was Tanyū's younger brother Kanō Naonobu (1607 to 1650). Closer both in spirit and technique to the Sung masters, he was particularly influenced by the great Zen painter-monk Ying Yü-chien. His finest surviving work is the pair of screens showing the Eight Views of the Hsiao and Hsiang Rivers (one of the celebrated subjects of Chinese painting) during summer and winter. The bold and free brushwork is characteristic of Naonobu, as is the skillful gradation of the ink tones, yet

147

it must be admitted that this work is exceptional even for Naonobu, and the hundreds of Kanō painters who followed these two masters during the rest of the Edo period were academicians who copied the traditional manner without Tanyū's versatility or Naonobu's inspiration.

A school which was far more original in character was the Sōtatsu-Kōrin school, which produced some of the greatest works of Japanese paintings. In contrast to the Kanō painters, who looked to China for their inspiration, Tawaraya Sōtatsu turned to the masters of the Yamato-e and the decorative painters of the Momoyama period. In fact, it has been said that he restored the Heian-period scrolls at the Itsukushima Shrine, and it is certain that he copied the famous Saigyō scroll of the Kamakura period. Little is recorded about his life, although we know that he was active in Kyoto and Sakai between 1615 and 1635. His masterpiece is the pair of six-fold screens in the Seikadō depicting scenes from *The Tale of Genji,* a choice of subject which in itself reflects his interest in the Japanese past *(Plate 83).* His style, which is both decorative and abstract, appeals greatly to the modern taste, and in recent years there has been a renewed interest in his work, while the Kanō school, once so prominent, has fallen in critical favor. In the Genji screen, his treatment of the narrative, with the courtiers of Prince Genji gathering around his royal cart, is clearly derived from Yamato-e, while the large, splendid pines and the gold of the foreground recall the style of Momoyama painting. However, the design of the whole is uniquely Sōtatsu, with its areas of flat, bright color arranged in a strong, over-all pattern. Curved shapes, such as the bridge and the long, serpentine band of the shore, are balanced by the pronounced verticals of the torii and the supports under the bridge, and the straight trunks of the pines in the background are contrasted with the curving, zigzag trunks of the pines in the middle and at the extreme right. Although the shapes and the colors are all so carefully balanced, the composition has a strong, rhythmic design which gives the whole a feeling of vitality.

Among his other works, probably the most remarkable are the screens in Daigo-ji, a temple with which he seems to have been connected. There are two pairs of two-panel screens, one set showing Bugaku dancers in a colorful and dramatic composition, while the other has painted fans pasted on the surface of the screens. The fan decorated with Japanese cottages, seen from above so that the heavy thatched roofs predominate, is the most famous. Its design, which is very original, is even more abstract, with a few large, simple shapes set at angles to one another on a white ground. One of his finest works, and one of the very few masterpieces of Japanese art to have left Japan, is the Matsushima screen in the collection of the Freer Gallery of Art in Washington. Here again the painting has a pronounced decorative design, and the use of strong shapes and rhythmic linear patterns creates a wonderful sense of the waves and the rocky islands.

His foremost follower, and the other master of this school, was Ogata Kōrin (1658 to 1716). He was born too late to have known Sōtatsu, who is believed to have died in 1643, but there can be no doubt that he based his style upon that of the older master. In fact he treated several of the same subjects Sōtatsu had painted, such as the Matsushima islands, and the deities of thunder and wind, but his painting lacks the imaginative power of Sōtatsu's, emphasizing instead more purely decorative elements. The result is often very pleasing, but his works, which have enjoyed great popularity both in Japan and in the West, lack the strong abstract design which make Sōtatsu's works so memorable. Indicative of his artistic temperament is the fact that Kōrin excelled not only as a painter but also as a potter, textile designer, and lacquer artist, showing that his genius was essentially decorative.

His most celebrated paintings are the pair of six-fold screens of irises originally in Nishi Hongan-ji in Kyoto and now owned by the Nezu Museum in Tokyo (*Color Plate 6*). The theme is based upon an episode from *The Tales of Ise,* a Heian-period novel, in which the hero composes a poem at the sight of the irises blooming around the bridge in Mikawa Province. The flowers, which are simplified and yet exquisitely varied, are grouped in a large, over-all design. The soft-green leaves and the dark-and-light blue flowers are set against a gold ground symbolizing water, and the effect of the richly massed blossoms and the intricate design of the long, narrow, sharply pointed blades is very striking. In contrast to the traditional Chinese-style painting of the Kanō school in which line was all important, Kōrin applies the color to the paper without first outlining the forms. Another of his masterpieces is the pair of two-fold screens in the collection of Mr. Tsugaru

149

of Tokyo. Between two large, blooming plum trees against a background of gold, there is a very artificial completely two-dimensional stream in silver leaf with curling ripples drawn in gold. The effect is gorgeous, combining, as the iris screens do, sheer pattern and richness of color with a close observation of nature. That he was just as capable of working in a more realistic style is demonstrated by his sketchbooks, in which his brilliant portrayal of nature anticipates the naturalism of Maruyama Ōkyo and his followers. After Kōrin's death his school languished, only to have a brief revival in certain works of the late eighteenth-century master Sakai Hōitsu (1761 to 1828), whose finest painting, which shows summer and autumn grasses, is on the back of the Kōrin screens of the gods of wind and thunder. In its decorative use of natural forms and its flat silver ground, this work recalls Momoyama masterpieces like the Chishaku-in screens, but it must be said that none of Hōitsu's other paintings live up to this wonderful work.

The school which more nearly approximated the point of view of the merchant class was the Ōkyo school which sprang up in the eighteenth century and dominated much of the art of Japan until fairly recent times. Its founder and greater practitioner was Maruyama Ōkyo (1733 to 1795), a farmer's son who was trained in Kyoto in the Kanō style but who developed a realistic manner which gave expression to the materialism of the bourgeoisie. This growth of realism, so contrary to the native Japanese artistic tradition and the type of Chinese painting which the earlier artists had admired, was the result of his study both of Western illustrations which had reached Japan through Nagasaki, and the more realistic Chinese painting of the Ming and Ch'ing dynasties. Yet above all it was his faithful copying of nature, best seen in his wonderful sketches of flowers and plants and animals, which helped him develop his own particular style. However, his finished paintings are by no means as realistic as his sketches, for, in spite of his attempt to produce "copies" of nature, he could not help but be influenced by the conventions of Japanese painting.

A good example of his style is the pair of six-panel folding screens in the Mitsui Collection *(Plate 84)*. The subject—pine trees in snow—is in itself rather conventional, and the composition with its large forms placed dramatically against a simple background is typical of Japanese decorative painting.

Color Plate 6. Iris Screen, by Ogata Kōrin. Edo period.

The pine in the reproduction is brought directly to the front, which cuts off both the top and the bottom of the tree and flattens the space by focusing upon the two-dimensional plane. Even more surprising is the use of gold in the background, although it is not the brilliant gold leaf so common in Momoyama paintings. The emphasis upon natural appearance would suggest that Ōkyo had studied Ming painting, while the use of modeling to bring out the roundness of the forms shows the influence of the West. In spite of the concentration on the foreground, there is an attempt to suggest space, and the pines themselves are rendered with a hard, naturalistic detail especially noticeable in the needles. Such works must have seemed astonishingly lifelike to his contemporaries, but today they seem little more than a kind of decorative realism. It would be impossible even to give an idea of the range of Ōkyo's work, whose output was tremendous both in scale and volume, nor would it be possible to list the innumerable pupils who imitated his manner. The most distinguished, perhaps, is Matsumura Goshun (1752 to 1811), who founded the Shijō school, which tried to combine Ōkyo's realism with Nanga, while the artist best known in the West is Mori Sosen, who is famous for his countless paintings of monkeys.

A reaction against the realism of the Ōkyo school is apparent in the other leading Kyoto school of the eighteenth century, the Nanga, or Southern school, thus named because its members wished to go back to the Chinese painters of the so-called Southern school, which depended upon inspiration rather than a studied technique. They were amateur painters in the best sense of the word, scholars, officials, soldiers, and literati of all types, who prided themselves upon the fact that they did not make their living as painters as the Kanō or Ōkyo-school artists did. Their work was called *bunjinga,* or gentlemen's painting, because it was done by men of education for their own enjoyment rather than for profit. As can well be imagined, this type of art, which originated in China of the early Ch'ing dynasty, where there was a similar school, was particularly popular with the aristocracy and the scholars of Kyoto, the old cultural capital, rather than the merchants of Osaka and Edo.

Of its numerous practitioners, many of them amateurs in the worst sense of the word, the best and most celebrated was Ike-no-Taiga who lived from

151

1723 to 1776. Typically enough for a Nanga painter, he was also a student of calligraphy and Zen, and he led a carefree life traveling about the mountains and the countryside, and associating with writers and painters. Of all his works probably the most outstanding is the set of album leaves, now in the collection of Mr. Kawabata in Kamakura, which he did jointly with his friend Buson. Called "Jū Ben Jū Gi," or the "Ten Conveniences and Ten Enjoyments of Rural Life," it illustrates poems by the Chinese Ch'ing poet Li Li-wêng, a fact which indicates the literary nature of this type of painting *(Plate 85)*. One of the finest of the ten scenes by Taiga is the one illustrating the joys of fishing, which in its reduction of the forms to a simple abstract pattern seems modern indeed, and it is not surprising that in recent years such work should have come into greater favor. What interests the artist is not the lifelike representation of the scene but the generalized forms of the boat and the three scholar-sages. The emphasis is upon the inspired, calligraphic line and the subtle tonal variations rather than the color or the realistic detail. Other works of his are more Chinese in character, with an even greater emphasis on the ink tones and the strong strokes of the brush. Of the many artists who followed Taiga, by far the greatest was Uragami Gyokudō (1745 to 1820), whose mountain landscapes are often inspired in their grand conception of nature.

The school of Japanese painting best known in America and most widely admired throughout the world is *ukiyo-e*. The term itself means painting of the "floating world," a name which is used for art dealing with the pleasures of ordinary people. This school, centered entirely in the capital and reflecting the growing importance of the merchant class, is a typical expression of Edo culture. At first, especially in the seventeenth century, it was a school of painting, but later it became a school largely devoted to the use of the woodcut and as such it is chiefly known today. This development was socially conditioned, for being an art of the people, the more modest the price was, the more widely the works could be distributed. They were the product of four different persons, the painter who designed the print, making a drawing and roughly indicating the colors, often only by inscription; the woodcutter who did the actual engraving; the printer, who, especially in regard to the color, had a good deal of influence; and the publisher who planned and financed the woodcuts. It has often been said that *ukiyo-e* prints are not the individual creations of the artists whose signatures appear on the print, but works produced by craftsmen working in close collaboration. There is certainly a good deal of truth in this, and the paintings of these artists are usually very disappointing, but their medium was the woodcut and in this realm the *ukiyo-e* masters are supreme. Conservative Japanese art criticism has tended to look down upon them as mere craftsmen who dealt with trivial and often licentious subjects in contrast to the Kanō painters, who portrayed scenes from China, or the Tosa-school painters, who dealt with events from Japanese history and literature. It is for this reason that they were first appreciated in the West, especially by the French Impressionists such as Manet, Degas, and Toulouse-Lautrec, and as a result the finest collections of Japanese prints are found not in Japan but in America and Europe. However, in recent times the Japanese themselves have come to admire them, and the masters of *ukiyo-e* are now considered among the most outstanding of Japanese artists.

The origins of *ukiyo-e* go back to the genre painting of the Momoyama period, for already at that time some of the Kanō-school painters treated scenes from the festivals and amusements of ordinary people. However, these works, which were painted on sliding or folding screens, were large compositions with many small figures in a landscape, while the genre painting of the early Edo period, which was often in the form of the kakemono, tended toward simpler compositions with a few isolated figures. The favorite subject was the beautiful women of the gay quarters, and the emphasis was wholly upon their worldly and sensuous appeal. It was an art by the common people for the common people or, to be more precise, the people of the big cities, for the bulk of the population were, of course, poor farmers, who had no opportunity either to create or to enjoy this kind of art. Significantly enough, the artists who painted these pictures are unknown, for their efforts were not considered important enough for their names to be recorded.

Among the works of this type, the most beautiful is probably the pair of large six-panel screens showing women in various activities, which is in the collection of the Yamato Bunka-kan in Osaka *(Plate 86)*. The figures, which are silhouetted against a gold background, create a strong, strikingly decora-

153

tive pattern. The forms are simplified, and the main emphasis is upon the ornamental design of the robes, and the arrangement of the figures and patterns. There are eighteen women shown in various poses and engaged in different activities, some dressing hair, others writing letters, still others smoking, or making music, or playing games. The painting combines two elements characteristic of *ukiyo-e,* the colorful abstract design and the interest in the charm and the activities of women, and it is works like this which were the forerunners of *ukiyo-e.*

The true founder of the *ukiyo-e* school and one of the most creative of the early Edo artists was Hishikawa Moronobu, who lived from 1618 to 1694. It was he who brought about the change from painting to woodcut printing, thus creating an art which could be produced in large enough quantities to satisfy the demand. His subjects were taken from the Kabuki theatre and the gay quarters in the Yoshiwara district in Edo, for these were the chief centers of escape from the represssions of society. It may seem strange to the Westerners that so much emphasis was placed upon the gay quarters, but during this period when all of society was strictly codified and there was no freedom for ordinary people the amusement district was the one place where men of wealth and men of culture could get together in the company of charming and educated women, and Yoshiwara became a kind of meeting ground not only for those bent upon sensual gratification but for those who were interested in stimulating conversation. One might well say that in this respect the teahouses of the pleasure district had the same role in Edo society that the cafés have traditionally had in Europe.

Moronobu worked in monochrome, using a strong, descriptive line, which creates a sensitive pattern in black and white. He also painted several colored kakemonos of beauties, but they are in a more traditional and less distinctive manner. In *ukiyo-e*-style paintings, Miyagawa Chōshun (1683 to 1753) was far more remarkable. He made no woodblocks but restricted himself to painting, and his *e-makimono,* or narrative scrolls, which are excellent in their draftsmanship and delicate color, are extremely interesting for the view they give of early eighteenth-century society. A contemporary of Chōshun's who was outstanding for his portrayal of the beauties of the pleasure district was Andō Kaigetsu who used both woodblocks and kakemonos. The women,

Color Plate 7. Girls Playing a Game, by Suzuki Harunobu. Edo period.

who are usually shown standing in coquettish poses, are dressed in gorgeous kimonos with large, decorative patterns. For strength of line and boldness of expression, his work has seldom been equaled, and although we know little about him and have few of his works, he must be considered one of the masters of this school.

The earliest *ukiyo-e* prints were made in black and white, but color was soon added, first by hand and later by using additional blocks which added red and green. The fully developed color print, called *nishiki-e,* or brocade picture, was the creation of the eighteenth-century artist, Suzuki Harunobu (1725 to 1770). By using many blocks, he was able to print in more than ten colors, including half-tones which could not have been produced before. He was a subtle colorist, using many subdued tones as well as areas of brighter shades, and he had, besides his color sense, a fine feeling for design. Instead of limiting his compositions to large figures against plain grounds, he put them in a setting, often an interior, which he used not only as a stage for his figures but also as a charming linear pattern. Besides his innovations in color and composition, Harunobu increased the range of the subject, for he did not restrict himself to scenes from the pleasure district but usually portrayed charming young girls of ordinary background. His work quickly revolutionized the art of the woodcut, and though recent critics have pointed out that others, notably Nishikawa Sukenobu (1671 to 1751), served as models for many of his prints, the importance of Harunobu in the development of *ukiyo-e* cannot be exaggerated. He is rightly considered the father of the Japanese color print and one of the six great masters of *ukiyo-e,* the others being Kiyonaga, Utamaro, Sharaku, Hokusai, and Hiroshige. The world Harunobu creates is an enchanted one in which slender, graceful girls write poems, play games, or look at the freshly fallen snow *(Color Plate 7).* The figures are never individualized and the atmosphere, which is usually quiet and intimate, is pervaded with a delicate sentimentality. Harunobu lacks the expressive power of Sharaku, or the artistic greatness of Utamaro, yet no other *ukiyo-e* artist has created such charming creatures, or used line and color with such subtlety. In addition to the prints admired today, he also made erotic pictures, as did almost all the *ukiyo-e* print-makers, but artistically they are quite inferior.

155

The earliest of the *nishiki-e,* or brocade pictures, were made in 1765, and for the rest of his short life Harunobu's style prevailed in this art form. However, after his death in 1770, new artists appeared whose work represented a kind of revolt against the dream-like atmosphere of Harunobu's pictures. The most gifted and by many critics regarded as the greatest of the Japanese woodcut artists was Torii Kiyonaga, who lived from 1752 to 1815. His most important period of activity falls into the Temmei era (1781 to 1788), and during this time the Kiyonaga-type women completely dominated the *ukiyo-e* prints. Although coming from a family which had specialized in portraits of actors, his art was devoted to pictures of tall, willowy beauties of the gay quarters. In contrast to the delicate and childlike girls Harunobu created, Kiyonaga's women are more realistic and more mature. His line is strong, and his colors are quiet, with browns and greys which are particularly beautiful. Characteristic of his work is the print showing three beauties of the Kyoto geisha district enjoying the cool of the evening *(Plate 87).* The figures, which are larger than Harunobu's, are placed in rather statuesque poses, and there is none of the gentleness or intimacy which fills the quiet scenes of Harunobu. The geisha smoke and talk and stand about self-consciously, and with their tall figures and calm faces, they create a kind of serene and classical beauty.

Even greater than Kiyonaga was the leading artist of the Kansei period (1789 to 1801), Kitagawa Utamaro, who lived from 1753 to 1806. At first he had been under Kiyonaga's influence, but after the older master retired from print-making Utamaro became the leader of the Ukiyo-e school with his portrayals of sensuous and sophisticated beauties. His chief innovation was the introduction of *ōkubi-e,* or large-head pictures, which concentrated upon the head and the upper part of the body *(Plate 88).* His figures are strong and simple, his lines sometimes delicate, especially in the face and the hands, and sometimes swelling, as in the garments. In contrast to the realism of Kiyonaga, Utamaro is very abstract, and usually the setting is eliminated altogether. Sometimes there is only a single large figure, seen close up so that the head and shoulders fill the picture, and the emphasis is not upon the atmosphere or the narrative, but on the formal elements such as the shape of the face and the lovely pattern of the hair. For sheer beauty of line and composition Utamaro has few equals anywhere, and yet it must be said that like all the *ukiyo-e* artists, he is limited both in subject matter and design.

Besides the beauties of the teahouses, the other favorite subject was the actors of the Kabuki stage. From the very start, this theater had been closely connected with *ukiyo-e,* and many print-makers specialized in portraits of the idols of the theatre. In fact we are told that print-makers often attended the dress rehearsal of a new play in order to make the picture of a popular actor in his newest role before any one else could, a fact which points up the gulf between artists like the print-makers, who were commercial in the best sense of the word, and the gentlemen-painters of the Nanga school, which was current in Kyoto. Among the artists who specialized in Kabuki scenes, the most famous were Torii Kiyonobu, Torii Kiyomasu, and Torii Kiyomitsu, all members of the Torii family, who traditionally designed the billboards and billets of the Kabuki theatre.

A far greater artist than any of these and one of the most astonishing phenomena in Japanese art was Tōshūsai Sharaku, who is believed to have been a Noh actor. His *oeuvre,* consisting of some one hundred and forty actor portraits, is in itself remarkable, but what is astonishing is the fact that he made all of these prints within the brief span of ten months (from May, 1794 to February, 1795). The style he used had first been developed by Katsukawa Shunshō, but he gave it an intensity and power which no other *ukiyo-e* artist possessed. The faces of Harunobu are little more than charming, undifferentiated masks, and though Kiyonaga's and Utamaro's faces are somewhat more individualized, they have very little expression. Their features are always composed, but in Sharaku the faces are contorted with the intensity of their expressions. There are no backgrounds—the figure is the whole theme, sometimes alone, sometimes with another figure. The poses are often dramatic, as in the plate shown, where the head is thrust forward, and at times the hands express the same tense emotion as the face *(Plate 89)*. It is interesting that Sharaku, who in Europe has always been a great favorite, is not highly regarded in Japan, for his fierce expressions are closer to modern Expressionism than to the Japanese artistic tradition. (The guardian figures of the Nara period would seem to be an exception, but they are Indian deities carved in a style which came from China.) Although it has often been said that Sharaku's prints are caricatures (he is supposed to have stopped because of the actors' resentment), no one familiar with Kabuki could maintain this, for they record the intense facial expressions one sees in the climactic moments of Kabuki.

With the death of Utamaro in 1806, the great period of Japanese prints had come to an end. Although there were many others who made innumerable woodcuts of the beauties of the Yoshiwara district and the actors of the Kabuki stage, none equaled the masters of the last decades of the eighteenth century. However, just at the point when *ukiyo-e* seemed to have exhausted itself, a great innovator appeared in the person of Katsushika Hokusai (1760 to 1849). An immensely creative artist whose total work is estimated at some thirty-five thousand designs, he devoted himself primarily to the depiction of scenes from the life of the common people and above all to landscapes. Of his numerous sets of prints and printed books, the finest are the "Thirty-Six Views of Fuji" published in 1829, when he was almost seventy. One of the most famous of these is the "Red Fuji," a print which brings out the shape of the mountain by silhouetting it against a furrowed sky *(Color Plate 8)*. Although the color lacks the subtlety of the earlier print-makers, its flat strong areas strengthen the abstract qualities of the design, in which the mountain appears as a cone balanced by linear and speckled patterns. These late works show a style combining features of Western art, the most striking of which is his mastery of perspective, with traditional Chinese and Japanese artistic conventions. The result is a rather abstract type of drawing and color pattern which, especially in late nineteenth-century France, was greatly admired. The world he portrays is no longer that of the pleasure district or Kabuki, but an everyday life in which he shows a cooper making a large tub, or carpenters working on a house, an indication of the new interest in the common people which was characteristic of the nineteenth century.

Even more popular in Japan is the second of the great landscapists of *ukiyo-e,* Andō Hiroshige, who lived from 1797 to 1858. His style is more realistic than abstract, more lyrical than strong. What he loved was the moods of nature—the different seasons, the different weathers, and he was a master in catching the atmosphere of the mist, the moonlight, the rain beating on the trees, the falling snow *(Plate 90)*. There is something soft and rather

Color Plate 8. Red Fuji, by Katsushika Hokusai. Edo period.

Daitoku-ji, Kyoto

Plate 82. Sliding Door with Landscape,
by Kanō Tanyū. Edo period.

Plate 83. Tale of Genji Screen,

by Tawaraya Sōtatsu. Edo period.

Plate 84. Pine Tree Screen,

by Maruyama Ōkyo. Edo period.

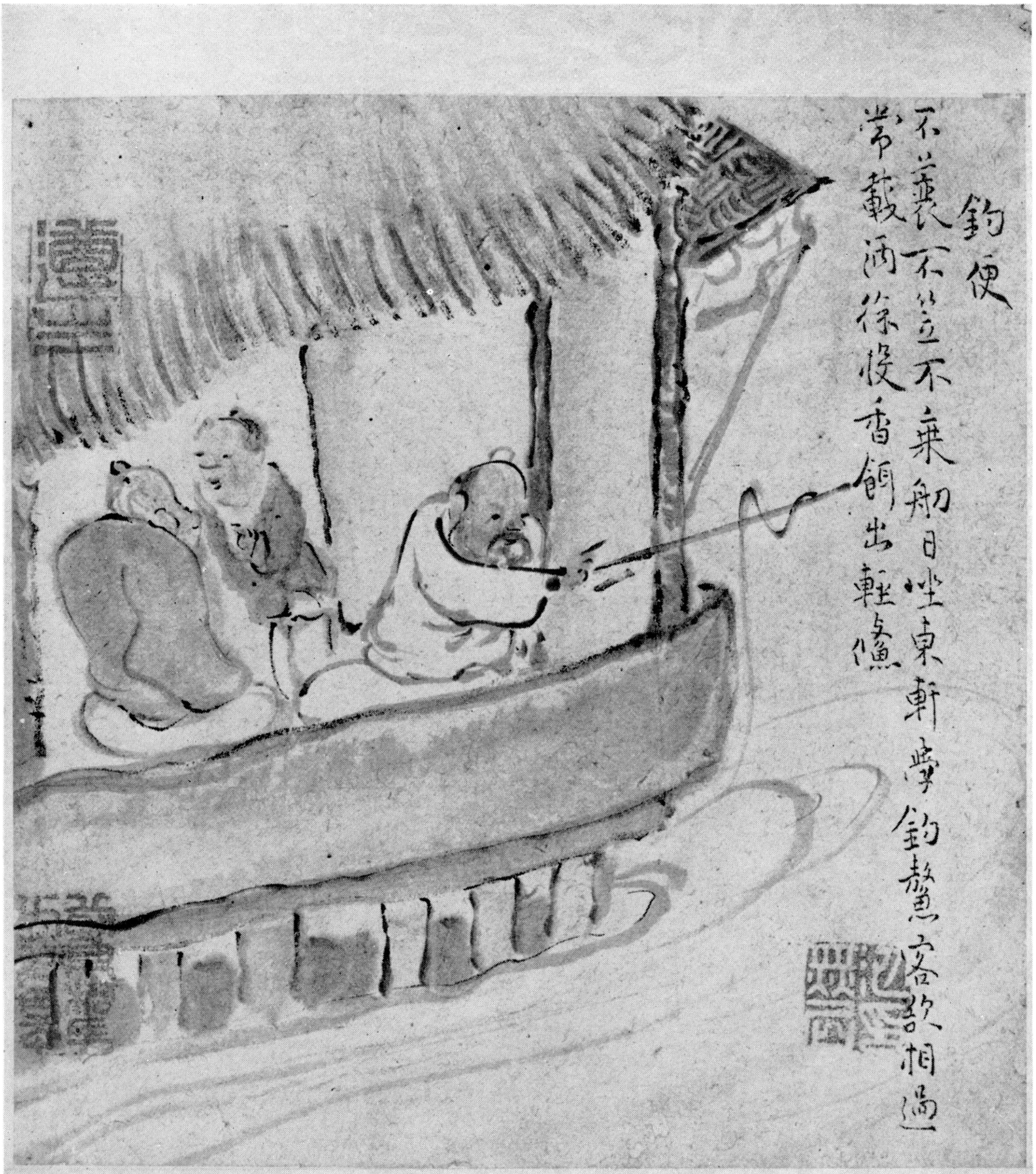

Coll. Kawabata, Tokyo

Plate 85. The Joys of Fishing,
by Ike-no-Taiga. Edo period.

Coll. Yamato Bunka-kan, Osaka

Plate 86. Genre Screen of Women.

Edo period.

Plate 87. Beauties Enjoying the Cool of Shijō River,
by Torii Kiyonaga. Edo period.

婦人相學十躰
浮気之相
相見　歌麿画

Coll. Tokyo National Museum

Plate 88. Japanese Beauty,
by Kitagawa Utamaro. Edo period.

Plate 89. Kabuki Actor,

    by Tōshusai Sharaku. Edo period.

Coll. Tokyo National Museum

Plate 90. Gion Shrine in Snow,

by Andō Hiroshige. Edo period.

Plate 91. Shin-Goten (New Palace),
Katsura Detached Palace, Kyoto.
Edo period.

Plate 92. Shōkin-Tei (Pine-Lute Pavilion),
Katsura Detached Palace, Kyoto.
Edo period.

Plate 93.   Tea House, Mitaka-shi, Tokyo.

Edo period.

Plate 94. Imari Bowl. Edo period.

Coll. Marquis d'Ajeta, Rome

Plate 95. Kakiemon Jar. Edo period.

Plate 96.   Nabeshima Dish.

Edo period.

Coll. Tokyo National Museum

Plate 97.   Tea Bowl,
by Ogata Kenzan.
Edo period.

Coll. Setsu, Kamakura

Plate 98. Ink-Stone Lacquer Box,
by Kōetsu. Edo period.

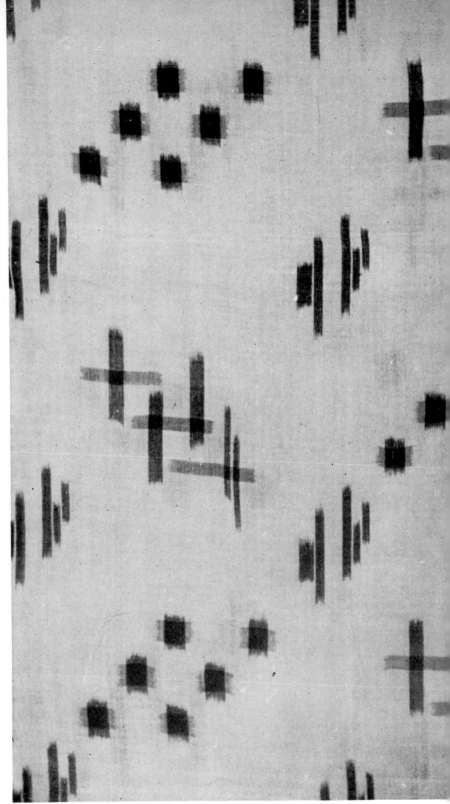

Plate 99. Okinawa Textile. Edo period.

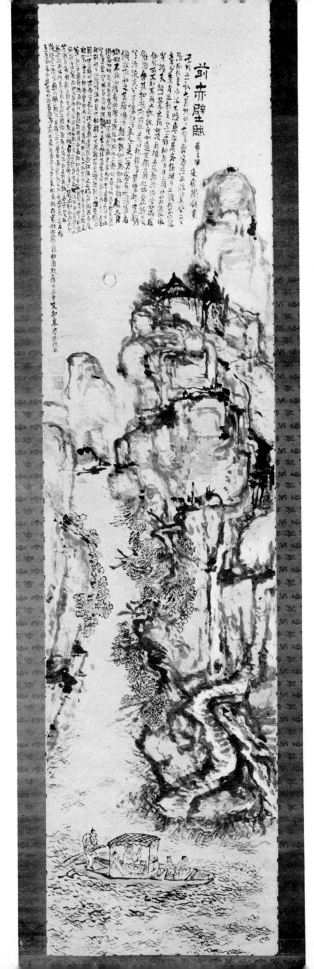

Plate 100.

The Red Cliffs, by Tomioka Tessai.

Taishō period.

Coll. Tatsuma, Nishinomiya

Coll. Art Research Institute, Tokyo

Plate 101. Enjoying the Cool of the Lake,
by Kuroda Kiyoteru. Meiji period.

Coll. Hayashi, Kyoto

Plate 102.   Cat, by Takeuchi Seihō.

Taishō period.

Plate 103.
Shijō Bridge, Kyoto,
by Maeda Seison.
Taishō period.

Coll. Tokyo
National Museum

Plate 104. Seated Nude,

by Umehara Ryūzaburō. Shōwa period.

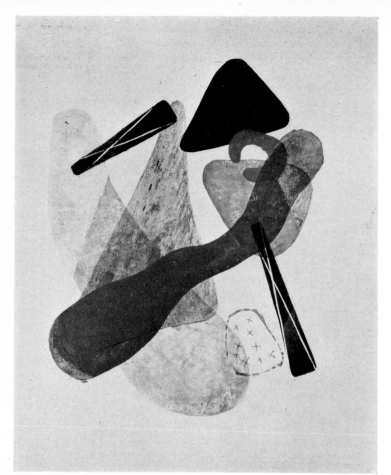

Plate 105.

Lyric No. 13, by Onchi Kōshirō.

Shōwa period.

Artist's Collection

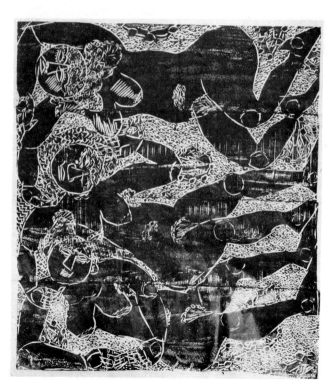

Plate 106. Women in Ecstacy,

by Munakata Shikō.

Shōwa period.

Artist's Collection

Plate 107. Tea Cup, by Hamada Shōji.
Shōwa period.

Artist's Collection

Plate 108. Vase, by Kawai Kanjirō.
Shōwa period.

Artist's Collection

Plate 109. Shino Wave Plate,
by Kitaōji Rosanjin. Shōwa period.

sentimental about his work, and though his quality is uneven—at his best he is really great, and no one who has lived in Japan can fail to recognize in him the supreme artist of the Japanese landscape. Among his many works the most famous is the set of the "Fifty-three Stages of the Tōkaidō Road," made in 1832 after a trip to Kyoto in the previous year. After his death in 1858 *ukiyo-e* deteriorated, and those who followed Hiroshige were vulgar in design and garish in color.

There remains one other school, that of the artists who worked in a Western manner, and although it was less prominent at the time and certainly not outstanding for its achievements, it was to prove very important in the development of Japanese art. When the policy of seclusion was relaxed a little in the early eighteenth century, Dutch scientific books were imported, many of them with illustrations done in copper engraving. The realism of these pictures made a deep impression upon the Japanese, and the naturalism in the work of men such as Maruyama Ōkyo was certainly due in part to them, as was the more realistic rendering of space in the prints of Hokusai and Hiroshige. Others who show Western influence are the Nanga painter Watanabe Kazan (1783 to 1841), whose portraits are strikingly Western in their naturalism, and *ukiyo-e* artists such as Okumura Masanobu who used linear perspective in scenes showing the inside of the Kabuki theatre.

The first person to use a wholly Western style, in contrast to the artists who only borrowed certain elements, was Shiba Kōkan, who lived from 1738 to 1818. He advocated an art which would reproduce nature exactly as people saw it, and he was particularly interested in the scientific rendering of space through perspective, and through modeling in terms of light and shadow. In his paintings and copper engravings he attempted to put his theories into practice, but the results, which lack spontaneous feeling, have very little merit as works of art. Nevertheless his influence was considerable, both through his own work and through that of his numerous followers. Compared to the West, however, even the work of Kōkan seems very stylized, and it was not until Meiji times that true realism appeared in Japanese painting.

THE ARCHITECTURE OF THE EDO PERIOD

Generally speaking, the architecture of the early Edo period followed the style of the Momoyama period, and after 1700 a great decline set in which led to an elaboration of detail and a loss of structural sense. The most original contribution of the age was the memorial-shrine structure, the best known and most flamboyant of which is the Tōshogū Mausoleum of Ieyasu at Nikkō. Tokugawa Ieyasu, the founder of the Tokugawa Shogunate, had been deified after his death in 1616 as Tōshogū Dai-Gongen, or Great Manifestation of Buddha Resplendent in the Eastern Region, and his grandson Iemitsu, who greatly venerated his divine ancestor, decided to build a mausoleum for him. A new style of building was created to do honor to the deity, and the result was buildings which were a mixture of a Buddhist temple, a Shinto shrine, and a stupa tomb. The whole of the shrine complex was executed with a garish splendor, and every part was embellished with the most elaborate sculptural detail. Red and green and blue and gold and white were used throughout the entire buildings, covering both the woodwork and the plaster with a confusion of staring colors. The most elaborate of all and certainly a great tour de force is the Yōmeimon or Sun-Bright Gate. It is a two-story structure with a roof gaudy and complicated beyond belief. Brightly colored, fanciful carvings showing all sorts of floral forms and animals, especially lions and dragons, cover the entire surface of the woodwork so that the structure of the building is completely hidden. The result has impressed many by its elaborate craftsmanship and profusion of ornamental detail, but in the last analysis it is not only vulgar in its ostentation, it is completely unsatisfactory from an architectural point of view.

The Katsura Detached Palace was built during the very same years (the second quarter of the seventeenth century) as the shrine at Nikkō, but it is the exact opposite in spirit as well as in structural detail, indicating once again the dual nature of the Japanese soul *(Plate 91)*. While the Tōshogū Mausoleum is all garish display, Katsura Rikyū is the very essence of simplicity, and it is only natural that modern architects should have dismissed the Nikkō structures as monstrosities and hailed the Katsura buildings as the masterpieces of Japanese architecture. In them the functional use of the building material and the beauty of the geometric design is carried to its ultimate perfection. Vertical and horizontal lines of unpainted wood, varied by rectangular areas, make a frame for the translucent white of the *shoji* paper and the opaque white of plaster, and crowning the whole is the large thatched roof, unornamented except for the design along the ridge.

The rooms have the same severe simplicity, with the plain *tatami* matting on the floor, and the sliding screens, with their lovely vistas as one room opens into the next and the outside partitions open onto the garden. (This flowing space is one of the characteristics of Japanese architecture, where the rooms are not cut up into cells, nor the building as a whole enclosed in solid walls. There is an interpenetration of the outer space of nature with the inner space of the building, and this free flow of space is one of the thnigs which has influenced modern Western architecture.) The most beautiful of the interior designs at Katsura Rikyū are the front rooms of the tea-house, the Shōkin-tei, or Pine-Lute Pavilion, so named because the wind in the pines outside is supposed to sound like a lute *(Plate 92)*. Here the designs and the colors and the materials are somewhat more varied than those of the exterior. The paper in the *tokonoma* and the *fusuma* has a pattern of large blue and white squares, and this geometry is repeated in the small rectangles of the *shōji* and the large rectangles of the *tatami*, where shape is brought out by the dark strips of the border. Particularly beautiful is the emphasis upon the texture and appearance of natural substances, such as the wood, the rush in the *tatami,* the bamboo, and the reeds. The functional clarity and simplicity which modern architects strive for was achieved at Katsura Rikyū three hundred years before the Bauhaus, and it is not surprising that Walter Gropius, when visiting Japan, thought that these buildings were the climax of Japanese architecture.

This love of unadorned beauty, which is so characteristic even today of Japanese domestic architecture at its best, is the result of the cult of Cha-no-yu, or the tea ceremony. The term used by the Japanese to describe the mood of Cha-no-yu is *wabi,* for which there is no English equivalent, but it includes the feeling of quietness, solitude, and simplicity. The buildings designed for the tea ceremony are called *chashitsu,* and significantly enough there are several of them at Katsura, indicating the close connection between

161

the spirit of Cha-no-yu and the architectural design of the palace. The teahouse is extremely simple, usually resembling a rural cottage in order to create a feeling of rustic simplicity. The first such tea rooms had been built during the Muromachi period, but they did not become common until the Momoyama and more particularly the Edo period.

Members of the nobility as well as rich merchants built teahouses on their estates, and, although they look rather unimpressive, fine old ones are made much of and carefully preserved. A good example may be seen on the campus of the International Christian University in Mitaka-shi, Tokyo, one which was built by the Edo-period scholar Hokkai Matsuura, who called it Kusa-no-ya, or House of Grass (Plate 93). It is beautifully situated on the side of a steep, wooded hill, half-hidden by trees and with the land rising directly behind it. This close relationship between the teahouse and the setting is very important, for it adds to the spirit of serenity and naturalness which Cha-no-yu tries to create. The building itself is a small, thatched cottage of a construction which is deliberately crude, since too high a finish would spoil its rustic charm. Inside there is a tea room, usually only four and a half mats large, with small windows admitting dim light, and a *tokonoma,* where a flower arrangement is set in front of a hanging scroll. The walls of these tea rooms are quite plain, their floor is covered with *tatami* mats, and there is usually a door for the host and a door for the guests, which is called *nijiri-agari,* or "wriggling-in entrance," because it is so low that the guests must crawl through it as a sign that worldly position and rank are left behind during the tea ceremony.

THE CRAFTS OF THE EDO PERIOD

With the growth of material wealth, the crafts, especially ceramics and lacquer, continued the rich heritage of the Momoyama period. At first the style was like that of the preceding period, but later new styles and new types of ware were developed by the Tokugawa craftsmen. However, as the aristocratic culture declined in the latter part of the Edo period, the standards of craftsmanship also declined, with cheap, mass-produced wares for plebeian consumption more and more the rule, and by the beginning of the nineteenth century all the crafts had suffered a serious deterioration. The most striking

162

developments were the decentralization of manufacturing, with many provincial centers springing up, and the production of porcelain by Japanese potters. This in turn increased the popularity of ceramics, and by the end of the Edo period porcelain was widely used even by the common people. Another outstanding development was the appearance of folk art, which was particularly important in the late Edo period. It might well be said that crafts were one of the principal manifestations of the age, and it was through the products of the Edo craftsmen that Japanese art was introduced to Europe. At first through Dutch traders, but later through other European merchants as well, Japanese decorative arts were exported to European countries, where they soon found wide favor. The first things sent abroad were the beautiful porcelains originating at Arita, and later on numerous small decorative art objects were sent. Such things as *netsuke,* or the little carved figures used to hold tobacco pouches or medicine containers in place, *tsuba,* or sword guards, lacquer boxes, Japanese textiles, and above all ceramics of various kinds were greatly prized by American and European collectors. In fact the West learned about Oriental art through its crafts and *ukiyo-e* prints long before it had discovered the older arts of Japan or China or India.

Although the coarse earthenware pottery produced during the Momoyama period continued to be made during the Edo period, the emphasis soon shifted to finer, harder porcelain wares with a pure white body decorated in colors. At first it had been necessary to import these prized porcelains from Korea and China, but after a Korean potter discovered porcelain clay in fine quality at Arita in Kyushu, this type of ware was made in Japan. It was fired at very high temperatures, and its fine white paste was covered with a transparent glaze under or above which painted designs were added. Many of these early porcelains were decorated in blue and white in imitation of Korean Yi-dynasty wares, but later, colored overglaze decorations in enamel colors became even more popular, a technique which had been imported from China.

The center of manufacture was the neighbourhood of Arita, but because the Arita wares were exported through the nearby port of Imari, these porcelains are usually called Imari ware, and as such have achieved great fame both in Japan and the West. Among these wares, the best known is *ko-*

Imari, or old Imari, some of which are blue and white, although the majority have brilliantly colored decorations. The most interesting among these, at least to Westerners, are the designs showing sailing ships and Dutch traders with pronounced noses and bright red hair *(Plate 94)*. A great variety of designs were used, some purely ornamental, others showing scenes from Chinese or Japanese mythology, and the elaborate decorations and rich colors, among which red was often predominant, are fitting expressions of the taste of the Edo period. This type of ware was made in large quantities both for home consumption and export, and as a result the quality varies greatly. Generally speaking the earliest ones are the best, and the mass-produced wares of the nineteenth century show a marked falling off in workmanship and design. Arita ware continues to be made today, but the output does not live up to the high standards set by the potters of the Edo period.

Of the colored porcelains made in the Arita district, the most celebrated are the so-called Kakiemon wares, which have been made by the Kakiemon family since the middle of the seventeenth century *(Plate 95)*. These porcelains have a pure white body with elegant decorations modeled upon the Chinese porcelains of the K'ang Hsi type of the early Ch'ing period. The colors are very beautiful with bright reds, blues, greens, yellows, and blacks, and there are charming decorations, bird-and-flower designs being the most common. Both the Imari and more particularly the Kakiemon porcelains enjoyed great popularity in Europe, and the European factories such as Delft in Holland and Meissen in Germany and Worcester in England made imitations of Kakiemon ware.

Another outstanding type of porcelain made in the Arita district is known as Nabeshima ware since it was made for the House of Nabeshima, the Lord of Saga. These porcelains, whose golden age lasted from the middle of the eighteenth to the beginning of the nineteenth century, are probably the most technically perfect porcelains ever made in Japan *(Plate 96)*. The most famous were the *iroe*-Nabeshima, or enameled Nabeshima. The designs, which are far more abstract than those of the Kakiemon ware, show a more purely Japanese taste, and the flat, simple decorative character of many of the ornaments reveal a marked influence of the dyed and woven patterns of contemporary textiles. The designs on the Nabeshima porcelains were usually outlined in blue and then filled in with color glaze, and the result is a regularity and perfection unique to Nabeshima ware.

Many other outstanding kilns could be mentioned as typical of Edo porcelains, the best of them being Kutani ware, which is outstanding for the strength of its designs often executed in bold, abstract patterns. Most striking among them are the *ao*-Kutani, or blue-green Kutani, named after the deep blue-green ground which gives them a very heavy, very impressive look. Other Kutani wares, modeled after Chinese porcelains, resemble Arita ware. Another center of ceramics manufacture was Seto near Nagoya, which became so important for its vast and diverse production that the term "Seto-mono" is used in Japan today in the same inclusive sense that the term "China" is used in the West. Another great center was in Kyoto, where Kiyomizu ware was made, but it would be impossible to list the many porcelain kilns which, especially during the later Edo period, sprang up all over the country.

Among the many potters of the age, there were two whose works are regarded as unique masterpieces, namely Ninsei (1598 to 1666) and Kenzan (1663 to 1743). The former is particularly famous for his use of gold-sprinkling and painting in gold, techniques which he adapted from the gold lacquer designs. He was also very much influenced by contemporary painting, and his designs are often pictorial in character. The colors are usually bright, and the effect of his works is gaudy in the same way that the Tōshogū Shrine in Nikkō is. A much finer potter was his disciple Ogata Kenzan, the younger brother of Ogata Kōrin, whose paintings have already been discussed. Kenzan's designs were freer and more abstract than Ninsei's and there is in his work a far greater respect for the basic shape and material of the vessels. His style, which is characteristically Japanese, resembles that of his brother Kōrin in its emphasis upon the decorative, and his set of plates with designs showing the four seasons is of unique beauty. A work of his which shows his style at its best is the lovely tea-bowl with cherry blossoms in the Setsu Collection *(Plate 97)*. The choice of the motif, so typical of Japan, is already characteristic of Kenzan, and the way in which he treats the branches and the flowers shows his ability to reduce the forms of nature to a simple ornamental design without sacrificing the natural appearance.

The lacquers of the early Edo period followed the style of the Momoyama

165

lacquers, but during the later part of the Tokugawa reign the designs became increasingly ornate and pictorial. By the end of the Edo period, lacquer production, although it had increased in quantity, had further declined in quality as it became mass-produced for popular consumption. The greatest of the early lacquer artists and one of the most gifted and versatile men in the history of Japanese art was Hon'ami Kōetsu (1558 to 1637). He was an extraordinarily creative genius who was outstanding not only in lacquer but in ceramics, painting, and above all calligraphy. Of the lacquer objects ascribed to him, most celebrated is the ink-stone box (now in the collection of the Tokyo National Museum) with a *maki-e* design showing a pontoon bridge at Sano *(Plate 98)*. The bridge is executed in lead against a gold background while the characters of the poem (which reads: "I wish to install a boat bridge at Sano on the road to the eastern provinces in order to reach you; I am always yearning for you and no one knows my sorrowful heart") are in silver. The bridge makes a broad, plain band across the squares of the pontoons and the linear pattern of the water. The raised characters are used as a part of the decoration, and the strong composition with its variety of squares and wave-lines shows the great gift of Kōetsu as a designer.

The most brilliant lacquer artist of the eighteenth century was Ogata Kōrin (1658 to 1716) who, like Kōetsu, was equally famous as a painter and calligrapher. Being a follower of Kōetsu and Sōtatsu in painting, he also imitated their style in *maki-e,* as may be seen in his famous ink-stone box, called Yatsuhashi, which shows a scene from the *Ise Monogatari*. It is named after the eightfold bridge, whose sections in Kōrin's design appear at right angles to one another. The bridge, as in Kōetsu's box, is done in lead, the supporting posts in silver, the iris blossoms in inlaid shell and the iris stalks in *maki-e*. In contrast to the rather ornate and intricate type of design which was generally prevalent in lacquerwork, Korin's design is very simple, with the flat abstract shapes combined in a strong decorative pattern. After his death lacquer production went on unabated, but none of the many craftsmen following Kōrin were able to equal his work.

During the Tokugawa reign, the textiles flourished as they had in the Momoyama period. The old weaving center in the Nishi-jin district of Kyoto continued to be the heart of the textile production, with both the cloth for

Color Plate 9. Kimono with Noshi Design. Edo period.

the Imperial Court and the shogunate made there, but centers appeared in the provinces as well. As with the other crafts, the style of the early Edo period was little more than a continuation of the Momoyama style, the middle Edo period had ever more gorgeous and elaborate decorations, and the late Edo period already showed a deterioration both in technique and in the artistic quality of the designs, which tended more and more towards mere display. Here again, as in the case of the ceramics and lacquer, it would suggest that mass production and a high artistic level were mutually exclusive, and that as quantity rises quality tends to fall.

Embroidery and weaving continued to be the principle techniques, but a new dye process known as Yūzen-style dyeing was also developed, an innovation attributed to a painter named Miyazaki Yūzensai, who was active in Kyoto during the Genroku era. With this process, in which a small stick and rice paste were used, it was possible to create free, multicolored designs, which could not be attained even in embroidery. The most subtle and at the same time most gorgeous effects could be achieved, which greatly appealed to the taste of the luxury-loving Edo people. This method could also be combined with other techniques, such as embroidery, weaving, tie-dyeing, and the use of gold and silver foil, as in the magnificent kimono with a *noshi* design in the collection of the Yūzen Historical Society in Kyoto *(Color Plate 9)*. Other Yūzen designs show scenes from the Yoshi-wara district, or gorgeous plant-and-flower patterns. In the end, however, it was the very magnificence of these designs which led to the decay of the textile art, for the essential nature of the material was disregarded, and it began to be treated as if it were a surface to be painted upon.

The Edo period was rich in folk art, and, although at the time it was not appreciated, its productions were among the best and most genuinely artistic of the age. In fact, during the nineteenth century when the so-called "fine arts" had become decadent, these simple craftsmen preserved a more truly artistic spirit. Today, when modern industry threatens to destroy folk art, Dr. Yanagi Sōetsu and the *mingei*, or folk-art, group have not only helped keep these arts alive, but have also preserved many of the finest specimens of this great artistic heritage of the common people. The artists who created these works were humble craftsmen whose names and careers are unknown, and who worked quite unself-consciously, most of them probably looking upon their craft as a side line rather than considering themselves professional artisans, and yet some of their work stands up well beside that of men who were recognized artists.

Among the many and diverse products of folk art, which includes children's toys and straw raincoats and everything else one could think of, the most impressive are the ceramics and textiles. The strong, plain tea bowls are particularly remarkable, as are the oil plates, with their spontaneous designs, which are treated very abstractly and rendered with quick, skillful strokes. Among the textiles, the most distinguished are those from Okinawa. Their designs are often wholly abstract, such as the one in the reproduction with its simple, skillfully varied geometric forms *(Plate 99)*. The colors are the strong, rather earthy tones of natural dyes, the yellows being particularly beautiful. These cloths with their simple, severe designs appeal more to modern taste than the gorgeous works of the Kyoto weavers which, for all their technical brilliance, seem fussy and over-ornate.

10

The Art of Modern Japan

THE opening up of Japan by Commodore Perry was followed by the overthrow of the Tokugawa Shogunate, and this led to a complete change in Japan's government. In 1867 the last of the shoguns resigned, and in the following year the Emperor Meiji, who moved his court from Kyoto to Edo (which was renamed Tokyo, or Eastern Capital), assumed direct control of the country, an event usually referred to as the Meiji Restoration. The Meiji period (1868 to 1912) was one of the most epoch-making in the history of Japan, and at its close Japan emerged as a modern military and industrial power. Only the Nara period, when Chinese civilization was introduced, can be compared to this age, which changed every aspect of Japanese life. Still, however complete the acceptance of foreign things seemed, the nation at heart remained true to its own traditions, a fact which many Western observers, contemplating the Western façade which the Japanese erected, tend to overlook. In modern as in ancient times, the Japanese were more than willing to learn what the foreigners had to teach, in the one case the Confucian philosophy of state and the Buddhist religion, in the other, European technology and science; yet there remained a core of native tradition which enabled the Japanese to preserve their identity as a people. Nevertheless, the changes which took place were extraordinary, and the spectacle of a backward, feudal society which had lived in almost complete isolation for over two centuries emerging within a generation as a modern Westernized nation is astonishing indeed, and a great tribute to the resourcefulness of the people and the able leadership of the Emperor and his advisors.

Most startling of all perhaps were the economic and technological advances. A few facts may illustrate the rapidity with which the development took place. In 1868 Osaka and Kobe, then known as Hyōgo, were opened up to foreign trade; in 1869 the daimyos returned their holdings to the crown; in 1871 the first daily newspaper was founded and the first regular postal service was inaugurated between Tokyo and Osaka; in 1872 the first railroad was opened between Tokyo and Yokohama; and in 1873 the solar Gregorian calendar was introduced to replace the traditional lunar one. Modern industry was developed, a modern merchant marine was built, and foreign trade became one of the main sources of revenue. The result of this economic growth was a phenomenal increase in population, and Japan, which for centuries had had an almost static population of about thirty million, numbered sixty million in 1930, seventy million in 1940, and eighty million in 1950.

Western ideas, particularly in regard to science, political philosophy, morality, and religion, also made their impact. Japanese students of government and science went abroad to learn from the Europeans, notably the Germans, and Westerners, especially English and Americans, came as missionaries and teachers to Japan. Two events of signal importance in this connection were, first, the founding of the Ministry of Education in 1871, which led to the establishment of universal education as well as of modern universities along Western lines, and second, the edict of religious tolerance of 1873, which opened Japan to Christian missionaries. Although the actual number of conversions was small, and has remained so even today, almost a century later, the influence of Christian ethics upon the thinking of the modern urban intelligentsia has nevertheless been very great, and the Christian church has had a profound effect in fields such as women's education, social work, and moral teachings.

In the arts the impact of Western civilization was almost overwhelming. Japan had always looked to China for guidance, and whether it was in architecture, painting, poetry, or music, the Chinese influence had been paramount. Now all this changed, and during the early years of the Meiji period there was a frantic rejection of everything traditional and Chinese in favor of the new fashions from the West. In some ways these early enthusiasts went even further than the Japanese today in their imitation of everything that seemed characteristically European. (In making such statements, it must, of course, be borne in mind that this revolution affected only a relatively small number of people in the great urban centers and that the mass of farmers and artisans continued in their time-honored ways.)

Among the writers of the period, it became fashionable to imitate the realistic manner of the great novelists of England, France, and above all Russia. The playwrights began producing dramas of modern life instead of the traditional tales of the feudal past, and the poets, feeling that forms such as the *haiku* were too short for the more complicated reactions of modern men, imitated the narrative poems of the great English poets. Outstanding among these Western-style writers were the novelists who dealt with the social problems of the age, such as Shimazaki Tōson (1872 to 1943), who wrote about the Eta, the outcasts of Japan. The greatest of the Meiji novelists was probably Natsume Sōseki (1867 to 1916), whose work is concerned with the routine life of ordinary people, and the most remarkable living novelist is Tanizaki Junichirō, born in 1886, whose early work reflects the influence of English literature but who in his mature work has returned to more traditional Japanese themes. He translated *The Tale of Genji* into modern Japanese, and his *Thin Snow,* which was influenced by *Genji Monogatari,* has been widely acclaimed as the masterpiece of postwar Japanese literature.

Along with the new ideals of freedom and human dignity, there came a concept which was to have disastrous consequences for Japan and for the rest of the world, and that was the idea of nationalism. The Japanese leaders who saw the Western powers grabbing colonies throughout Asia and demanding extraterritorial rights and trading concessions soon imitated their teachers and as time went on even surpassed them at their own game. In 1872 universal military service was introduced, and in the same year the Japanese tried out their armed forces by sending a military expedition to Formosa demanding indemnity for some Ryukyu Islanders who had been killed there. Twenty years later, in 1894, Japan took on a full-fledged war with China,

171

which ended in complete success for the Japanese, and in 1895 Formosa and the Pescadores were added to the Japanese Empire. Next came the Russo-Japanese war of 1904 to 1905 which to everyone's surprise proved a great military victory for Japan, and as a result Japan was recognized as the dominant power in Korea, which was annexed in 1910.

The Taishō period, which followed the death of the Emperor Meiji in 1912 and lasted until 1926, was one of relative democracy and peace. While a group of oligarchs, the most famous of which were Itō, Yamagata, and Saionji, had ruled during the Meiji period, party politicians now became more powerful and trade unions began to appear. The First World War enabled Japan to build up her own industries as well as annexing the former German colonies in the South Seas, and by the end of the period Japan had emerged as one of the great world powers. The new reign which started in 1926 and ironically enough was called Shōwa, or Clear Peace, led to excess which the more moderate Meiji leaders would have avoided. The evergrowing influence of the military was greatly strengthened after their successful conquest of Manchuria in 1931, followed by the pact with Nazi Germany and Fascist Italy in 1936 and the so-called China Incident in 1937. The outbreak of the Second World War and the initial German victories made it seem as if the time were ripe for Japan to seize control in Asia. The events which followed are only too well known, and the war resulted in the destruction of many of Japan's cities and the annihilation of her fleet and her merchant marine and much of her industry.

Astonishingly enough, this total war, followed by total defeat, had far less effect than might be supposed. Only ten years after her surrender, Japan has once again emerged as the most powerful industrial nation in Asia. The population increase has more than made up for the losses suffered during the war, the cities have been rebuilt, and, although rearmament has as yet made very little progress, Japan is potentially a great military power. The Westernization which had been discouraged by the militarist circles during the thirties and even more during the war years, has been resumed at an accelerated pace, and today Japan in many respects is closer to the Western countries than to her Asian neighbors. Perhaps this was inevitable in the long run—perhaps it represents little more than the continuation of tendencies

172

which had been dominant ever since Japan was opened by Commodore Perry, yet it must be said that the enlightened and on the whole benevolent character of the American occupation had much to do with the fact that the youth of Japan welcomed Western ideas and customs instead of withdrawing in sullen resentment.

It is difficult to predict the future, but there are certain phenomena which undoubtedly will continue unabated. The most important is the increasing loss of prestige of Chinese culture among the younger generation. Confucianism and the Chinese classics, which only fifty years ago were still a part of every educated man's heritage, have been replaced by Western political philosophy and Western literature, and democracy, although far from complete, has made a deep impression upon the youth of Japan. Industrialization and the growth of the cities must inevitably continue because of the population pressure, and modern science and technology, which have already transformed so many aspects of Japanese civilization, are bound to be of ever greater importance. Japanese art and literature and music are likely to become more and more a branch of the Western arts which, as years go by, may make their own contribution, but they will be contributions which are closer in spirit to Paris than to the old China, and to Europe than to the old Japan.

THE PAINTING OF THE MODERN PERIOD

The Japanese artistic traditions, which by the end of the Edo period had already been running dry, could not withstand the impact of European art. The last of the great Edo painters, Watanabe Kazan, who had died in 1841, and Andō Hiroshige, who had died in 1858, had, in their emphasis upon naturalism, already shown the influence of Western painting, but now, when the Western influences no longer merely trickled in through Nagasaki but literally flooded the country, there was a complete revolution in Japanese art.

The counterreaction began to set in almost at once, strangely enough under the leadership of an American scholar, Ernest Fenollosa, who had come to Tokyo in 1878 as a professor of political philosophy at Tokyo University. It was to his credit that he stimulated interest in the ancient art of Japan at a time when the Japanese intelligentsia were rejecting the art of their country

173

as unfit for the modern age. However, his attempt to revive the style of Ashikaga ink-painting met with little success. Although he and Okakura Kakuzō, the famous Japanese critic and author of *The Book of Tea,* were instrumental in forming a society for the propagation of traditional Japanese art, which attempted to infuse new life into the Kanō school by using the more plastic forms and brilliant colors of Western painting, all that came of this endeavor was a hybrid art which was neither Japanese nor Western. Its most celebrated practitioners, Kanō Hogai (1828 to 1888) and Hashimoto Gahō (1835 to 1908), enjoyed great fame after Fenollosa had discovered them, but today it is clear that they were simply the last proponents of a dying tradition.

The work of these artists showed that any attempt to revitalize Japanese painting simply by adapting some of the mannerisms of Western painting was doomed to failure, and that Ashikaga ink-painting, which in its own day had been a vital expression of the spiritual and cultural climate, could not be resurrected in the nineteenth century. However, there was one contemporary of theirs who was able to breathe new life into the old forms, and that was Tomioka Tessai (1836 to 1924), although it must be added that his most powerful works were all made during the last years of his life, already well into the twentieth century. He was a true eccentric, a uniquely gifted and vigorous artist who went his own way regardless of the prevailing taste. Tessai was a typical exponent of the Nanga school, and characteristically enough he was a Kyoto rather than a Tokyo man, and a student of Confucian philosophy, Buddhist teachings, and Shintoism. His artistic training was also typical for a man of his temperament, for he first studied Yamato-e and later Nanga, but in his maturity he developed a unique style, which for vigor of expression and inspired brushwork has not been equaled in Japanese art. His dashing and forceful way of applying ink and the beauty of his color are very remarkable, and even those who do not care for his undisciplined manner of painting are willing to grant the power of his genius. His work, unlike that of Hogai and Gahō, shows no influence of Western perspective or plastic form, but continues the more abstract traditions of Oriental art, as in the painting illustrating the famous Chinese poem about the red cliffs by the great Sung poet Su Tung-p'o *(Plate 100)*. This work exemplifies

174

both his vigorous brushwork and the literary inspiration of his art, yet it must be said that however brilliant Tessai was, he was the last in the line of Nanga painters following Taiga and Gyokudō, rather than the beginning of a new tradition in Japanese art.

Far more influential in their own day as well as being more representative of the dominant trend of modern Japanese painting were the Western-style painters, among whom Kuroda Kiyoteru (1866 to 1924) was the most outstanding *(Plate 101)*. He was one of the first in the long line of Japanese artists who went to Paris, where he spent ten years, returning to Japan in 1893. The result was a style based wholly upon the Realists and Impressionists and which, except for occasional Japanese motifs, would never be recognized as Japanese painting. As has been said before, these early Meiji artists often went even further in their Westernization than later generations, and it was obviously Kuroda's intention to divest himself of everything Japanese in order to become a modern, that is European, artist, a goal in which he was completely successful. A skillful painter, he produced works which are striking in their realism, and, although of little interest to Westerners, they were startling to the Japanese, upon whom they made a tremendous impression.

While Kuroda was primarily a Realist, the more purely Impressionistic style of the late nineteenth century found an even more gifted exponent in Fujishima Takeji (1867 to 1943), who, although born at about the same time as Kuroda, lived much longer and was able to carry this Western style further. An artist of great sensitivity, his work is artistically superior to that of Kuroda, and his rendering of light and atmosphere is superb indeed. Yet he too was merely an imitator of European painting, who also spent ten years abroad, where he stayed from 1906 to 1916 in Paris and Italy. Arriving a decade later than Kuroda, it was Monet by whom he was most influenced, yet, like Kuroda, he simply absorbed what he found in Paris without adding anything Japanese. He too, however, had a profound effect upon Japanese painting and even today is a very influential artist.

While Kuroda and Fujishima were being hailed as leaders of the modern-style oil painting in Tokyo, Kyoto, always far more conservative, continued to admire the traditional Japanese-style masters. Among them the most famous was Takeuchi Seihō, who, born in 1864 and dying in 1942, was an almost exact contemporary of Kuroda and Fujishima. Unlike Tessai, who was an offshoot of the Nanga tradition, Seihō traced his ancestry back to the Shijō school, which was closely related to Maruyama Ōkyo and had developed a very realistic style during the eighteenth century. Seihō, however, did not restrict himself to the manner of this school. He traveled in China and was deeply influenced by Chinese-style ink-painting, and he also went to Europe, where he could not help but be affected by the work of the European masters—in fact, he did a painting of Venice in a completely Western style which recalls Turner, whom he greatly admired. Yet above all he was a brilliant eclectic, a man who possessed a marvelous technical skill and who could do almost anything he set his hand to. In his own day he enjoyed an immense reputation—in fact, he was probably the most successful and celebrated artist of his time, yet like his American contemporary, John Singer Sargent, who had a similar kind of gift, his work has not stood up too well, for it lacks depth of feeling and intensity of expression. His painting of the cat is a perfect illustration of his style *(Plate 102)*. The animal itself is portrayed with the most vivid realism, but the fine linear detail, the relative flatness, and the isolation of the form against an empty background are all within the Japanese tradition. The skill with which the cat is rendered shows Seihō's brilliance as a craftsman, yet at the same time the painting lacks intensity, the very quality which marks the work of Tessai.

The Japanese-style painter Yokoyama Taikan who, although born in 1868, is still alive today, is probably the most famous living artist of the conservative tradition. A man of great gift and tremendous energy, he has been a leader in the attempt to establish a new Nihon-ga, or Japanese-style painting. He studied under Okakura and Hashimoto Gahō, and as a professor at the Tokyo Art Academy and one of the founders of a Japanese artists' group, the Nihon Bijutsu-in, Taikan has been a powerful force in contemporary Japanese painting. His virtuosity and productivity are remarkable, indeed, and one cannot help but be impressed with him as a phenomenon. Yet his style, a mixture of Chinese, Japanese, and Western methods like that of his teacher Gahō, is eclectic in the extreme, and his work, although skillful, lacks vitality and

176

expressiveness. The series of big paintings depicting Mt. Fuji, the national symbol of Japan, which he painted in his old age, when most men have lost their vigor, shows his virtuosity and creative power at their grandest, yet somehow these paintings do not ring true, for they lack the simplicity and sincerity of the old masters.

A painter who is far less grandiose than Taikan, but who in his mature work has proved himself one of the masters of Japanese-style painting is Maeda Seison, who was born in 1885. Seison's early work, which was not very promising, consisted of rather bombastic paintings of historical subjects, often of great size and rendered in a detailed realism which is not in keeping with the subject. Other works show his close study of the artists of the Momoyama period as well as many other aspects of the Oriental tradition, such as Chinese painting, Buddhist painting and sculpture, Sōtatsu, and Yamato-e. There are even works of his which show a distinctly Western influence, reflecting his trip to Europe, but in his finest work he is able to fuse these various sources and create something which shows a unified and original style. Outstanding among these is the set of eight kakemonos representing views of Kyoto, which he painted on the occasion of a trip to Kyoto in the company of his friend and fellow painter Kobayashi Kokei. The theme is the traditional one of the eight views except that he substituted those of Kyoto for the customary ones of the Hsiao and Hsiang Rivers in China or of Lake Biwa in Japan. The technique is also traditional, namely *sumi-e,* but the style clearly reflects his knowledge of European art. This is particularly true of the painting of the Shijō Bridge, which is strikingly reminiscent of Pissarro, who in turn had taken his motif from Hiroshige, so one might say that it is a return to Japanese painting as seen through Western eyes *(Plate 103).* The severity of form and the beauty of the abstract pattern of light and dark make this kakemono and the others in the series, especially the one showing an air view of rows of Kyoto houses, very rewarding. Equally remarkable is one of his most recent works, a screen representing a blooming peach tree, in which traditional Japanese decorative painting is combined very successfully with modern abstract design. However, it must be granted that these paintings are by no means characteristic of Seison's work, which, taken as a whole, is very uneven.

Another well-known Japanese-style painter is Kobayashi Kokei, born in 1883, who also combines a profound knowledge of the Oriental tradition with an understanding of modern abstract art. His still-lives showing a few pieces of fruit in a dish are very Oriental in their economy and suggestiveness, and yet they also show the mark of modern painting. Perhaps his finest and certainly his most characteristically Japanese work is his narrative scroll illustrating the story of the Dōjoji Bell. The *makimono* form as well as the style recall Yamato-e, while Sōtatsu's influence is evident in the emphasis upon the clear outlines, the abstract forms, and the beauty of the color design, yet the work is not merely a patchwork of the styles of the ancient masters but an original creation, which combines elements derived from the past with elements of modern design. His best-known work is the picture showing a kneeling girl, whose long black hair is being combed by her younger sister, who is dressed in a lovely kimono *(Color Plate 10)*. Like the *ukiyo-e* artists of the past Kokei glorifies the characteristically Japanese type of female beauty, but instead of depicting the geisha girls of the Yoshiwara district, he chooses ordinary girls engaged in simple daily tasks. Although one of them is half nude, the treatment of the subject is very chaste, in spite of the intimate nature of the scene. The firm yet delicate lines and the clear, subtle colors are lovely, and there is a feeling of simple beauty about the painting which reflects the Japanese ideal of feminine gentleness and charm.

However great the achievements of the best of these Japanese-style painters were, they are today a group of old men, the youngest of whom is already seventy, while Taikan, the oldest, is almost ninety. The younger artists have for better or worse turned to Western-style oil painting, and even those who persevere in the Japanese tradition have adapted more and more Western characteristics, so today it is often very difficult to decide if an artist should be regarded as Japanese- or Western-style. The future of Japanese painting, unless all indications are misleading, lies with the Western-style artists, and it is upon their contributions that the position of Japanese painting in the development of twentieth-century art must rest. Of course the great mass of Western-style painters are mediocre artists who simply imitate whatever seems fashionable in Paris, but there are at least two whose work compares favorably with the best of contemporary Western art.

Calor Plate 10. Combing the Hair, by Kobayashi Kokei. Shōwa period.

Color Plate 11. Landscape, by Yasui Sōtarō. Shōwa period.

The first and perhaps the greatest painter in Japan today is Umehara Ryū-zaburō, who was born in Kyoto in 1888. He began as a student of the oil painter Asai Tadashi, and then in 1908 he went to Paris, where he studied under Renoir. His early work mirrors the great French Impressionist in sensuously beautiful nudes and soft, sunlit landscapes; yet, even then, as a young man in his twenties, Umehara's extraordinary gift as a painter was clearly evident. During the following decade the influence of Cézanne was increasingly pronounced, and his landscapes became more architectural, and his still-lives were painted in the abstract and plastic style of the great post-Impressionist. However, it was not until the mid-thirties and forties that Umehara reached his artistic maturity, evolving a style which, although ultimately derived from Renoir, Cézanne, Van Gogh, and Gauguin, is never-theless peculiarly Japanese, for like the novelist Tanizaki in recent decades he has become increasingly interested in his Japanese heritage. The subjects he treats, like his seated nudes and his magnificent series of mountain land-scapes, are certainly derived from French painting, but the strong linear contours, the areas of flat, brilliant color, and the pronounced sense of design recall the Japanese native tradition without slavishly imitating it *(Plate 104)*. At the same time he brings to his work an intensity of emotion which is quite exceptional in Japanese art. Umehara has succeeded in merging the two traditions, and from this fusion he has created something original which takes its place in world art as an international and yet distinctly Japanese contribution.

The other great Western-style painter is Yasui Sōtarō, who was also born in Kyoto in 1888, the same year as Umehara and died in 1955. He too studied first with Asai and then went to Paris, where he came under the influence of Pissarro. His earliest work consists of plastically rendered nudes and Impres-sionist landscapes, and like Umehara, he was profoundly affected by Cézanne, which is particularly noticeable in his still-lives. In his later years Matisse seems to have exerted a great influence upon him, which is apparent in his use of abstract decorative effects and rhythmically moving lines. Altogether Yasui, who seems closer to the School of Paris, appears not to have made as conscious an effort to go back to the Oriental tradition as Umehara has. Yet in his most recent work, especially in the mountain landscapes with the great variety of greens ranging from deep blue-greens to light yellow-greens, he at least gives a distinct feeling of the Japanese landscape *(Color Plate 11)*. He is perhaps even better known for his numerous portraits, the best of which are strong in design and vivid in their revelation of personality, but it is in his landscapes and still-lives of the 1950's that he has created his finest works.

It is impossible to do justice in a brief survey to the innumerable artists who work in oil. Every possible style from the Impressionism of Monet and Renoir to the latest phase of Abstract Expressionism finds its equivalent in Japan. Many of the artists are extremely talented and the great artistic gift of the Japanese manifests itself in our age as in times past by the multitude of able painters. Still, one can not help but feel that the the School of Paris has not quite been digested. Umehara has been able to absorb what there was to learn, but most of these artists are little more than weak imitators of Matisse or Picasso, Braque or Klee, Modigliani or Bonnard, to name a few who are particularly popular. Perhaps this is inevitable at this stage of development, and it is certainly equally true in America and other parts of the world, but it must be hoped that something more authentic will emerge, although this in no way implies that there should be a return to the traditional Japanese manner, or even less a revival of Chinese-style ink-painting, both of which are forms that are no longer relevant in today's world. A more fruitful approach and one which shows surprising vitality is the school of modern *shodō,* or calligraphy, whose artists combine in a very effective way the beauty of traditional Japanese writing with the inventiveness and intensity of feeling found in twentieth-century art. Trained in calligraphy, they have also absorbed much from Klee, Miro, and Kline, who in turn were influenced by Oriental calligraphy. The result is an art which is traditionally Japanese, especially in the prominence of brush and ink, and yet at the same time very modern.

Another form of artistic expression which has been revived in recent decades is the art of woodblock printing, or *hanga.* The tradition of *ukiyo-e,* which had been one of the great artistic achievements of the Edo period, had come to an end with the death of Hiroshige in 1858, and in Post-Meiji Japan, the social conditions and the craftsmanship which had once made it possible no longer existed. Only one modern artist, Hashiguchi Goyō

180

(1880 to 1921), successfully revived *ukiyo-e* woodblock printing. However, even his prints, which were of Japanese beauties, show Western influence in the more plastic treatment of form and the more realistic detail, for he was also an oil painter, and it must be said that however charming his works were, they are few in number and printed in very small editions.

The prints of Kawase Hasui (born 1883) and Yoshida Hiroshi (1876 to 1950) were not only more successful but a far more characteristic expression of the taste of modern Japan. Hasui studied Japanese-style painting and then turned to woodblock printing, to which he devoted himself exclusively. His subjects are almost always landscapes, and he traveled all over Japan and Korea in search of suitable scenes. His output was tremendous, and his style, which is very realistic and detailed, was based upon careful preparatory sketches and reveals a close study of Western painting. This is even more true of Yoshida, who actually started his artistic career as a painter of Western-style water colors, and his prints are little more than English nineteenth-century water colors representing Japanese scenes engraved and printed by Japanese craftsmen. The primary interest of his works lies in their colorful content, for in addition to the Japanese scenes, he also portrays scenes from China, India, and even the West.

A very different kind of woodblock print has been created by a group of artists organized in 1918 into a society called Nippon Sōsaku Hanga Kyōkai, or Japanese Woodcut Artists' Association. They were greatly influenced by Western art; in fact most of the leading members of the group have studied oil painting and admire Western prints. Under the influence of the latter, they not only design but also cut and print their pictures themselves, and yet in spite of their Western outlook many of them in their choice of subject matter and style reflect their Japanese heritage as well. Here again the number of artists involved is very large, and it is difficult to select one or two as the outstanding for they vary all the way from completely Western-style abstractionists to traditional Oriental artists. Among the former, by far the most remarkable and the grand old man of Japanese *hanga* was Onchi Kōshirō (1891 to 1955), who was the pioneer of non-objective painting in Japan, for under the influence of Kandinsky, he produced complete abstractions as early as 1910 *(Plate 105)*. Yet, in spite of his Western orientation, his sensitivity

181

to subtle tones of color and his interest in textures show his Japanese background. His work is imaginative and lyrical, flowing freely from his sub-
conscious like that of Kandinsky, and at his best Onchi was the finest abstract
artist in Japan.

Hiratsuka Un'ichi, born in Matsue in 1895, is much more in the main
stream of Japanese art both in choice of subject matter and technique. From
the very start he was primarily a craftsman and even today he is considered
the finest woodcut artist in Japan. His black-and-white prints representing
Japanese scenes and Buddhist temples are particularly beautiful, combining
very effective modern design with traditional Japanese technique. The most
powerful and expressive of the print-makers is the somewhat younger Munakata Shikō, born in 1903, who recalls Tessai in his intense vision and eccentric
personality. Unlike Hiratsuka, who is always the careful craftsman, Munakata works very rapidly and often carelessly but with great freedom and
power. His subjects are usually Buddhist ones derived from Central Asian
wall paintings, but they are interpreted in a highly subjective manner, and
his work at its best is strong and inspired (Plate 106). There are many other
print-makers who are fine artists, such as Saitō and Sekino, but it would be
impossible in a work of this length to discuss them all.

THE ARCHITECTURE AND SCULPTURE OF THE MODERN PERIOD

The architecture and sculpture of Japan underwent as profound a revolution as the painting. Unfortunately the influence of the West coincided with
the most debased and eclectic period in the entire history of European
architecture, and the result was that Japanese architects copied with little
understanding a great variety of revival styles which prevailed in the West.
European architects such as Josiah Conder came to Japan, and Japanese
architects went to Europe, where they studied Western designs and building
practices. The big public buildings, like government offices, museums, depart-
ment stores, and theatres were almost invariably built in a Western manner,
and the styles used ranged all the way from Classic Revival, as for example
in the Bank of Japan building in Tokyo, to English Gothic, German Renaissance, Italian Baroque, and almost any other style which can be imagined.
One of the most amazing examples is a replica of Versailles on a somewhat

reduced scale, which is now used as the Diet Library. The only significant structure built during the period up to the great earthquake of 1923 is Frank Lloyd Wright's Imperial Hotel, which even today is the most interesting piece of modern architecture in Tokyo. From 1925 the International Style has made itself felt, and men such as Gropius, Le Corbusier, Taut, and Wright have exerted a tremendous influence. Many of these buildings are very fine examples of modern architecture, although it cannot be said that the Japanese practitioners have made any very important contributions to this style.

By and large, domestic architecture has continued to be built in the traditional manner, and it is here that more genuinely Japanese types of modern building have been attempted. The most outstanding architect who combines the contemporary Western style with traditional Japanese design is Horiguchi Sutemi (born 1892). Sensing the affinity between the simplicity and economy of modern architecture and the old Japanese way of building, he has tried to merge the two, often with very pleasant results, and his Hasshōkan, a Japanese-style inn in Nagoya, as well as his private houses and tea rooms is of great beauty.

Along with Buddhism, which had been its chief patron, the sculpture of the Edo period had shown a marked deterioration. Only the miniature art of the *netsuke,* which had flourished throughout the Edo period, continued to enjoy a certain popularity even after the little objects no longer had a function. Western collectors furnished a new market for the small animal and human figures, which were carved, often with great vividness and care, in ivory, bone, and wood. With the beginning of the Meiji period, monumental sculpture as an independent artistic expression without religious purpose began to be produced, and Japanese sculptors, like their fellow painters and architects, made the usual trip to Paris. The sculptors, including those who never got to Paris, were greatly influenced by Rodin and one of them, Fujikawa Yūzō (1883 to 1935), even succeeded in becoming a pupil and assistant of the great French master. The works they produced, which never go beyond mere competence, are little more than a weak echo of European art of the nineteenth century.

Today every Japanese sculpture exhibition still abounds with minor Rodins, but others, such as Bourdelle, Despiau, Maillol, Kolbe, and more recently true moderns like Moore, Lipchitz, Brancusi, and even Calder, have their followers in Japan. Among those working in the abstract twentieth-century idiom, the most gifted is Kasagi Sueo, but even he contributes little of his own. Far more creative is the American-born Isamu Noguchi, who has gone back to ancient Japanese *haniwa* for his inspiration, and who has also used traditional Japanese lantern designs to make some of the most beautiful lamps of our age. Even more impressive in the wealth of his artistic ideas is the famous master of the Sōgetsu school of flower arrangement, Teshigawara Sōfu, whose grandiose and often very beautiful recent flower arrangements are really not flower arrangements at all but fantastic pieces of modern sculpture used in conjunction with a few flowers, sculptures which reflect the full range of modern art from Brancusi to Arp, and from Moore to Calder.

The Crafts of the Modern Period

The most outstanding achievements of the modern movement in Japan are not to be found in architecture or sculpture or even in painting but in the crafts, a field in which the Japanese have always had a great gift and a great interest. Whatever critics may say about the eclecticism in other fields of artistic creativity, in ceramics, at least, Japan is the leading country in the world, and it is America and Europe who are the imitators. The very fact that hundreds of Western potters have made the long trip to the Far East in order to study under the great Japanese potters speaks for itself, but the high esteem in which famous Japanese potters are held both in Japan and abroad, and the success which their exhibitions have had not only in Tokyo but in New York and Paris and London is a clear indication that they are not only traditional artisans but true artists who are the equals if not the superiors of the celebrated contemporary painters.

There are several groups of potters, the best known of which is probably the *mingei*, or folk-art, group, which under the dedicated leadership of Dr. Yanagi Sōetsu has given rise to one of the most significant movements in present-day Japanese art. Leading among the *mingei* potters are Hamada Shōji (born 1894) and Kawai Kanjirō (born 1890). Hamada spent some years in England, where he was influenced by English folk art, but he was primarily a traditional Japanese artisan who was able to absorb the foreign influence and produce a pottery which is wholly modern and yet also wholly Japanese. The heavy, rather coarse appearence of his ware, the abstract designs and the somber colors, in which browns prevail, are not only typically Japanese but also very beautiful in their strength and simplicity *(Plate 107)*. Kawai's work is similar in style, but freer and less traditional both in shape and design. He too prefers heavy pottery to porcelain, and simple shapes and abstract designs, all of which join elements of the Japanese tradition with those of modern art *(Plate 108)*.

While the members of the Mingei group show a Western influence in one degree or another, there is a school of modern ceramics which is wholly based upon ancient Japanese models. Many of the potters do nothing but imitate the older wares as faithfully as they can, and there are others who derive their style from the late Edo period and produce monstrosities of vulgar ornateness which is really surprising in a country like Japan, where there is such a strong tradition of restraint. However, there is at least one potter who towers above all the others working in native styles, and who, although restricting himself to a traditional framework, is nevertheless a great creative artist in his own right, and that is Kitaōji Rosanjin (born 1881). His magnificent tea bowls and plates and jars and vases are ostensibly Japanese pottery of the Shino, Oribe, Bizen, and Karatsu types, but, perhaps because these Momoyama wares appeal so strongly to contemporary taste, they seem peculiarly modern. Rosanjin, although following a traditional style, is able to infuse the old forms with new vigor, and he has created some of the most beautiful and most typically Japanese works of our times *(Plate 109)*.

Not only in pottery but also in textiles there are signs of new life, and weavers such as Yanagi Yoshitaka, and dyers such as Serizawa Keisuke, bring fresh vitality to their craft. Like Hamada, Serizawa combines traditional techniques and designs with a keen understanding of modern abstract art, and from these two elements spring creations which are at once truly Japanese and truly modern. Other crafts flourish besides pottery and textiles. The paper-makers of Japan continue to be the most exquisite in the world, the basket-makers, and bamboo artists carry on their time-honored crafts, and the calligraphers, both traditional and modern, still create masterpieces. The Western critics who, often after a superficial glance at a few Western-style painting exhibits, throw up their hands in despair and say that with the death of Hiroshige a hundred years ago the great artistic tradition of Japan had come to an end, should turn to the craftsmen of Japan, as artists the world over have been doing in increasing numbers. It is here that the soul of Japan is expressed at its purest, and in a manner which has a particular appeal to modern taste.

BIBLIOGRAPHY

GENERAL HISTORIES OF JAPANESE ART

Hōshu Minamoto. *An Illustrated History of Japanese Art.* Kyoto, 1935.
(Good treatment of painting and sculpture but no discussion of architecture and crafts.)

Tsuda Noritake. *Handbook of Japanese Art.* Tokyo, 1935.
(Good general discussion of all phases of Japanese art; especially useful for listing the famous sites and collections.)

Pageant of Japanese Art, 6 vols. (edited by Staff Members of the Tokyo National Museum) Tokyo, 1952–54.
(This is the most recent and most complete discussion of Japanese art available. The text is written by leading Japanese authorities and there are numerous excellent plates.)

Langdon Warner. *The Enduring Art of Japan.* Cambridge, 1952.
(Popular introduction into Japanese art by one of America's leading scholars in this field.)

JAPANESE PAINTING

Lawrence Binyon. *Painting in the Far East* (4th ed.), London, 1934.
(Well-written but rather outdated discussion of the various schools of Japanese painting, and few illustrations.)

Henry P. Bowie. *On the Laws of Japanese Painting.* London, 1911; reprinted New York, 1951.
(A detailed technical discussion of traditional Japanese ink-painting, with many diagrams.)

Arthur Morrison. *The Painters of Japan.* 2 vols. London, 1913.
(Very much outdated and poorly illustrated but still the most complete discussion of this subject by a Westerner.)

Hugo Munsterberg. *The Landscape Painting of China and Japan.* Tokyo, 1955.

(A complete discussion of this specialized branch of Far Eastern painting.)

Pageant of Japanese Art, Vols. I-II. Tokyo, 1952,

(This is the most complete and up-to-date discussion of Japanese painting, although it omits the modern period entirely.)

Kenji Toda. *Japanese Scroll Painting.* Chicago, 1935.

(Very good and scholarly discussion of this important phase of Japanese art with some good color reproductions and Japanese references.)

JAPANESE COLOR PRINTS

L. Binyon and J. J. Sexton. *Japanese Color Prints.* London, 1923; reprinted New York, 1955.

(Excellent discussion of the *ukiyo-e* school arranged chronologically. Good plates.)

Arthur D. Ficke. *Chats on Japanese Prints.* London, 1916; reprinted several times.

(Popular but very good and learned treatment of the subject with artists' seals.)

Shizuya Fujikake. *Japanese Wood-Block Prints.* Tokyo, 1954.

(A small volume in the Tourist Library particularly useful in dealing extensively with modern prints.)

James Michener. *The Floating World.* New York, 1954.

(Lively and well-done discussion by the famous novelist. Poor plates.)

Waldemar von Seidlitz. *History of Japanese Color Prints.* London, 1910.

(A pioneer work by a German expert, but still useful.)

Basil Stewart. *Subjects Portrayed in Japanese Color Prints.* London, 1922.

(Very learned and useful work giving a clue to the subjects of *ukiyo-e* prints.)

JAPANESE SCULPTURE

Japanese Sculpture, 6 vols. (by various editors and photographers) Tokyo, 1952.

(Collection of magnificent photographs with brief text dealing with Japanese sculpture from the prehistoric period to the Kamakura age.)

Pageant of Japanese Art, Vol. III. Tokyo, 1953.
  (Scholarly discussion and excellent plates.)

Langdon Warner. *The Craft of the Japanese Sculptor.* New York, 1936.
  (Good discussion of the technical aspects of Japanese sculpture.)

JAPANESE ARCHITECTURE

Jirō Harada. *The Lesson of Japanese Architecture* (Rev. ed.), London, 1954.
  (Many good pictures of Japanese houses but brief text.)

Pageant of Japanese Art, Vol. VI. Tokyo, 1954.
  (Scholarly discussion and excellent plates.)

A. L. Sadler. *A Short History of Japanese Architecture.* Sidney, 1941.
  (A scholarly discussion based on Japanese sources but illustrated only
  by line-drawings.)

Alexander Soper. *Buddhist Architecture in Japan.* Princeton, 1942.
  (A definitive scholarly work but not for popular consumption.)

Bruno Taut. *Houses and People of Japan.* Tokyo, 1937.
  (Interesting discussion of Japanese domestic architecture by one of
  Europe's leading modern architects.)

Tetsurō Yoshida. *The Japanese House and Garden.* New York, 1955.
  (Excellent discussion of Japanese houses by a Japanese architect. Magnificent plates.)

JAPANESE CRAFTS

H. L. Joly. *Japanese Sword Guards.* London, 1910.
  (A very scholarly catalogue of a famous *tsuba* collection.)

G. Koizumi. *Lacquer Work.* London, 1923.
  (A practical guide to the art of Japanese lacquer. Poor illustrations.)

Tadanari Mitsuoka. *Ceramic Art of Japan.* Tokyo, 1949.
  (A small but excellent volume in the Tourist Library. Poorly printed.)

Yuzuru Okada. *Netsuke, A Miniature Art of Japan.* Tokyo, 1951.
  (A small but good volume in the Tourist Library.)

Okada, Koyama, and Hayashiya. *Japanese Ceramics.* Tokyo, 1954.
  (Only brief English text but many magnificent plates.)

Pageant of Japanese Art, Vols. IV-V. Tokyo, 1952 and 1954.
  (These volumes deal with ceramics, metalwork, textiles, and lacquer.

Scholarly discussion and excellent plates.)

A. D. Howell Smith and A. Koop. *A Guide to Japanese Textiles,* 2 vols. London, 1919–20.
(A scholarly and detailed catalogue of Japanese textiles in the Victoria and Albert Museum.)

Soetsu Yanagi. *Folk Crafts in Japan.* Tokyo, 1949.
(A brief but excellent introduction into Japanese folk art with some plates.)

INDEX

191